# MOROCCO

**SPIRAL**GUIDE

AA Publishing

C000024795

# Contents

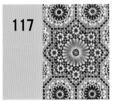

Written by Sylvie Franquet
Revised and updated by Sylvie Franquet

Project Editor Sandy Draper
Project Designer Alison Fenton
Series Editor Karen Rigden
Series Designer Catherine Murray

Published by AA Publishing, a trading name of AA Media Limited,
whose registered office is Fanum House, Basing View, Basingstoke,
Hampshire, RG21 4EA. Registered number 06112600.

ISBN: 978-0-7495-6247-2

The contents of this publication are believed correct at the time
of printing. Nevertheless, AA Publishing accept no responsibility
for errors, omissions or  changes in the details given, or for the
consequences of reader's reliance on this information. This does
not affect your statutory rights. Assessments of attractions, hotels,
restaurants and so forth are based on the author's own experience
and contain subjective opinions that may not reflect the publisher's
opinion or a reader's experience. We have tried to ensure accuracy
in this guide, but things do change, so please let us know if you
have any comments or corrections.

A CIP catalogue record for this book is available from the
British Library.

Cover design and binding style by permission of AA Publishing
Colour separation by Keenes, Andover
Printed and bound in China by Leo Paper Products

Find out more about AA Publishing and the wide range of travel
publications and services the AA provides by visiting our website at
www.theAA.com/bookshop

A03805
Maps in this title produced from map data © New Holland
Publishing (South Africa) (Pty) Ltd, 2008

# The Magazine

A great holiday is more than just lying on a beach or shopping until you drop – to really get the most from your trip you need to know what makes the place tick. The Magazine provides an entertaining overview to some of the social, cultural and natural elements that make up the unique character of this engaging country.

# A Cold Country
## with a Hot Sun

**Arab geographers called the highlands of North Africa "Jzirat el-Maghreb" – the Island of the West or Sunset. This "island" was surrounded by the Atlantic, the Mediterranean and, in the south, by a vast sea of sand – the Sahara.**

Morocco, on the westernmost tip of this "island", has many draws: from verdant valleys to arid sand dunes and barren mountains; from cool rivers and lakes in the Middle Atlas to sunny beaches on its Atlantic coast. Even in the middle of the countryside there is stunning architecture to discover.

The landscape alternates between lush fields in the Middle Atlas, and stark desert in the south. Many people are lured by the expansive, barren beauty of the desert. Marshal Lyautey, the French colonial administrator who laid the groundwork for modern Morocco, described it as "a cold country with a hot sun". It is an appropriate description, as it is a common misconception that temperatures are always soaring in Morocco. In the mountains, which form a considerable part of the country, the temperature swings between boiling hot summer days and icy winter weather when most of the peaks are under snow. In the summer months, the desert is blazing during the day but cools down considerably when the sun drops. The Atlantic coast, particularly near Agadir, enjoys pleasant temperatures all year round: in summer it is a lot cooler than Marrakech and the desert towns, while in winter it is still hot enough for sunbathing.

**Small train of camels crossing the Erg Chebbi sand dunes into the Sahara**

## Beach Delights

Morocco has 2,800km (1,750 miles) of coastline facing the Atlantic and 530km (330 miles) on the Mediterranean. The coast, backed by the fertile Sous and Sebou plains, is the most densely inhabited region and the richest. Much of the Atlantic coast is considerably rougher and windier than the Mediterranean, but it has some fantastic surfing beaches, among them Sidi Kaouiki (► 94), Sidi Ifni and Dar-Bouazza (► 94) near Casablanca. Tangier (► 100–103) is the country's largest passenger harbour, while Casablanca (► 79–80) has the largest industrial harbour.

## Spectacular Mountains...

About one seventh of the country lies more than 2,000m (6,500 feet) above sea level, and the Atlas Mountains consist of three ranges. The High Atlas, the most famous, has more than 400 peaks above 3,000m (9,800 feet) and ten above 4,000m (13,000 feet), including Jebel Toubkal (► 146), at 4,167m (13,671 feet) the highest mountain in North Africa.

The Middle Atlas is a range of high plateaux, where many Berber live in traditional tribes, herding sheep and goats. The highest point here is Jebel Bounaceur at 3,340m (10,960 feet).

The Anti Atlas, featuring Jebel Sarhro at an impressive 2,712m (8,898 feet), is a barren mountain range skirting the desert alongside the Draa Valley. The Atlas mountains are made of sedimentary rocks with intrusions of granite and quartzite. The northern coast is separated from the rest of Morocco by the Rif Mountains (➤ 109), an extension of the cordillera of southern Spain.

### Just Right for Skiing

The French introduced skiing to Morocco in the 1930s and now two resorts cater for all abilities. Skiing is a bit of a lottery in Morocco, as some winters have seen only a dusting of snow, but more recently there has been plenty of powder. The best time to go is from mid-January to mid-March and you will need to climb to around 2,000m (6,500 feet) to find snow. Oukaïmeden (➤ 162), the country's foremost ski resort only an hour's drive from Marrakech, sits at 2,400m (8,000 feet) and has Africa's highest cable lift going to the top of Jebel Oukaïmeden (3,273m/10,738 feet). The resort is under Saudi development to turn it into an upmarket all-year-round resort with five-star hotels, ski lifts and artificial snow. More experienced skiers can hire a highly trained Berber guide to go skiing in the Tazaghart area. The more modest ski pistes of Mischliffen, Azrou (➤ 132) and Ifrane (➤ 138) are popular weekend destinations.

> "Expect verdant valleys, arid sand dunes and high mountains, sunny beaches and cool lakes"

### Waiting for the Rain

Water manifests itself as a quandry in Morocco: there is either too much or too little. During the last 25 years, droughts have been more frequent and severe than in previous decades and yet there have also been floods (for instance, in May 2006). In Morocco, agriculture is a fundamental part of the economy and approximately 85 per cent of the crops are irrigated by rain water. Even though the government has invested heavily in drought-prevention measures in recent years, Morocco experienced an exodus of around 450,000 people, including many farming families, in the 1990s. The authorities have redoubled their efforts to mitigate against the vagaries of the weather in Morocco.

### Barren Desert Delights

Beyond the Draa Valley and the Anti Atlas lies the vast Sahara Desert. Most of the desert in Morocco consists of *hamadas* – barren, windswept

**Jebel Toubkal is popular with snowboarders**

rocky plateaux – and, less commonly, of *ergs* – picturesque sand dunes that sometimes rise to spectacular heights. Many *oueds* (rivers) cross the sands, brought to life by rainstorms but quickly drying up again. Oases are rare, except near the Draa and Ziz valleys (➤ 154, 155), which are fed by water from the Anti Atlas. The Western Sahara near the Atlantic does see a little more rain and some mist coming off the ocean, making the area greener and less barren. The only other riches of the desert are the phosphates hidden beneath its surface.

## On the Shoulders of a Giant
In Greek mythology, Atlas was a magnificent Titan who revolted against the gods. As a punishment they placed the burden of the heavens on his shoulders. When his load became too heavy he begged to be turned into stone and was transformed into Mount Atlas.

### VITAL STATISTICS
- Morocco covers 710,850sq km (274,480sq miles) including the Western Sahara, and has a population of nearly 33 million people.
- The government's ambitious "Vision 2012" strategy aims to raise the annual number of tourists to ten million by 2012. Many tourist developments are under construction all over the country but particularly along the Atlantic Coast and around Marrakech.
- Less than 40 per cent of the population now work the land, compared to more than 90 per cent at the beginning of the 20th century.
- Morocco contains 75 per cent of the world's phosphate reserves and is the world's largest exporter of the substance.

# Matters of
# Belief

**Religion is no simple matter in Morocco. Although the
majority of Moroccans are Muslims, the Berbers have
maintained some of their older pagan customs, particularly
a large number of *marabouts* (shrines to holy men).**

So, while orthodox Islam insists there should be no intermediary between
man and Allah, holy men still play a large part in Morocco's spiritual life.
In addition, the *chorfa* (plural of *cherif* or *sherif*) – descendants of the
Prophet Mohammed – are venerated as wise men. Morocco's Alaouite
dynasty of kings are *chorfa*.

## The Basics of Islam
Muslims believe in the "Five Pillars" of Islam: the Shahaada (the
confirmation that there is only Allah and Mohammed is His messenger);
Salaat (prayers five times daily); Soum (fasting during Ramadan); Zakaat
(giving alms to the poor) and Hajj (making a pilgrimage to Mecca).
Muslims live by their holy book, the Koran (or Qu'ran), believed to be the
direct word of Allah given to the Prophet Mohammed.

**The decorative five-fingered Hand of Fatma is a symbol of good luck in Morocco**

The Hadith, the sayings of the Prophet, together with the Koran, form the basis for how Muslims should conduct their lives. They should pray five times a day, facing the Kaaba in Mecca (Saudi Arabia). Some go to the mosque, while others pray in shops, at home, at work or at the roadside – wherever they happen to be. Most men go to a mosque for Friday noon prayers and to hear the weekly sermon, so businesses and museums usually close at that time.

> "Muslims believe that all things happen because Allah wants them to happen"

During the Holy month of Ramadan, which commemorates the revealing of the Koran to Prophet Mohammed, Muslims refrain from eating and drinking from sunrise to sunset. Children, travellers, the sick, the elderly and pregnant women are excused from fasting.

### *Inshallah*, *bismillah* and *el hamdu lillah*

The name of Allah is constantly invoked. The most common phrase is probably *inshallah*, literally meaning "God willing", although it can also mean "maybe", "yes", "no", "could be", "for sure", or variations on that theme. Muslims believe that all things happen because Allah wants them to happen; no human should presume to know Allah's will. Before a meal or a departing on a journey Muslims say *bismillah*, short for *bismillah*

**The dome-and-merlon shaped battlements of the Almoravid Koubba ruins in Marrakech**

**The Karaouiyne Mosque in the Fez el-Bali district of Fez, rebuilt in the 12th century**

*er rahman er rahim* – "in the name of Allah the compassionate and merciful". To express surprise or in times of trouble Muslims whisper *Allahu Akbar* ("Allah is great"), and to express pleasure or relief they may say *el hamdu lillah* ("Praise be to Allah").

## White Koubbas and Moussems
Pilgrims visit the *koubbas* or *marabouts* (tombs) of their wise holy men (though there are a few women) to pay respect, seek advice or a find a cure for a disease. Some people tie strips of fabric to the grilles of tombs to bind their contract with the saints. Others put oil inside the tomb, where it becomes infused with the saint's *baraka* (blessing) and is then used to heal a sick person. Women in particular seek help and advice from *marabouts* about infertility, psychological problems and childbirth.

Where Sufi brotherhoods have formed around particular saints, the tomb is called a *zaouia*. The most important *zaouias* are in the Aïssaoua in Meknes, the Gnaoua (▶ 82), the Regraga in Essaouira, and the Taïbia in Ouezzane. The birthday of the holy man is celebrated with a *moussem* (▶ 26), which involves several days of feasting and prayers.

# *Bismillah*
## A Moroccan Feast

**A real Moroccan feast is not for the faint of heart or weak of stomach. The many courses of rich food may be unfamiliar to Western palates, but it is a feast in every sense, with bright colours, rich aromas and tastes from sweet to hot and sour.**

### Hospitality Reigns

The sharing of food – a big bowl of couscous or a steaming tagine, for example – is a social affair; but in Morocco it is also an expression of solidarity, of family or tribal bonding. Hospitality is an honour for the wealthy but also a way of survival for the poor.

To evoke this spirit of hospitality, Moroccans like to tell a pre-Islamic story that celebrates a prince who spent his fortune on entertaining passing guests honourably. Even simple travellers who had lost their way were given grand hospitality, until in the end the host had nothing left. One day the king visited him, having heard that the prince owned a fantastic horse. At the end of the meal when the king finally mentioned the delicate subject of purchasing the animal, the prince admitted that in order to fulfil his duty of hospitality he had to kill the animal. The irony is that the tradition of hospitality led to both host and guest losing out.

**A popular family-run food store at Djemaa el-Fna meeting place in Marrakech**

## A Veritable Feast

Moroccans eat at low, round tables, while sitting on cushions or a sofa. Before a meal, a bowl of water, perfumed with orange blossom or rose essence, is usually brought to the table to wash hands before eating. Traditionally, only the right hand is used for eating, and food is scooped up with a chunk of bread from a central bowl. The invitation to eat is *bismillah*, after which the host will take the first bite, and will then often hand out the choice pieces of meat to the much-honoured guests.

As a guest you should try to taste each of the dishes, though you don't have to eat everything as it is considered polite to leave some food, as well as to belch to show you've eaten plenty. Guests should talk very little as they eat, and avoid touchy or exciting subjects that might distract people from the numerous pleasures of the table.

> "Listen to our stories like you drink tea with little sips, so you get its full flavour"

The meal starts with a soup, such as *harira*, a rich chick pea, meat and tomato soup, often eaten with dates. This might be followed by a selection of salads, then by several *tagines* (stews), grilled meat or fish. As if this isn't plenty enough the next dish is a pyramid of couscous with vegetables and broth, and followed by fresh ripe fruit.

Tagine is a traditional dish served in restaurants all over Morocco

The meal ends with a much-needed digestive mint tea, served with almond and honey sweets. Take your time to enjoy the tea: as the people from the High Atlas say: "Listen to our stories like you drink tea, with little sips, so you get its full flavour." This very Moroccan drink was first introduced by the English. They brought teapots and green tea, which the Moroccans thought too bitter so they added mint and sugar to it.

## Ras el Hanout

*Ras el Hanout* ("Head of the Shop"), the most exotic Moroccan flavouring, is used on special occasions, and winter stews. It is a pungent blend of 27 spices: including cardamon, mace, galangal, guinea pepper, nutmeg, pimiento, cantharide, Indian and Chinese cinnamon, cyparacée, long pepper, cloves, curcuma, grey and white ginger, oris root, black pepper, lavender, rosebuds, Chinese cinnamon, ash berries, belladonna, fennel flowers, *gouza el asnab*, asclepiadic fruit, cubeb and monk's pepper.

**Previous page and below: Mint tea is refreshing and has excellent digestive properties**

# A very important
# **date**

**The elegant silhouette of the palm tree is not only beautiful but it's also an essential element in both Arab and Berber culture.**

As the Berber proverb says, "It is good to know the truth and speak the truth, but it is even better to know the truth and speak about palm trees". The country has a wide variety of palms, but the date palm (*phoenix dactylifera*) is the most important. It is said that the date palm needs to have its feet in the water and its head in the fire, so it's perfectly adapted to the Moroccan south and is the only crop in the region. It is vital to Morocco's economy and environment for several reasons:

- Palm trees are incredibly fertile and can bear fruit for more than 150 years.
- They protect the soil from erosion by the desert wind and provide protection from the blistering sun, both for humans and for the crops grown in their shade.
- Every part of the palm tree is used: dates are a key ingredient in the Moroccan diet, the flowers provide a popular aphrodisiac, the trunk and leaves are used as building materials, the sap makes an inebriating liqueur and the fibres are woven into ropes.

However, things are not all rosy in Morocco's palm groves. In recent years, North Africa has lost three-quarters of its palm trees due to an (as yet) incurable fungal disease called *bayoud*. In addition, groves in southern Morocco are also jeopardised by drought, demographic pressure and the demand for land from foreigners buying houses in Marrakech.

**Dates grow in abundance in Morocco and are a tasty treat**

**Date palms growing in the fertile gardens of Agdal Jardin in Marrakech**

## Religious Dates

The trees also have a religious importance in Islamic, Christian and Jewish traditions. The Prophet Mohammed was born in a palm grove. To remember this, Muslims traditionally break the Ramadan fast each night with a date and a spoonful of water.

North African tradition has it that the date palm originated in the Garden of Eden when a full-grown tree bearing ripe fruit sprang from the spot where Adam had just cut his nails and hair. The angel Gabriel appeared behind the tree and told Adam that it was to be his food. When Adam had to leave the garden he took the palm with him.

When the ancient Jewish leader Moses led his people out of Egypt, they were hungry and thirsty until they came to the palm grove of Elim. The Bible also mentions the beauty, mythology and usefulness of palm trees.

---

### NOTABLE DATES

- The sweetest dates are found in Zagora (▶ 154).
- The *boussekri* has firm flesh and, eaten with mint tea or milk, is the usual snack of shepherds.
- Many places now have 90 per cent *deglet nour* date palms because the large, sweet dates fetch high prices in the West, but they are not similarly appreciated locally.
- The oblong *boutoub* also keeps well, while the soft *boufggous* date is dipped in cumin-flavoured water.
- In villages, dates are kept in earthenware jars and buried in the ground – *akbourn* or buried dates have a strong smell and bitter taste because of their fermentation.
- Less tasty dates are not wasted but fed to goats and sheep.

---

# Conquests and Dynasties

**Morocco has a long and colourful history. The earliest identified inhabitants are the Berbers, whose origins and history are not well-known but they are thought to have originated from Central Asia.**

One of the many mosaics used by the Romans to adorn their buildings in Volubilis

The most influential invasion came when the Arabs descended from the Arabian peninsula at the end of the 7th century, conquered Morocco and converted the Berbers to Islam. Later on it was mainly Europeans who came, attracted by the country's riches and strategical position.

### Early beginnings

In the 12th century BC the Phoenicians from Lebanon established trading posts along the Moroccan coast, and were followed by the Carthaginians from Tunisia. After the fall of Carthage in the middle of the 2nd century BC, the Romans took control and made the north of Morocco the province of Mauretania Tingitane (from Tingis which gave the name of Tangier). The country enjoyed a period of great economic and cultural advancement, particularly under the local king Juba II, who was educated at the court of Augustus, and married the daughter of Anthony and Cleopatra. Volubilis (► 126–127) was the centre of culture and wealth at this time.

## The Arab Conquest

From AD 640 onwards the Arabs moved west to conquer land and convert people to Islam, but Morocco wasn't entirely conquered until AD 705, as the Berbers offered strong resistance. It is said that when the Arab military leader Oqba ben Nafi reached the Atlantic Ocean at Massa, he rode his horse into the sea and declared that God was his witness that the ocean was the only thing that could stop the conquest. From Morocco the Arabs moved on to conquer Spain.

## Great Berber Dynasties

In AD 788–974 Moulay Idriss I (▶ 131), the political refugee and founder of Fez, headed Morocco's first Muslim dynasty – the Idrissids.

The Almoravids, the first Berber dynasty was founded in the 11th century, in the Sahara by Ibn Yaasin. His successors Abu Bekr and Youssef ben Tachfine, founder of Marrakech, expanded the empire to include Muslim kingdoms in Spain. From 1147 onwards the Berber Ibn Toumert preached war against the Almoravids and the resulting Berber Almohad dynasty, founded in the High Atlas, marked the high point of Moroccan history. It dominated Northern Africa and Muslim Spain, with Yacoub el-Mansour who later declared himself sultan of Seville.

## The Arabs Again

During the 16th to 17th centuries Morocco flourished under the Saadians. Abu el-Abbas Ahmed el-Mansour, the most famous Saadian king (reigned 1578–1603), was named "el-Mansour" – the Victorious – after he defeated the Portuguese in the battle of the Three Kings in 1578.

## The Alaouites

In 1666 Moulay Rachid took control of Morocco, followed by the notorious Moulay Ismail (▶ 128–130), who founded the Alaouite dynasty which rules today. Mohammed V took over after independence from France in 1956. His eldest son Hassan II (1929–99) reigned from 1961 for 38 years and his image is still seen all over the country. In 1975, he organised the Green March, in which 350,000 Moroccans walked south, determined to "recapture" the Western Sahara from the Spanish.

The current king, Hassan II's son, Mohammed VI, is well loved and has been a modernising force. The official capital is Rabat, but King Mohammed V spends much time in Marrakech, promoting the city as a tourist destination and a film location.

**The Roman ruins at Volubilis**

# An Architectural
# Mosaic

**Many of the traditional architectural features originally came from further east in the Islamic empire. Similar types of buildings are found all over Morocco, and what follows is a glossary of architectural terminology.**

**Karaouiyne Mosque in Fez (left);** *hammam* **baths at Dar Mnebbi in Marrakech (right)**

## Agadir

The *agadir* or *irherm*, such as *Irherm n'Ougdal* (➤ 172) built in elaborate pisé work (packed clay from the riverbed), looks like a kasbah but is used as a communal fortified granary in southern villages.

## *Djamaa* (mosque)

With a couple of exceptions, Morocco's most obvious Islamic monuments are closed to non-Muslims. Built in Moorish style, and modelled on the 8th-century Grand Mosque of Córdoba in Spain, most Moroccan mosques have simple exteriors, with only the minaret and ornate entrance gate attracting attention. The mosque always has a *sahn* (courtyard) with an ablution fountain and at least one prayer room along one of its sides, with a *mihrab* or *qibla* (niche facing Mecca). The muezzin calls believers to prayer from the top of the minarets, most of which are modelled on the great Almohad minarets of the Koutoubia Mosque in Marrakech (➤ 61).

### Fondouk

The *fondouk* or caravanserai is an inn where travelling merchants slept and ate, stored their wares and stabled their animals. One of the most impressive surviving examples is the restored 18th-century Fondouk Nejjarine in Fez (► 124).

### Hammam (steam bath)

Physical purity is fundamental to Islam. Prayers are preceded by ablutions, so *hammams* were usually built near mosques and supervised by them. As well as practical (private bathrooms are comparatively recent), they were also popular meeting places. Men and women are always kept separate. One enters a *hammam* covered by a towel, moving from the cold room to the tepid room then the hot room. The restored Hammam Mounia in Essaouira (► 81–83) is a good place to be tempted by the steam.

Ironwork for sale (left) in Marrakech; the tiled courtyard of Karaouiyne Mosque (right)

## Kasbah

The *ksar*, or kasbah, is a fortified tribal village, traditionally belongs to one important family, and are often very grand, despite the fact that their pisé work just "melts" during the rains and the community simply moves on. The Route des Kasbahs (► 148–149) is lined with them.

### Medersa (Koranic schools)

*Medersas*, such as Medersa Bou Inania in Fez (► 122), played an important role in old Morocco, as an education based on Islamic theology, law and rhetoric led to higher political, judicial or religious careers.

### Marabout

*Marabouts* or koubbas are domed, square, usually whitewashed, tombs of saints, which can be elaborate as the Tombeaux Saadiens in Marrakech (► P62), or as simple as Sidi Chamarouche in the High Atlas (► 169).

## Medina

The medina is the old part of the city, a labyrinth of narrow alleys enclosed within thick ramparts. Its main arteries are clogged with souks, workshops and sacred buildings and bustle with noise. The quieter residential back streets provide its inhabitants with a calmer and safer environment. The medina of Fez el-Bali (▶ 122–124) is an example of a classic medina: every quarter has its main mosque, *hammam*, bakery, market and school. The word "medina" comes from the town Medina in Saudi Arabia where the Prophet Mohammed fled after his persecution in Mecca.

## *Riad*

The hip place to stay in Morocco is the *riad* hotel. *Riad* literally means an enclosed garden, but now also refers to the house it surrounds. Most rooms overlook the garden and may only have small windows facing the outside of the building. *Riads* once housed extended families, each with their own apartment. Marrakech has more than 600 *riad* hotels (▶ 64–65) and restaurants (▶ 66–67), and more are being restored all over Morocco.

Towers of the kasbah, Aït Benhaddou (left); exterior of a *Hammam*, Marrakech (right)

## Souk

Souks (market and shopping streets) are some of the main attractions of Moroccan cities. Often pedestrianised and sometimes covered, souks are arranged by speciality, so there are souks for carpets, spices, vegetables or wool, and for dyers, leatherworkers, and so on. The result is an exotic riot of colours, smells and noises. Listen out for the word *balek!* It might be warning of a passing donkey or porter. Marrakech has some of Morocco's largest souks (▶ 52–53) and Fez (▶ 122–125) some of the finest, but for more relaxed trading try Essaouira (▶ 81–83) or Rabat (▶ 76–78).

## *Zellij*

Most courtyards in Morocco are decorated with *zellij*, a mosaic work of small coloured ceramic fragments arranged in geometric patterns.

# Berber first,
## Moroccan Second

**Berbers, Morocco's original inhabitants, still form more than half of the population. The Romans called these fierce and proud tribes "the Barbarus", which became "Berbers", but they themselves prefer to be called "Amazigh".**

The Berbers are a proud race and consider themselves to be Berber before Moroccan. Their most identifiable feature is their language, the country's second most spoken language after Arabic. A growing cultural awareness among Berbers, supported by King Mohammed VI, has given greater importance to their language. It is believed to be the oldest language in North Africa, and written for more than 3,000 years, however, most Berbers today have no written language as it was forbidden in school and they studied in Arabic or French.

### Language Conservation
Since 2008 Berbers are allowed to be schooled in their own language, but so far they don't have enough teachers. In Morocco there are three main dialects: Riffan, spoken in the North to Fuguig; Tamazight, spoken in the High and Middle Atlas; and Soussi or Chleuh spoken in the South.

**A woman of the Berber Gheghaia tribe weaving carpets in the hamlet of Imlil**

### The Sound of the Berbers

Berber music has a long tradition, which is very different from Arab music. The village music is performed by the men and women in the village who sing and dance together. The rhythmic ritual music performed with drums and flutes is only performed during *moussems* or exorcist rituals. Groups of professional musicians often travel from village to village in the High Atlas to perform their songs and poems. Raï music has its roots in traditional Berber music, but has been influenced by Western music, particularly in the use of synthesizers and rhythm guitars. The word *Raï* means "opinion" and the songs express concerns of North African youths uprooted in Europe.

### Berber Life and People

In the mountains, the Berbers live in stone houses perched on rocky slopes, overlooking their cultivated terraced fields. Some Berbers, like the Aït Atta of Jebel Sahro and the Draa plains, are still nomadic, living in low tents made of goat skins and camel hair.

Berber women are unveiled and more open in public than women in the cities and plains of the north. They herd and graze goats and cattle, and carry huge loads of firewood or provisions on their heads. The weekly souks, often established on tribal borders, are a central part of their lives, particularly for the nomads, because as well as produce, this is where news and views are exchanged. Berbers in the plains built ksar (► P21), fortified villages, as protection against surrounding tribes, but in the hills, where they were more able to defend themselves, they only protected their *agadirs* or *irherms* (granaries).

Berber musicans, Essaouira (above); drums in Souk Smarine, Marrakech (right)

# Festivals
## and *moussems*

*Moussems* have been celebrated in towns and villages since around the 16th century, and there are still about 750 each year. In recent years some of the larger *moussem*s attract many tourists, and are accompanied by a music festival.

### The Original *Moussem*

Spread all over the countryside are the white tombs and *marabouts* of the *chorfa*, the descendants of prophet Mohammed, and master Sufis or pious men, the local 'saints'. Once a year, a festival is held around the tomb to celebrate their birthday. This is a very much a North African tradition, as the orthodox Sunnis forbid the veneration of any one except Allah. It often falls at the end of the harvest period, and is very often the only occasion that the inhabitants of the dispersed villages in the Atlas mountains get together for celebrations, to hold a huge market to trade produce, to meet for possible marriages and to stock up before the winter when villages can be cut off for several months. Festivities start on a Friday, day of prayers and last up to a week. A visit to the tomb of a big saint can replace

A Berber woman dressed up for a *moussem*

the recommended pilgrimage to Mecca, and is often called 'the hajj or pilgrimage of the poor'. Apart from religious rituals the festival always includes a large market, traditional dancing and singing, acrobats, and *fantasias* with horses and music.

## The Most Famous *Moussem*

The best known *moussem* is undoubtedly the one in Imilchil, in the High Atlas. The local tribes get together in September before the snow closes them off, to honour the local saint Sidi Ahmed Oulmaghni, to stock up for the winter and last but not least to get married. Here men and women can meet and talk and arrange a wedding, and if it doesn't work out during the year, they can come back and try someone else. In El-Jadida more than 300,000 people gather for the *moussem* to celebrate the 12th-century saint Moulay Abdellah Amghar, as well as almost 1,000 horsemen from all over the country who represent their tribe during the *fantasia*. The evening before the birthday of prophet Mohammed, a procession is held in Salé to the tomb of the patron saint Sidi Abdellah ben Hassoun when the inhabitants carry huge multi-coloured candles.

## The Festivals

In recent years some of the sacred element of the *moussem* has been lost, particularly in the cities, and the music has taken over. Essaouira has a big *gnawa* and world music festival every summer that attracts many international performers. In early June a more subdued Festival of World Sacred Music takes place in Fez, with international performers of spiritual music. Ouazarzate has the Ahouache, a Berber dance and music festival in September, while Casablanca has a festival of street music in June. In the south several festivals take place where the Touareg tribes make peace and music, including in Dakhla.

*Fantasia* at Ain el-Aouda featuring music and horses

# Pirates
## and Corsairs

**When, in 1610, the devout Catholic king Philip III expelled all Muslims and Jews from Spain, many headed for Morocco. Some were skilled craftsmen who applied their art, but others took their revenge by becoming pirates or corsairs.**

The corsairs of Tetouan and Bou Regreg were much feared, venturing as far north as England and Iceland. Piracy continued in Morocco until bombardment by Austria, in revenge for the loss of one of their ships, seriously damaged Rabat and other coastal settlements in 1829.

### The Salée Rovers
The richest of the corsair states was the Republic of Bou Regreg. More than 300,000 Moriscos (Muslims expelled from Spain) settled on either side of the Bou Regreg river, in Rabat and Salé. Many of them took to piracy, mainly as revenge against the Spanish ships. The notorious Salée Rovers, as they became known, soon also attracted European adventurers and renegades. Their language was a lingua franca, a mixture of Spanish, Italian, French and Portuguese. They specialised in plundering ships returning to Europe from West Africa and the Spanish Americas. One of the most successful Rovers was Mourad Reis, a German originally called Jan Janz who converted to Islam. Mourad Reis attacked villages in Cornwall (England), Ireland and Iceland, taking hundreds of captives who were sold in slave markets in North Africa.

### The Pirate Queen of Tetouan

Like Salé and Rabat, the city of Tetouan saw an influx of Moriscos from Spain and soon the city grew rich on the profits of their piracy. In 1512, upon the death of Tetouan's founder el-Mandari, his dynamic 20-year-old wife, Fatima, assumed power and became the corsair queen. Her corsairs were much feared, and she even had alliances with the fearsome Ottoman pirates of Barbarossa. Fatima ruled for more than 30 years and used her ill-gotten wealth to patronise artists and intellectuals at her court.

### Sir Henry Mainwaring

The 16th-century Englishman Henry Mainwaring worked for all the big pirate bosses, including the Sultan of Morocco, the Bey of Tunis and the Duke of Tuscany. Based in Mehdiya (▶ 84), he looted ships and sold his captives in slave markets in France and North Africa. Later on he returned to England, where he became a naval officer and eventually a politician, arguably not much of a career change.

### Built with Corsair Money

Under the rule of the Alaouite sultan Moulay Rashid, and his successor Moulay Ismail (▶ 128–130), the corsairs of Tetouan and Salé were encouraged to attack Christian ships mercilessly. Many of the slave captives were forced to help build Moulay Ismail's new capital at Meknes. As the sultan took about 60 per cent of this profitable business, the corsair republic soon went into decline.

The American writer, translator and composer Paul Bowles (▶ 30–31) dominated Tangier's post-war artistic and intellectual life. His fascinating novels, short stories and translations have helped to shape Western notions and ideas of Tangier and other Moroccan cities. Contemporary Moroccan writers continue his tradition by writing down many of the traditional stories.

# Literature
## in Morocco

**Telling stories is still a strong tradition in Morocco, as anyone visiting the Djemaa el-Fna at night or a weekly rural souk can testify. Many of these stories told were recorded and written down by the writer Paul Bowles in the 1950s.**

### The Original Travel Writer

The 14th-century explorer and geographer Abu Abdallah Mohammed (1304–77), known as Ibn Battutah (or Battuta), was called the "Traveller of Islam". He was born in Tangier but in 1325 his intended pilgrimage to Mecca resulted in a journey of almost 30 years across the Middle East, North Africa, Asia Minor, Africa and China. His book *Rihla* (Travels) contains vivid descriptions of the different cities, landscapes and people he encountered. His adventures are brilliantly and accurately captured by the British writer Tim Mackintosh-Smith in fascinating books *Travels with a Tangerine: A Journey in the Footnotes of Ibn Battutah* (John Murray 2001) and the follow-up *Hall of a Thousand Columns, Hindustan to Malabar with Ibn Battutah* (2005). Battutah's modest *marabout* lies in the medina of Tangier, and is located in the street named after him.

### Paul Bowles

After studying music in Paris, Bowles headed for Tangier in 1931 and was immediately enchanted, though he didn't come to live in Morocco until several years later. Unlike many foreigners, Bowles was self-effacing and fascinated by his exotic, new environment. Although he and his artistic friends were at the heart of the foreign expat community, his real interest lay in Moroccan life and culture, and he befriended many local people.

**Paul Bowles in Tangier**

French President Nicolas Sarkozy awards Moroccan writer Tahar Ben Jelloun in 2008

Bowles married the writer Jane Auer, but spent his early years in Tangier living with the Moroccan painter Ahmed Yacoubi. Later, he became friends with the author Mohammed Mrabet, whose work he translated.

His evocative first book, *The Sheltering Sky*, attracted many visitors to Morocco, including the author William Burroughs and assorted hippies. The story was filmed by Bernardo Bertolucci in 1989, and starred Debra Winger and John Malkovich, with Bowles himself as narrator, and the movie attracted a new wave of visitors to the country.

Bowles also spent the 1930s and 1940s composing music, and recording traditional Moroccan music. Paul Bowles died in 1999, but his works remain influential on modern Moroccan writers.

## Moroccan Writers

Tahar Ben Jelloun, the country's most famous author, was born in Tangier but now lives in Paris. He writes very Moroccan stories in French, in which dreamlike narratives tell of the harsh reality of daily life. His most acclaimed book, *The Sand Child* (1985), tells of a girl from the south who is brought up as a boy in order to circumvent Islamic inheritance laws regarding females. Mohammed Mrabet (born c1940) was also influenced by Morocco's storytelling tradition and has written many novels and short stories, most of which have been translated by Paul Bowles. His works include *M'Hashish* (1969) and *Chocolate Creams and Dollars* (1993).

# Best experiences

**In Morocco you become immersed in the country: its hustle and bustle, its spirituality, its pungent flavours and smells.**

**Baskets and souvenirs for sale at Souk la Criee Berbere in Marrakech**

- Become addicted to the syrupy mint tea served at all times of the day, poured from spectacular heights to make it bubbly.
- Shop till you drop in Morocco's marvellous and colourful city souks like Marrakech (► 52–53), Fez (► 122) and Essaouira (► 82–83), or visit the picturesque rural weekly markets like Asni (► 144), where locals gather to buy food, cattle, clothes and sunglasses.
- Wander around Fez el-Bali (► 122-123), and *"baalak"* (Arabic for "watch out") for busy porters and persistent donkeys with their heavy loads, in what is perhaps the ultimate medina.
- Catch the surf along the beautiful and exhilarating Atlantic coast at Essaouira (► 82–83), Taghazout (► 87) or Mirleft (► 152), and head south for some dune boarding in Merzouga (► 155).
- Admire the spectacular varied landscapes and get closer to Berber culture while hiking in the High Atlas mountains (► 141–162).
- Get ultra clean in the traditional *hammam* (steam bath) and indulge in a long loofah massage to exfoliate old skin.
- Watch the pink flamingos at the peaceful nature reserve of Moulay Bousselham (► 116).
- Start the evening with a dinner at the Djemaa el-Fna in Marrakech (► 50–51) before hitting the city's exciting night spots (► 70).
- Experience the silence and spirituality of the desert on a walk or tour from M'Hamid (► 154).
- Luxuriate in the shade of palm trees at the oases of Tinerhir (► 154–155), Figuig or Akka.

# Finding Your Feet

# First Two Hours

Morocco has 12 international airports, the important one are Casablanca, Marrakech, Agadir, Fez and, to a lesser extent, Tangier. The Straits of Gibraltar (14km/9 miles wide) separate Morocco from Europe. Regular ferries operate from Algeciras and Tarifa (Spain) to Tangier or Ceuta, from Sète (France) to Tangier, Almeria and Málaga (Spain) to Melilla.

## Aéroport Marrakech Menara

- The airport is **6km (4 miles) from town**. Bus 11 runs to Djemaa el Fna, but services can be erratic. Alsa City bus runs between the airport terminal every hour between 7am–midnight (20dh) to Djemaa el-Fna and Guéliz.
- **Taxis** cost about 80dh to the medina, 100dh to Guéliz (the new town) and 150dh to the Palmeraie, but insist on the meter being switched on.
- There's a **bureau de change** and several **car-rental** desks.

## Aéroport Mohammed V, Casablanca

- Morocco's largest airport is **30km (19 miles) from town**.
- **Trains** from the airport to the train stations of Casao-Port and Casa-Voyageurs run hourly between 6:50am–10:45pm and cost 35–50dh.
- The **Aérobus** (40dh) runs between the airport and the major hotels between 7:30am–10:30pm. Another bus goes to the main CTM bus station between 7:30am–midnight.
- *Grand taxis* costs about 250dh to the centre (fixed prices from the airport).

## Agadir al-Massira Airport

- Agadir's airport is **25km (16 miles) south of the city**.
- No public transport. *Grand taxis* charge a fixed rate (150dh) into town, taking six people.
- 24-hour bank and several **car-rental** agencies.

## Fez Saïss Airport

- The small airport at Saïs, **15km (9 miles) south of the city**, handles international flights from Paris and London, including RyanAir flights.
- **Bus 16** goes to the railway station or a *grand taxi* should cost 100dh between 6am–8pm.
- No ATM, only a bureau de change.

## Aéroport Ibn Battouta Tangier

- The airport is **15km (9 miles) from the centre**.
- Local **buses** 17 and 70 to Grand Socco in the centre leave from the main road, 2km (1 mile) away from the airport. Otherwise try to negotiate a price for a *grand taxi*; the official charge is 150dh per car for up to six people, but drivers often try to charge per person, and will ask for extra money if you're carrying luggage.
- Car-rental desks in the arrivals hall and bureau de change.

## Tangier Port

- Passport control in Tangier Port is notoriously slow, so expect a long queue. Make sure you get a departure card on the boat and have your passport stamped before getting off, or the wait will be even longer.
- There are bureaux de change inside and outside the port.
- Tangier centre is within walking distance, but if you have a lot of luggage take a *petit taxi* (10–15dh per person).
- The port area is notorious for its **hustlers**, who may tell you that you need a guide because the city is dangerous. It is best to ignore them.

## Tourist Information Offices

While tourist offices in Morocco are not always very helpful, they can provide you with a few leaflets and sometimes maps. They can also help with dates of festivals, addresses or put you in touch with official guides. All staff speak Arabic, French and English. Visit www.visitmorocco.org for information.

### Agadir
✚ 184 A3
✉ Immeuble A, place Prince-Héritier-Sidi-Mohamed
☎ (048) 84 63 77

### Casablanca
✚ 182 C3
✉ 55 rue Omar Staoui
☎ (022) 27 95 33
(Syndicat d'Initiative)
✉ 98 boulevard Mohamed V
☎ (022) 22 15 24

### Essaouira
✚ 182 A1
✉ 10 rue du Claire
☎ (024) 78 35 32

### Fez
✚ 183 F4
✉ Place Mohammed V
☎ (035) 62 34 60

### Marrakech
✚ 182 C1
✉ Place Abdelmoumen ben Ali, Guéliz
☎ (024) 43 60 57

### Meknès
✚ 183 E3
✉ Place Batha L'Istiqlal, Ville Nouvelle
☎ (035) 52 44 26

### Ouarzazate
✚ 185 D3
✉ Avenue Mohamed V
☎ (024) 88 24 85

### Rabat
✚ 183 D4
✉ Corner of rue Zellaga and rue Oued al Makhazine
☎ (037) 67 39 18 / 67 40 13

### Safi
✚ 182 B2
✉ 26 rue Imam Malik
☎ (024) 62 24 36;
www.safi-ville.com

### Tangier
✚ 183 E5 29
✉ Boulevard Pasteur
☎ (039) 94 86 61

## *Faux Guides*

- Hustlers and *faux guides* can be a problem for the first time visitor, mainly in the medinas of tourist cities, but also at airports and, particularly, in Tangier port. The authorities have dealt with most of them, but some remain and should be avoided.
- They may tell you that there is no public transport into town in the hope that you take their car, or that your hotel has recently closed so you can go and stay at their "cousin's" hotel, where they get a percentage of the cost.
- They may also tell you (falsely) that medinas are dangerous places where you will get lost. They will then offer to guide you around and lead you to shops where they will receive a commission on whatever you buy from the shopkeeper.
- Be aware that if you try to shake them off they will often accuse you of being racist or a paranoid tourist, but just ignore all that.
- If you do want assistance exploring a medina, then it is best to look for the officially accredited guides recommended by your hotel or by the tourist office.
- One drawback of the clampdown on hustlers and *faux guides* is that it has now become more difficult to walk around town with a Moroccan friend, as this may attract police attention.

## Drugs

- The Rif Mountains are a pretty lawless region, as their main crop is *kif* (cannabis). Although its cultivation is legal, it's strictly illegal to buy, sell or be in possession of cannabis or hashish.
- Many foreigners are in Moroccan jails for getting involved in the business, so beware. Local gangsters, particularly around Ketama, often target vehicles passing through, especially foreign or rented cars.
- Visitors are quite likely to come across marijuana in various forms and in related traditional by-products such as *majoun* and honey. Beware, however, that you are more likely to find yourself in trouble for buying some than the locals.

---

**Admission Charges**
The cost of admission to museums and places of interest mentioned in the text is indicated by the following price categories:
**Inexpensive** under 30dh     **Moderate** 30–50dh     **Expensive** over 50dh

---

# Getting Around

The public transport system works well in Morocco. An efficient train service links the main towns in the north with Casablanca, Rabat and Marrakech; elsewhere you can travel by bus, or by *grand taxi* (communal taxi).

## Urban Transport

- The best, and often the only, way to **explore the medina is on foot**, but you may need some transport to visit sights further away.
- *Petits taxis* can travel only within the city, and carry no more than three people. They are relatively cheap and all have meters, but do insist that the driver switches it on after departure. The normal rate doubles after 8pm. It is standard practice, particularly with a single passenger, for the driver to pick up more passengers on the way.
- *Grands taxis* (➤ 37) operate in cities like normal taxis but, as they have no meters, you need to negotiate the price before you set off.
- Tourists rarely use local buses because **taxis are reliable and inexpensive** and you can do most things on foot.
- Where a bus is useful it has been indicated in the text.

## Trains

- The rail network covers only a small part of the country, but if it is available, it is usually the **best way to travel**. Trains are comfortable, reliable and efficient.
- **Two main lines** run from Tangier to Marrakech via Fez, Meknès and Casablanca and from Oujda to Marrakech, joining the Tangier line at Sidi Kacem.
- **Timetables** are available at main stations and tourist offices or online at www.oncf.org.ma.
- It's best to **book tickets in advance**, but very often you can just turn up and get a seat, as there are frequent trains.
- **Second-class tickets** are usually a little more expensive (just over 3dh per 10km/6 miles) than a similar journey by bus, while **first-class** tickets offer a more comfortable journey with air-conditioned carriages. It costs more but is still very reasonable.

## Buses

- The **bus service is very good**, and slightly cheaper than *grands taxis*, at around 2–3dh per 10km (6 miles).
- The national bus company **CTM** has the fastest and most reliable buses with fixed departure times, numbered seats and loud videos to watch on the longer routes.
- All major towns have a *gare routière* (bus station), but **CTM buses leave from their own offices**, which are not necessarily near by. For longer journeys and CTM buses try buying tickets in advance.
- In summer you might consider taking **night buses** for longer journeys to avoid the midday heat.
- Services run by some of the **smaller companies** leave only when they are full up, and they stop when flagged down.
- The train company ONCF also runs fast and efficient **Supratour Express** buses to connect larger cities like Essaouira, Agadir and Tetouan with their rail network.

### Grands Taxis

- Collective *grands taxis* (service taxis) operate almost everywhere in Morocco, and they are the **fastest way to get around**. Big Peugeot or Mercedes cars will carry up to six passengers and operate all day, particularly on popular routes, departing as soon as they are full.
- Just turn up at the *grands taxis* terminal and **state your destination** to get a seat in a car.
- **Prices are fixed per seat**; just ask the other passengers. If you do not want to wait you can pay the price of all six seats.

### Sample Journey Times

- **Marrakech–Casablanca:**  3 hours (train)
  3 hours 30 min (CTM bus)
  2 hours 30 min (*grand taxi*)
- **Tangier–Casablanca:**  6 hours (train/bus)
- **Fez–Casablanca:**  4 hours 10 min (train)
  5 hours 30 min (bus)
  3 hours (*grand taxi*)
- **Agadir–Casablanca:**  9 hours (bus)
- **Essaouira–Casablanca:**  5 hours (bus)
- **Essaouira–Marrakech:**  3 hours 30 min (bus)

### Domestic Flights

- **Royal Air Maroc** (RAM) operates from Casablanca to the major cities in Morocco (tel: (022) 51 91 00/31 11 22; www.royalairmaroc.com). For most flights you have to change in Casablanca.
- **Book all domestic flights in advance** and make sure you reconfirm them 72 hours before departure (24-hour information line: (090) 00 08 00) as there are often changes to the schedules or even cancellations of flights.

### Driving

- Driving is fairly easy in Morocco, but **accidents are quite frequent**, particularly because people often walk in the road without looking out for traffic. Always watch out for pedestrians or cyclists, particularly in villages or towns.
- **Roads are generally good and well kept**, and there is relatively little traffic out of urban areas.
- **Police checks are very frequent**, especially for speed offences.

**Finding Your Feet**

- **Driving in the dark can be dangerous** as many people cycle or walk in the middle of the road, or even drive without lights.
- To drive on **pistes or unsurfaced roads** – in remote areas or in the desert – you need an appropriate vehicle (preferably four-wheel-drive) and some experience of similar environments.

## Driving Essentials

- The **minimum age** for drivers is 21 years.
- **Speed limits**: on motorways 120kph (75mph)
  on main roads 100kph (60mph)
  on urban roads 30–40kph (20–25mph).
- Drive on the **right**.
- **Seatbelts** are compulsory for drivers and passengers, and you may be fined if caught not wearing one.
- **Filling stations** are common in and around towns, but there are fewer in rural areas and in the south, so always fill up when you can.
- Premium is the standard brand of fuel for cars, and unleaded fuel is available at most stations. Prices are similar to those in Europe, but the duty-free fuel in Melilla and Ceuta is less expensive.

## Car Rental

- A car is especially rewarding in the **south of Morocco**, where there is less public transport, and the traffic is light.
- **Renting a car is easy** as there are many agencies in Morocco, but it is relatively expensive. International agencies tend to be more expensive than local ones, but are cheaper when booked before arrival or with a flight. With local firms you can usually bargain a little over the fare, but you should ensure that you check the quality of the vehicle before use.
- To rent a car you must be aged **over 21**, and you need a **passport** and **driving licence**. An international licence is not required but can be useful if your normal one does not carry a photograph.

## Breakdowns

- **Moroccan mechanics are usually good** and very resourceful. Most small towns have a garage but, as most spare parts are for French makes such as Peugeot or Renault, it may take a while to order anything else.
- If you break down far from a garage **you may have to pay a truck driver to tow you** to the garage.

## Parking

- In almost every town centre or at every sight someone will offer to be a *gardien de voitures*, sometimes officially, but very often self-appointed. In either case you should offer them about 5–10dh for looking after your car before driving off.

## Police Checks

- As a result of the large number of deaths on Moroccan roads, the police have become increasingly vigilant and there are usually **checks** outside cities. Foreigners are usually flagged through, though you may be asked to show your papers.
- If you are stopped for **speeding** or for some other reason, always remain calm and polite. A quick apology may get you off a fine of up to 450dh.
- Major roads have **radars** to check speed – but drivers coming in the opposite direction will usually warn others by flashing their lights.

# Accommodation

This guide includes a wide, though carefully selected, choice of places to stay, ranging from simple but charming bed-and-breakfasts to sumptuous royal palaces. Coastal areas are busiest in summer, while Marrakech is now busy almost all year round, and particularly during the school holidays.

## Hotels

- Moroccan hotels are usually either classified, with tourist board star-ratings, or unclassified, less expensive places with very few comforts.
- Morocco has been criticised for not using international ratings for its hotels. But, although in the past many of its "five-star" hotels were not up to standard, they now have improved services and amenities. Many new hotels are being built, and medinas all over the country (but in Marrakech in particular) have excellent *riad* hotels.
- Morocco has a fair number of luxurious palace hotels, as well as numerous well-kept and friendly budget hotels, but be warned that the middle categories can be quite grim.

### Riads

- For an authentic Moroccan experience, the best place to stay is a **riad** (► 22), which are often hidden in the medina. Large old houses or palaces are increasingly being converted into restaurants, bed-and-breakfasts or luxurious hotels.
- *Riads* are smaller and more intimate than ordinary hotels, with only a few rooms, usually centred around a tranquil, leafy courtyard near the markets and intriguing alleys of the medina. It is a great way to experience Morocco, and it is often possible to arrange home-cooked dinner as well. This is not an easy option if you have small children, as safety and noise levels are an issue.
- Prices vary from budget to very expensive.

## Youth Hostels

- Morocco has 11 quite **well-run and clean youth hostels** (*Auberges de Jeunesse*) in the major cities.
- A membership card is not required, although members get a reduced rate. Prices range from about 30–50dh per person per night in a dormitory.
- Information is available from Fédération Royale Marocaine des Auberges de Jeunesse, parc de la Ligue Arabe BP 15998, 2100 Casablanca; tel: (022) 47 09 52; www.iyhf.org

## Camping

- There are very basic and inexpensive (about 35-60dh per person) **campsites** (*muhayyem* in Arabic) in all major cities and along the coast. Most have fairly rudimentary washing and lavatory facilities, but a few are well kept and some better-quality sites even have swimming pools.
- Camping outside sites is not illegal, but it's not advisable, unless you are looking for adventure.

## Mountain Refuges

- Walkers can stay at the many mountain refuges for 15–50dh per person per night. Lists are available from Moroccan tourist offices or from Club Alpin Français (50 boulevard Moulay Abdekkahman, quartier Beauséjour, 20200 Casablanca; tel: (022) 98 75 19; www.caf-maroc.com).

## Booking Accommodation

Useful websites for information and bookings include:

**www.ilove-marrakech.com/www.ilove-essaouira.com** *Riads* and boutique hotels
**www.boutiquesouk.com** Select list of *riads*, palaces and boutique hotels
**www.marrakech-riads** *Riads* and guest houses in Marrakech and around
**www.fesmedina.com** Historic properties for rent in Fez medina.

---

**Accommodation Prices**

The price categories indicated in this guide are for a double room per night, including breakfast and taxes:

£ under 600dh          ££ 600–1,600dh          £££ over 1,600dh

---

# Food and Drink

You can eat well in Morocco. The cities in particular have a large choice of restaurants to suit all tastes and budgets. Women usually prepare Moroccan cuisine, and recipes are handed down from mother to daughter. Men traditionally make the mint tea, and are only allowed near the stove in a restaurant. If you are not so lucky to receive an invite to a Moroccan home, then the nearest thing to home cooking is one of the splendid *riad* restaurants. A meal here is not for the faint hearted, as it usually involves an elaborate set menu of several courses with a selection of salads, *pastilla* (pigeon pie), couscous or tagine, desert and fruit. Dinner in your own *riad* is as good as home cooking, as the lady of the house will prepare it just for you.

## Eating Out

- During **Ramadan** many restaurants in tourist areas remain open, but visitors should be discreet when eating or drinking during the day.
- **Breakfast** is usually from 7:30 to 10am, **lunch** from noon to 2:30pm and **dinner** from 8 to 11pm, although opening hours can be vague.
- A **meal** usually starts with raw and cooked salads, followed by a tagine (stew of vegetables or fruits with meat, chicken or fish) or couscous. Dessert is usually fresh fruit, or Moroccan pastries with mint tea.
- **Some Moroccan food takes a long time to prepare** and so needs to be ordered 24 hours advance, when you book the table.
- In most places **the dress code is relaxed**, although in more stylish places in Marrakech and Casablanca it is a good idea to dress up for the occasion.
- **Menus** are generally written in French and Arabic, and in English at more touristy places.
- Traditionally a Moroccan meal is eaten with two fingers and the thumb of the **right hand**. Bread is served in large quantities and is often used as cutlery to scoop up food.

## Moroccan Restaurants

- Most **quality hotels** have both an international and a Moroccan restaurant, serving well-prepared dishes, decorated in traditional style with banquettes circling low, round tables.
- Moroccan restaurants are usually the precinct of **tourists**, as locals prefer to eat Moroccan food at home, and French or Italian food when they go out. A meal in these places is often accompanied by a floor show with musicians and a belly dancer.

- Some *riad* restaurants in Marrakech charge a **fixed price** for an evening of delights, which include a steady flow of culinary pleasures, wine, an exotic décor and a live traditional music and dancing shows.
- If you are staying in a *riad* you can usually order dinner in advance, which is served in a cosy dining room, and often cooked by the Moroccan lady who looks after the house.

## International Cuisine

The French legacy is still strong, and French eateries range from old-style colonial dives to upmarket restaurants. In the big cities like Marrakech and Casablanca the hip places serve fusion and Asian food.

## Vegetarian Cuisine

- A large selection of **salads** are based on vegetables only, and the choice is very wide. **Tagines** can be served without meat, but are often cooked in meat stock or meat fat.
- If you are eating in someone's home, **your hosts will usually serve you meat** even if you have told them you do not eat it, as they will assume that you do not eat meat because you cannot afford it. Leave the meat if you must, but eat something so as not to offend your hosts.
- **Markets** have plenty of fresh fruits and vegetables, as well as excellent **yoghurt** to supplement your diet.

## Street Food

- Moroccans like to eat at *gargottes*: street kiosks and cafés that sell inexpensive snacks such as *harira* soup, salads and *brochettes* (skewers of meat), *merguez* (spicy sausages) and simple tagines.
- The most obvious place to sample street food is on **Djemaa el-Fna in Marrakech** (➤ 50–51) or the stalls outside **Essaouira harbour** (➤ 81).
- Tourists are often wary of the **hygiene standards** in these places, but if it's popular with the locals then the food is usually fresh.

## Drinks, Wine and Beer

- **Green tea** with mint is the national drink, but Arabic coffee is also served. Morocco has wonderful oranges so most places sell fresh **orange juice** in season. **Almond milk** and **banana with milk** are also popular.
- **Soft drinks** and bottled **mineral water** are available everywhere.
- Morocco is a Muslim country so, while **alcohol** is widely available in tourist hotels, restaurants and bars, it is generally not easy to buy in medinas or in rural areas.
- Moroccans who do drink alcohol often prefer a cool **local beer**, either Casablanca or Flag. Hotels usually have **imported beers**, though at double the price of the local brew.
- Moroccan **wines**, mostly from the Meknes region or from Haha near Essaouira, are a little heavy but very drinkable. The most common wines are the red Cabernet. Président, Guerrouane, Ksar, Siraoua, the rosé Gris de Boulaouane and the dry white Special Coquillages. Beauvallon and CB Initials are better quality and delicious.

---

**Restaurant Prices**
Price guides are for a three-course meal per person, excluding drinks but including taxes and service:
**£** under 200dh          **££** 200–400dh          **£££** over 400dh

# Shopping

Morocco is a shopper's delight, with a wide variety of good-quality crafts at reasonable prices. There is only one rule in the souks: bargain hard. Almost every city and large town has an ensemble *artisanal* (government shop) that makes and sells regional crafts at fixed prices. The prices tend to be a bit higher than in the souks, but these shops are perfect places for those who don't like bargaining, as you can get an idea of the sort of prices you'll expect to pay, before venturing into the souks.

## Shopping Hours
- **Shops in the *Ville Nouvelle*** (new town areas) usually open Mon–Sat 8:30am–noon and 2–6:30pm; in the summer they may close for longer during the afternoon and stay open later; during Ramadan they don't close for lunch, but do close earlier in the afternoon.
- **Shops in the medina** tend to be open from 8 or 9am to around 8pm or even later in tourist areas. Many shops are closed on Friday for prayers at the mosque.
- **Souks** usually start at around 6am.

## Bargaining
Bargaining in Morocco is as normal as saying hello, and is expected wherever you shop. There are no real rules about how much of the initial price you should pay as some vendors start with ridiculous mark-ups, while others stay close to their final price. It is often a good idea to check out prices before you start buying. The main rule is to take your time and not be intimidated: it can be a fun game! But never mention a price you are not prepared to pay. If you go shopping with a guide he will take you to shops where he will earn a percentage of your purchases, which will be added to your bill.

## Souk Days
- Many villages are named after their weekly market day.
- There are no markets on Friday as it's a day for rest and prayers.
- Arrive early in the morning when the market is in full flow, as it usually finishes by lunchtime.

| | |
|---|---|
| Souk el-Had | Sunday market |
| Souk el-Tnine | Monday market |
| Souk el-Tleta | Tuesday market |
| Souk el-Arba | Wednesday market |
| Souk el-Khamees | Thursday market |
| Souk es-Sebt | Saturday market |

## Spices and Toiletries
- Spices and natural toiletries are plentiful and make inexpensive presents.
- The most common **spices** are cinnamon sticks or powder, nutmeg, powdered ginger, paprika, curcuma, cumin, *ras el hanout* (➤ 15) and saffron. The best and most genuine strands of **saffron** come from Taliouine; the powder is fake.
- **Toiletries** sold in the spice market include kohl (black eye make-up also used to protect the eyes), *ghassoul* (clay to wash the hair or skin), henna (to dye hair), small clay pots imbued with poppies (lipstick), amber, musk (perfume), and almond or olive oil soap. More upmarket stores sell aromatic oils, natural bath products and perfumes.

- **Honey** is widely produced and is often found in village souks, but also in specialist shops in Essaouira and Agadir.
- Essaouira is also famous for its rich and sweet nutty argan **oil** pressed from argan nuts (▶ 93), used both in food and cosmetics.

## Minerals and Fossils

- Everywhere in the Atlas you will come across vendors selling minerals and fossils at very tempting prices; but beware of fakes, particularly the brightly coloured ones.
- Often these fossils are just found in the desert, riverbeds or mountains, and so their trade is not harmful to the environment.

## Jewellery

- When most of the Jewish population left the country, they took a lot of authentic Moroccan silver jewellery with them. As a result, the majority of the jewellery found on sale in Morocco today comes from **India, Indonesia and Niger**.
- The **best jewellery souks** are in Essaouira, Tiznit and Marrakech. Silver jewellery is sold by weight, except for very rare old pieces. Many craftsmen reproduce some antique designs beautifully, particularly in the Tiznit region, but do not be tempted to pay antique-level prices for them.
- Most genuine **Berber jewellery** is very heavy and chunky.

## Crafts

- **Craft traditions** are stronger than ever in Morocco, and even a lot of tourist tat is still pretty tasteful and well made.
- Among the main tourist souvenirs are *babouches* (slippers), the traditional footwear in Morocco, made by craftsmen who pass their skills down from father to son.
- Moroccans excel at **woodwork**, especially in Essaouira, where beautiful thuya or cedar inlay work is produced.
- Fez is famous for its blue-and-white designs of **pottery**, while Safi, Morocco's major ceramic centre, produces colourful pottery houseware, as does Salé.
- **Leather** is also an excellent buy, typically as *babouches* or pouffes, although places like Marrakech also have good-quality leather clothing and handbags.
- **Carpets** tend to be expensive in Morocco, but good-quality rugs and kelims (flat-woven carpets and rugs) are more reasonable. The best kelims are made by the Berbers of the Middle and High Atlas, and are available in village souks such as Midelt, Azrou or Asni near Marrakech. Berbers (particularly in the Rif mountains) also weave beautiful *fouta*, woollen blankets in natural or bright colours.

## 10 Best Buys from Marrakech

- **Spices** (Marché Central or Rahba Qedima)
- **Slippers** (souk des Babouches)
- Custom-made **kaftans** Au Fil d'Or, Aya's (▶ 68)
- **Shopping baskets** with leather handles (Rahba Qedima)
- Thick felt-wool **handbags**, dyed with saffron (Souk des Teinturiers)
- **Fabric man with fez** to handle a hot teapot (Maison d'Été)
- **Nike trainers** half the European price (alleys around rue Bab Agnaou)
- **Love potion** (Rahba Qedima)
- **Moroccan music** cassettes (off Djemaa el-Fna, Marrakech)
- **Mejdoul dates** from the oases (between Djemaa el-Fna and Souk Smarrine)

# Entertainment

Most cities in Morocco have a few bars, mostly for men, and discos (often in tourist hotels), but the main entertainment is a meal and a good show in a wonderful Moroccan restaurant. There are few spectator sports, but the country offers a wide range of outdoor activities.

## Sport

- **Golf** was made popular by King Hassan II, and Morocco now boasts spectacular courses near every major city. For more details, contact **Royal Moroccan Golf Federation**: Dar es Salaam Golf Club, Rabat; tel: (037) 75 59 60; www.golf-maroc.com.
- The Atlantic coast is usually good for **surfing**, and spots like Sidi Kaouki near Essaouira and Dar-Bouazza near Casablanca are especially popular. **Royal Moroccan Surfing Federation**: tel: (022) 25 95 30.
- During the winter it is usually possible to **ski** near Oukaïmeden in the High Atlas or near Fez and Meknès in the Middle Atlas. You can cross-country ski in the High and Middle Atlas, as well as in the Rif Mountains. Contact **Royal Moroccan Ski and Mountaineering Federation** in Casablanca: tel (022) 47 49 79; www.frmsm.ma (in French).
- Moroccan horses are superb and, with wonderful landscapes to explore, **riding** here can be very rewarding. **The Atlas Mountains in particular are an impressive place to ride** (► 162).
- **Hiking** is popular all over the country, but particularly in the Atlas range around Mount Toubkal. Contact **Club Alpin Français**: tel: (022) 98 75 19; www.caf-maroc.com **Royal Moroccan Ski and Mountaineering Federation** (see above).
- In the toughest **long-distance run** in the world, competitors in the annual Marathon des Sables cover 243km (151 miles) of sand dunes and rocky desert terrain in six days. Check the website: www.darbaroud.com, or for runners from the UK (www.saharamarathon.co.uk).
- **Hunting** is a popular activity, particularly with the Moroccans and the French, and mainly in the Middle Atlas. The season for wild boar and for birds such as quail, pigeons, partridges and ducks runs from the first Sunday in October until early spring, every Sunday and on public holidays. Licensing is strictly controlled. Contact **Royal Moroccan Hunting Federation**: tel: (037) 70 78 35.
- Deep-sea **fishing** is popular in the Atlantic, with trips available from Essaouira, Safi and Asilah, and for wilder shores from Dakhla and Laayoune. Trout and other freshwater fish can be found in the lakes of the Middle Atlas, near Azrou, Ifrane, Beni Mellal and Ouirgane. Contact **National Fisheries Office**: tel: (022) 24 05 51.

## Traditional Music and Dance

Major hotels and restaurants may host traditional music and belly dancing. Don't miss the spectacular parties known as *fantasias*, traditionally held at Berber *moussems*, but also staged for tourists in Marrakech.

## Festivals (see also ► 26–27 Magazine)

Religious festivals are movable occasions according to the Islamic lunar calendar, but popular annual events include the Moulay-Idriss *moussem* (► 131), the Wedding Festival in Imilchil (► 133), Erfoud's Date Festival (► 155) and the Festival of Sacred Music in Fez (► 138).

# Marrakech

# Getting Your Bearings

The Red City of Marrakech has become one of the hippest destinations on Earth. Only a short plane hop from Europe, it is infinitely exotic, offering gorgeous Islamic architecture and old traditions but at the same time it has a vibrant nightlife. On top of that it's a great place to hide away and relax, in lush gardens, sumptuous *riad* restaurants and great hotels.

**Above:** Red pisé ramparts encircle Marrakech
**Previous page:** Carpets for sale, Souk La Criee Berbere (left); plaster carver at work, Souk Talaa (centre); fountain in Marrakech Museum (right)

RUE IBN AICHA

VILLE NOUVELLE

AVE MOHAMMED V
AVE MOHAMMED ABDELKRIM ELKHATTABI

Gare

**14** Guéliz

PLACE DU 16 NOVEMBRE

AVE HASSAN II

HIVERNAGE

0 ——— 500 metres
0 ——— 500 yards

**5** Jardins de la Ménara

AVE DE LA MENARA

**5** Beldi Country Club

Marrakech is set spectacularly against the High Atlas Mountains. At its heart is Djemaa el-Fna, a hub of entertainment for tourists and Marrakechis alike, particularly at dusk. Behind it lies the medina, an intriguing maze of alleys and souks enclosed by thick mudbrick walls.

The Almoravid conqueror Youssef ben Tachfine founded Marrakech around 1070. Legend has it that he ate so many dates that he created a large palm grove, the Palmeraie, and Marrakech still boasts many beautiful gardens.

The city can be overwhelming at first but staying in a *riad* in the medina, wandering around the streets, sipping mint tea and chatting to the friendly locals is incredibly rewarding.

## ★ Don't Miss

## At Your Leisure

The sun sets over Jardins de la Ménara Gardens in the Hivernage area of Marrakech.

# In Three Days

If you're not quite sure where to begin your travels, this itinerary recommends a practical and enjoyable three days in Marrakech, taking in some of the best places to see using the Getting Your Bearings map on the previous page. For more information see the main entries.

## Day One

### Morning

Start at the **6 Mosquée de la Koutoubia** (Koutoubia Mosque right; ➤ 61) and then stroll over to **1 Djemaa el-Fna** (➤ 50–51) for some refreshments. Head for the northern medina via **souk Smarine** (➤ 52), which turns into **souk Chaaria**, with **Musée de Marrakech** (Marrakech Museum, ➤ 61–62) and the **Dan Bellarj** on the left. Further along the street is the **3 Ben Youssef Medersa** (➤ 54) and near by is the **7 Koubba Ba'adiyin** (➤ 61). Have lunch on the roof terrace of **Le Foundouk** restaurant (➤ 67).

### Afternoon and Evening

For some proper shopping, return to the Koubba Ba'adiyin and head south into the **2 souks** (below), such as **des Babouches** and **des Teinturiers** (➤ 53), and then west in the chic shopping area around **rue Mouassine** and the **place de Bab Ftouh**. Return to the main drag of **Souk Smarine** and end up at the **Rahba Qedima** (➤ 52). Watch the sun set over the city and behind the mountains from the rooftop of the **Café des Épices** (➤ 66).Have dinner at the stalls on Djemaa el-Fna or in one of the *riad* restaurants in the medina, such as **Le Kosybar** (➤ 67). Book ahead.

# Day Two

**Morning**
Walk from the gate of
**Bab Agnaou** (➤ 57) to
the **9 Tombeaux Saadiens**
(Saadien Tombs, left,
➤ 62), then continue to the
**10 Palais el-Badi** (➤ 62).
Note the bustling place
des Ferblantiers, the main
square of the **mellah** (Jewish
quarter). North of the square
follow Riad Zitoun Djedid,
a street of large mansions,
including the palace and
museum of **11 Palais de
la Bahia** (➤ 62–63). Eat
a delicious lunch at the
splendid **Riad Tamsna**, off
rue Riad Zitoun el-Djedid.

**Afternoon**
Join the Marrakechis and go for a stroll in the delightful **Palmaraie** (➤ 59)
or take a taxi ride to the **Jardin Majorelle** (below; ➤ 59).

**Evening**
Have a drink at the popular **Grand Café de la Poste** (➤ 66), followed
by dinner at **Villa Rosa** (➤ 67) then stroll down to **Oliveri** (9 Boulevard
Mansour Eddahbi, tel: 024 44 89 13) for the best ice creams in town.
Later, go dancing at **Pacha Marrakech** (➤ 70).

# Day Three

**Morning**
Eat breakfast at **Café du Livre**
(➤ 66) and enjoy some great
shopping in **Guéliz** (➤ 63).

**Afternoon**
Take a taxi to the **Beldi
Country Club** for lunch and a
swim, a walk in the gardens
or a hammam in their spa
(➤ 70). Alternatively relax
in a steam bath at the **Bains
de Marrakech** or **Hammam el
Bacha** in the medina (➤ 70).

**Evening**
Dress up and go to **Le
Comptoir** (➤ 66) for dinner
and belly dancing.

# Djemaa el-Fna

It all happens in the Djemaa el-Fna, one of the world's most extraordinary meeting places, and the living heart of the city. By day it's a rather sleepy transit towards the souks. At dusk the spectacle starts as locals and visitors gather to eat great food, hear ancient tales from storytellers, have their fortune told or buy a recipe for a magic potion from the herbalists.

"Without the Djemaa el-Fna Marrakech would just be a city like any other." There is perhaps some truth in the words of the writer Paul Bowles (▶ 30–31).

The open-air theatre and restaurant that is Djemaa el-Fna is so unique that UNESCO had to create a new category – it's the first to be recognised as "Immaterial Heritage of Mankind". Nobody is sure how it all started, or where its name came from. But, sitting just at the entrance to the medina, it seems always to have been the city's focal point, a place of spectacle, trade, encounter and even execution – heads rolled here until well into the 19th century.

The square reverberates with the overwhelming sounds of snake charmers, water carriers, dancers, singers, acrobats, and the enthusiastic reactions of their audiences. It disappears under the smoke from the many food outlets that entice passers-by to eat freshly prepared snail soup, sheeps' brains, fried sole or grilled sausages.

**Opposite: Dancers performing to the crowd at the busy Djeema el-Fna meeting place**
**Below: At night Djemaa el-Fna becomes an open-air restaurant, theatre, circus and hospital**

## ANCIENT TALES

The exciting adventures of the Arab hero Antar, as told by a storyteller in the Djemaa el-Fna, begin:
"From the story of the black knight, the lion with pennant and standards, with the flag and the horse, defender of the Bani Abs Adnane, from Fizara and Dibane, intrepid knight with the reckless heart, snake in the river bed, burning without fire, the one for whom the bravest heroes bowed down, in full battle, courageous conqueror of the grandest warrior, and of Noujeir the son of Giants, master of Mourad and Zaid, Antara ibn Chaddad..."

### TAKING A BREAK

The food in Djemaa el-Fna is freshly prepared, smells great and definitely worth trying. **Juice vendors** set up early in the morning, and **Les Terrasses de l'Alhambra** (➤ 67) is a good place for lunch, while the rooftop of the **Café de France** is recommended as somewhere to stop for refreshments including mint tea, especially at sunset, when there are great views over the medina and the mountains.

✚ 182 C1

---

### DJEMAA EL-FNA: INSIDE INFO

**Top tips** Bring plenty of **loose change** for the street entertainers, especially if you want to photograph the colourful performers. The snake charmers in particular can be quite aggressive and ask for exorbitant amounts if you take a picture, but how much you pay is up to you.
■ If you have problems with **hustlers** or pickpockets seek help from the tourist police stationed there.

**One to miss** Definitely the dentists who pull out teeth in the square, and the **henna-tattooists** who use chemicals in their dye that often irritates the skin.

**In more depth** Read the **story** of Djemaa el-Fna in *Cinema Eden: Essays from the Muslim Mediterranean* by long-time Marrakech resident Juan Goytisolo.

# 2 Souks

The souks of Marrakech are a feast for the senses: the labyrinth of alleys, the mixture of people, the variety of wares, the colours, the smells and the play of light and shadow through the roof can be overwhelming. Take it slowly on your first visit, starting with the main drag. When you return, remember that one of the attractions is to get lost, so wander into side alleys where craftsmen make and sell their traditional wares in small workshops.

The easiest way into the souks is through the alley opposite the Café de France on **Djemaa el-Fna** (➤ 50–51). In the first covered part of the souk nuts, dried fruits and hand-woven baskets are sold. At the end of this is the main arched entrance to rue **Souk Smarine**, the area's principal artery. Souk Smarine is broad and dominated by merchants selling fabrics, kaftans and circumcision outfits for boys, though this is also a good place for quality antiques and serious carpets. Some 200m (220 yards) down on the right, two alleys lead into the **Rahba Qedima**, an open square lined with spice and apothecary vendors. At the end a passage leads into the **Criée Berbère**, the Berber market where slaves were sold until 1912. Now you can buy carpets from all over Morocco at auctions held at around 4–6pm.

**The busy scene at Souk Teinturiers in Marrakech**

Some of
the superb
ironwork for
sale at Souk
Haddadine in
Marrakech

## Craft Souks

Beyond the market, Souk Smarine forks in two: to the right
**Souk el Kebir** leads through the busy leather souk to the
**Ali ben Youssef Medersa** (➤ 54–55). The left fork Souk
el-Attarin leads through the **Souk des Babouches** (slippers)
to the **Souk des Teinturiers**, where dyers hang wool to
dry, the **Souk Chouari** (carpenters) and the smoky **Souk el
Haddadine**, where the blacksmiths work. The area between
the two streets is known as the **Kissaria**. Mouassine has
several antiques shops and funky boutiques, while the parallel
streets Riad Zitoun el Qedim and el Jedid offer sub Saharan
and locally made souvenirs, antiques shops and clothes
boutiques (➤ 68).

### TAKING A BREAK

The obvious place to stop for a drink is at the **Café des
Épices** (➤ 66) on the Rahba Qedima. Alternatively, go for tea
in one of the wonderful riads, such as the literary café-gallery
**Dar Cherifa** (derb Chorfa Lakbir, Mouassine, tel: (024) 42 64
63), or head for the Terrasse des Èpices (➤ 67).

➕ 182 C1
🕐 Shops/stalls: daily 9–7 or 8; many closed Fri 11–4 and public holidays

---

## SOUKS: INSIDE INFO

**Top tips** The souks are **liveliest around 4–5pm** as the temperature cools, tourists
finish sightseeing and Marrakchis go for their early evening stroll.
■ To get an idea of top prices in Marrakech visit the **Ensemble Artisanal** (avenue
Mohammed V, daily 9am–1pm, 3–7pm) before bargaining in the souks.
■ Until recently it took some skill to **enter the souks on your own**, but now
with the tourist police at the gates it's much easier. Bear in mind that if do
decide to take a guide or *faux-guide* into the souk then prices will be higher to
include the guide's commission on everything you buy.
■ Souk el Khemis, just outside Bab el Khemis is a **great junk market** where *riad*
owners source a lot of their furniture.

**In more depth** To see an authentic souk where Marrakchis shop, take a *petit
taxi* to **Bab Ailen**. No one will try to sell you anything aggressively, but you can
stroll among fishmongers, butchers and greengrocers, past tiny cafés, women
catching up on the news and children playing in the streets.

# 3 Ben Youssef Medersa

The largest *medersa* (Koranic school) in Morocco rivals the *one* in Fez in splendour. Its perfectly proportioned courtyard is a marvel of Moorish architecture, striking an amazing balance between plain surfaces and elaborate decoration.

The school took its name from the nearby Mosque of Ali ben Youssef, which was built in the 12th century, but almost entirely rebuilt in the 19th century at half its original size. The *medersa* was part of the Merenid Sultan Abou Hassan's extensive educational plan, which included the Fez *medersas* (► 122), but in 1564 it was completely restored and enlarged by the Saadian Sultan Abdullah el-Ghalib. It follows the traditional plan with its central courtyard and a prayer hall, but unlike other *medersas*, Ali ben Youssef's is entered via an inconspicuous portal and a long, dark corridor. This undoubtedly heightens the pleasure of discovering the large courtyard bathed in sunlight at the end of the passage. The

**Left: Fine cedar-wood screens cover windows overlooking the courtyard**

space, centred on a large fountain pool and flanked by two rows of pillars, is intended to inspire a sense of peacefulness. Although rich and elaborate, with colourful *zellij* mosaic, stucco and cedar carving, the decoration never disturbs this tranquillity.

At the back, a beautiful ornamental portal gives way to the prayer hall. Divided into three aisles by fine marble columns, the room is covered by a cedar dome surrounded by 24 small windows with detailed stucco work. The *mihrab* is decorated with lace-like sculpted plaster.

**The central courtyard and pool at Ben Youssef Medersa**

The *medersa* was built to house more than 900 students in 150 or so spartan cells on its first floor. Most cells were grouped around smaller interior courtyards, lit purely by skylights, but the favourite or most promising students were treated to the best rooms, overlooking the magnificent central courtyard.

### TAKING A BREAK

Drink a glass of fresh juice or a mint tea with Moroccan sweets at the stylish cafeteria in the courtyard of the nearby **Musée de Marrakech (Marrakech Museum)** (➤ 62).

➕ 182 C1
✉ Place Ben Youssef, turn left at the end of Souk el Kebir
🕐 Daily 9–6  🎟 Moderate

### BEN YOUSSEF MEDERSA: INSIDE INFO

**Top tips** You can keep your shoes on during the visit, but **wear modest clothing**. Make sure your arms are covered and don't wear short skirts or shorts.
■ Tickets include Ben Youssef Medersa, Musée de Marrakech (Marrakech Museum) and Kouba Ba'adiyin (P61).

**Hidden gems** Look at **the lavatories** at the end of the corridor opposite the entrance: you'll see that master craftsmen were employed even here.

# ④ The Ramparts and Gates

A tour of the city's 16km (10 miles) of ramparts reveals the superb, well-preserved *babs* (gates) and *pisé* walls and also offers glimpses of the real, less familiar Marrakech. Some stretches of wall run through a cemetery, while others cut through a busy souk or a crowded public square. The colours of the mud walls change with the light of day, from light pink to ochre to red to deep purple.

In 1126, the Almoravid sultan Ali ben Youssef began the magnificent walls, which were 10km (6 miles) long and 9m (30 feet) high, with 200 defence towers and 20 entrance gates. Within a year his workmen had finished them. The walls were frequently restored and enlarged by the Almohads and Saadians, but they still basically follow the 12th-century plan.

The massive square towers of **Bab Doukkala** are no longer used to enter the medina since a modern gate was built beside them. These gates once guarded the road to Doukkala, the Berber region between el-Jadida and Safi, but now the area is dominated by a busy bus station. Nearby is the **cemetery of el Hara** with the **Koubba (tomb) of Sidi Bennour**. Behind the gate rises the elegant minaret of the **Bab Doukkala**

*The essence of Marrakech: The red pisé of the walls, the palm trees lush gardens, and always the beautiful backdrop of the High Atlas Mountains*

**Mosque**, built in the 16th century by Lalla Messouada, the mother of Ahmed el-Mansour (➤ 19).

Past the small gate of **Bab Moussoufa** is the **palm grove of Sidi Bel Abbès**. On the other side of the wall is the **Zaouia of Sidi Bel Abbès**, containing the tomb of the city's great 12th-century patron saint, who is particularly venerated by merchants, farmers and blind people.

There is a daily market at **Bab el-Khemis** that is especially lively on Thursday mornings when livestock is bought and sold. Just before the gate is the **Koubba of Sidi el Babouchis**, patron saint of the slipper makers. Beneath the Almoravid towers of **Bab Debbarh** is the entrance to the **Tanners' Quarters**, but beware – the smell is unpleasant and can be overwhelming in the afternoon. Inside **Bab Ailen** is the shrine and Mosque of **Qadi Ayad**, another of the city's seven patron saints. Further along you will find the vast **cemetery of Bab Rhemat and Bab Ahmar** with the Aguedal Gardens (Jardins Agdal) to the south (➤ 58).

Go through Bab Ahmar to Bab Irhli, passing several *méchouars* – processional squares where festivals were celebrated. **Bab er Rob** has a good food and pottery souk, behind which is **Bab Agnaou**, the gate to the imperial city. In the cemetery beyond Bab er Rob is the tomb of **Sidi es Soheili**, another of the Seven Saints. The tour ends at Bab Jdid with the wall surrounding the Hotel La Mamounia.

### TAKING A BREAK

End the tour with a picnic in the **Jardins de la Ménara** (➤ 59), or with a drink on the terrace in the elegant Hotel Saadi.

➕ 182 C1
✉ Start at Djemaa el-Fna
🚗 Rented bike, calèche or taxi

---

## RAMPARTS AND GATES: INSIDE INFO

**Top tips** Although it is possible to walk around the walls in about 4–5 hours, it is **not advisable because of the heat and the traffic.**
- The most pleasant way is to **rent a calèche** (horse-drawn cab) from the stand in Djemaa el-Fna (➤ 164–166).
- You can rent bikes from the **Hotel de Foucauld** (place de Foucauld; tel: (024) 44 54 99) at about 70dh for half a day but the traffic is increasingly busy.
- Do the tour in the **late afternoon** when it's cooler, and the traffic is calmer.
- The **best-preserved stretches** are between Bab Ailen and Bab Rhemat, and near l'Hivernage.

# 5 Gardens of Marrakech

Enjoy the peace and soft afternoon light in one of Marrakech's peaceful gardens, which say as much about the city's history as its monuments do. From its creation in the 11th century until the 1920s, Marrakech was a garden city – two-thirds of the medina was given over to gardens and orchards. Recently, the municipality has made the restoration of existing gardens, and the creation of new green zones a priority.

The 12th-century Almohad sultans surrounded the Koutoubia Mosque (▶ 61) with splendid rose gardens, which have been restored to their former glory. Outside the city walls they created other glorious gardens. The largest of all is the Jardins Agdal (Aguedal Gardens) created by Sultan Abdel Moumen and enlarged by the Saadians. The royal court held lavish parties in the shade of these olive groves and near the large reservoirs filled with water from the Ourika River. The main reservoir is Sahraj el Hana (Tank of Health), beside the beautiful 19th-century Dar el Hana pavilion, which gives superb views from the terrace over the High Atlas. It is hard to

**The vibrant blue of Majorelle's house was inspired by the French workers' overalls**

believe that sultan Mohammed IV drowned here in 1873, when his boat capsized. The other pavilion, Dar el Beida, is closed when the King is in residence.

## Jardins de la Ménara

Also built by the Almohads, but rebuilt by the Alaouites in the 19th century, are the **Jardins de la Ménara (Ménara Gardens)**. Mohammed IV constructed an elegant green-tiled pavilion overlooking the large water basin and set in a cypress garden surrounded by olive groves. Walk around the reservoir to admire the reflection of the pavilion in the water.

## Palmeraie

The Almoravids established the vast palm grove of the **Palmeraie**, originally covering 13,000ha (32,000 acres) and planted with more than 150,000 trees. The circuit (22km/14 miles) in the groves was a popular excursion from the centre but, although it is still worth seeing, the grove has seriously dwindled – due to disease and redevelopment. Ethno-botanist Gary Martin created an ecological garden at his

**Flowering cactus at the Museum of Islamic Arts at Jardin Majorelle**

guesthouse in the Palmeraie, the Jnane Tamsna (P64), with palm, guava, orange and lemon trees, bougainvillea, olive trees and a rose garden.

## Jardin Majorelle

No less impressive is the **Jardin Majorelle**, planted between 1922 and 1962 by the French painter Jacques **Majorelle** (1886–1962). Against a background of bright blue walls he created a fabulous, unusual garden of cacti, giant bamboos and slender palms. After his death the garden was neglected until it was bought and restored by the French fashion designer Yves Saint Laurent, who is now buried here.

## Contemporary Gardens

The restored gardens of the Alaouite prince and poet, Moulay Abdel Salam, known as the **Cyber Park Arsat Moulay Abdel Salam**, part olive grove, part contemporary garden with an internet café, are the perfect place to cool down at the end of a hot afternoon. One of the newer gardens is at the **Beldi Country Club** and include a roseraie of 12,000 rose bushes, an organic vegetable garden that supplies the restaurant, several swimming pools and a spa (► 70).

### TAKING A BREAK

Have a delicious lunch and a swim in the gardens of the **Beldi Country Club**. The small café in the Majorelle garden serves breakfast until 11:30am, as well as light lunches. Less expensive is the small cafeteria in the **Jardins de la Ménara**, or take a **picnic**.

### Jardin Agdal
➕ 182 C1
✉ Bab Irhli and Bab Ahmar ⏰ Fri, Sat, closed when King is in residence.
🚌 Rented bike, calèche or taxi 💰 Free

### Jardin Majorelle & Museum of Islamic Art
➕ 182 C1
✉ avenue Yaqoub el-Mansour ☎ (024) 30 18 52; www.jardinmajorelle.com
⏰ Jun–Sep, daily 8–6; rest of year 8–5, 💰 Moderate

### Jardins de la Ménara
➕ 182 C1
✉ 2km (1 mile) from Bab Jdid ⏰ Daily 8–6:30 💰 Inexpensive

### Beldi Country Club
➕ 182 C1
✉ 6km (3.75 miles) south of Marrakech, Route du Barrage, Cherifia
☎ (024) 38 39 50; www.beldicountryclub.com 💰 Free, pay fixed price for lunch, or lunch and pool

### La Palmeraie
➕ 182 C1
✉ 8km (5 miles) from town on the Fez road ⏰ All the time 💰 Free

Looking across the still water to the pavilion at Jardins de la Ménara with the snow-capped Atlas Mountains in the distance

## GARDENS OF MARRAKECH: INSIDE INFO

**Top tips** The best time to visit the gardens is **late afternoon** when the air is cooler and the light warmer.
■ The best and most pleasant way to get to, and around the gardens is by **calèche or rented bike** (► 58 for rental information).

**Hidden gem** Jacques Majorelle's house has been turned into a beautifully arranged museum containing some of his colourful paintings, and Yves Saint Laurent's collection of traditional Moroccan crafts.

# At Your Leisure

## 6 Mosquée de la Koutoubia (Koutoubia Mosque)

Towering above the medina and the new town is Marrakech's main landmark, whose 70m (230-foot) minaret was finished by Sultan Yacoub el Mansour during the late 12th century. It's the oldest and most complete Almohad tower and served as a model for the classic Moroccan minaret that still visible in the country's mosques. Legend has it that the three golden balls on the top were made from the jewellery of one of el-Mansour's wives, donated and melted down as penance because she had broken her fast during Ramadan by eating three grapes. The whole minaret was originally covered in plaster, but when it was restored in 2000 it was the decided to keep it bare. The minaret is beautifully floodlit at night. Nearby is the tomb of Lalla Zohra, daughter of a 17th-century religious figure, who was believed to be a woman by day and a white dove at night. Local woman believe that she will protect their children. South of the Koutoubia are the tranquil Koutoubia gardens with roses, palm and olive trees, are perfect for an afternoon stroll.

🚹 182 C1 ✉ Place Youssef ben Tachfine ⏲ Closed to non-Muslims

## 7 Koubba Ba'adiyin

It might not be obvious from the outside, but this small two-storey kiosk – the only surviving Almoravid monument in town – is one of the highlights of Islamic art. The 12th-century ablution hall, with its variety of arches and exquisite interior decoration, is the earliest known example of the typical Moorish style that later became so popular in Andalucia and North Africa.

🚹 182 C1 ✉ Off place Ben Youssef ⏲ Daily 9–7 💰 Moderate, joint ticket with Dar Menebhi and Ali ben Youssef Medersa (P54)

## 8 Musée de Marrakech (Marrakech Museum)

This large, late 19th-century palace built by Menebhi, defence minister during the reign of Moulay Abdelaziz, is a perfect example of the Arab-Moorish style. The building was used as a school for many years, until it was restored in the late 1990s by the collector Omar

**Wherever you are in Marrakech you can see the minaret of Koutoubia Mosque**

Only the vast spaces within the walls today suggest the former grandeur of Palais el-Badi

Benjelloun and it's now a gallery for contemporary art and a space for exhibitions from private collections of Islamic and Moroccan art. Happy with its success, the Omar Benjelloun Foundation is now funding other restoration projects in the medina.

**182 C1 Place Ben Youssef (024) 39 09 11; www.museedemarrakech.ma Daily 9–7 Moderate, joint ticket with Ben Youssef Medersa (▶ 54) and Koubba Ba'adiym**

## 9 Tombeaux Saadiens

The Saadian kings were buried in these grand tombs, built during the late 16th century by Ahmed el-Mansour. Moulay Ismail built a large wall around them a century later and eventually they were "lost" until the French rediscovered them by accident in 1917. The flower-filled cemetery has several *koubbas*, but the first one, containing the tomb of Ahmed el-Mansour, is the most remarkable. He was buried in its magnificent central hall, surrounded by his sons. El-Mansour also built a magnificent mausoleum for his mother Lalla Messaouda.

**182 C1 Bab Agnaou Daily 8:30–11:45, 2:30–5:45 Inexpensive**

## 10 Palais el-Badi

When this 16th-century palace – "the Incomparable" – was built by the Saadian sultan Ahmed el Mansour, it became the marvel of the Muslim world. Workmen from all over the country took part in its 360-roomed construction; the marble came from Italy, and the walls and ceilings were decorated with mosaics, stucco and gold leaf from Sudan. A hundred years later, it took Moulay Ismail (▶ 128) ten years to strip the place of its splendour in order to build Meknes. Nonetheless, the *pisé* walls, vast pools, sunken gardens and summer pavilions are still impressive. The palace comes to life again in September, when it is the main venue for the international film festival.

**182 C1 Bab Berrima, near place des Ferblantiers Daily 8:30–noon, 2:30–6 Inexpensive**

## 11 Palais de la Bahia and museum

This royal palace, whose name means "the Brilliance", was built in the late 19th century by the vizier Bou Ahmed, a slave rose up in the world. He is said to have lived here with his four wives and 24 concubines.

Compared with the exquisite style of the nearby Tombeaux Saadiens (▶ 62) and the Palais el-Badi (▶ 62), some of the decoration may appear vulgar and over the top. The guided tour takes in vast reception rooms with sculpted ceilings, the harem and a garden planted with fruit trees, jasmine and date palms.

**182 C1 Rue Bab Rhemat, off rue Riad el Zitoun el Djedid (024) 38 95 64**

**⊙ Daily 8:30–11:30, 3–5:45 💷 Inexpensive plus tip for obligatory tour guide**

## 🔟 Maison Tiskiwin

The Dutch art historian Bert Flint opened his beautiful townhouse to show off his marvellous collection of Moroccan crafts and textiles, which he has lovingly gathered since the 1950s. The permanent exhibition takes visitors on a journey from Marrakech to Timbuctu, as Flint is convinced that it is the only way to understand the culture and heritage of Marrakech. The detailed basketwork, textiles, woodwork, carpets and exotic jewellery are arranged by the area or tribe you pass through on the journey.

**➕ 182 C1 ✉ 8 rue de la Bahia, just off Riad Zitoun Djedid ☎ (024) 38 91 92 ⊙ Daily 9:30–12:30, 3:30–5:30 (knock for entry) 💷 Inexpensive**

## 🔟 Dar Si Said Museum

The palace of Dar Si Said (➤ below), a smaller version of Palais de la Bahia, was also built by the vizier Bou Ahmed, but this time for his brother. Today it houses the Museum of Moroccan Arts, with a particularly good collection of Berber jewellery, carpets, woodwork taken from the kasbahs and a marble basin from the Ben Youssef Medersa (➤ 54–55).

**View from *riad* to the museum rooms of Dar Si Said**

**➕ 182 C1 ✉ Off Riad Zitoun Djedid near Maison Tiskiwin ☎ (024) 38 95 64 ⊙ Wed–Mon 9–noon, 3–6 💷 Moderate**

## 🔟 Guéliz

Guéliz is the heart of the modern town (Ville Nouvelle) of Marrakech. The main avenue Mohammed V connects Guéliz with the medina and is lined with airline offices, café-terraces, restaurants and the city's trendiest shops. Just off the avenue on avenue des Nations Unies is the new Marché Central, a good food market. The side streets, particularly around rue de la Liberté have great Western-style shops and some of the funkiest restaurants in town.

The whole quarter also has some stunning art deco architecture to admire as you wander around, look out for the small villas and the Eglise des Martyrs on rue de l'Imam, a 1930s catholic church built by the French. South of Guéliz, Hivernage was built as a sunny garden suburb. Many resort-style hotels and sumptuous villas are here, and it makes for a pleasant afternoon walk with a stop at one of the many café-terraces for refreshments. Morocco's famous architect Charles Boccara built the new Théâtre Royal on the Avenue de France, where occasional performances take place.

**➕ 182 C1 ✉ Tourist office: corner of avenue Mohammed V and place Abd el Moumen ben Ali ☎ (024) 43 61 31**

# Where to... Stay

## Prices

Expect to pay for a double room per night, including breakfast and taxes
£ under 600dh     ££ 600–1,600dh     £££ over 1,600dh

Marrakech has a vast range of hotels, from the luxurious Jnane Tamsna to the fleapits popular with hippies in the 1970s. Guéliz has mid-range hotels, while package tourists head for hotels with swimming pools in Hivernage. The ideal holiday would be a combination of an authentic *riad* in the medina, followed by a more luxurious hotel in the Palmeraie.

## Dar Sara £

One of the simpler *riad* B&Bs. Dar Sara's six rooms have whitewashed walls, bright blue shutters, and are simply decorated with locally made furniture and rugs. There are plenty of corners to relax with a book.

🚩 182 C1 ⊠ 120 derb Arset Aouzal, Bab Dakkala, medina ☎ (044) 42 64 63; www.villanovo.com/Dar-Sara

## Gallia £

This wonderful little *riad* hotel in two houses has been run by the same French family since 1929. It's in a quiet alley near place Djemaa el-Fna, and has a rooftop terrace. The rooms are simple but spotless, and breakfast is served in a beautiful courtyard with a fountain, birdsong and tortoises. Book in advance.

🚩 182 C1 ⊠ 30 rue de la Recette ☎ (024) 44 59 13; www.ilove-marrakech.com/hotelgallia

## Hotel La Mamounia £££

This grand old hotel was once the haunt of celebrities, and has the air of an elegant, sumptuous palace. The hotel is closed for restoration but will reopen to visitors summer 2009.

🚩 182 C1 ⊠ Avenue Bab Jdid, just outside the medina ☎ (024) 38 86 00; www.mamounia.com

## Hôtel du Trésor £

This is a wonderful and charming budget option whose Italian owner has revamped a 1950s *riad* hotel with humour and style. He kept the tiles in the rooms and the traditional courtyard with plunge pool and orange tree tiles, while adding funky art objects and interesting furniture finds from junk markets and auctions. The quiet rooms are set around the courtyard.

🚩 182 C1 ⊠ 77 Sidi Bouloukat, off Riad Zitoun el Qedim ☎ (024) 37 51 13; www.hotel-du-tresor.com

## Jnane Tamsna £££

The Jnane Tamsna, a creation of Senegalese-Parisian designer Meryanne Loum-Martin, comprises four houses with their own pool, with 17 ultra-stylish and luxurious bedrooms, set in a perfumed garden, designed by her husband Gary Martin, and a palm grove. Its seclusion and relaxed atmosphere, combined with friendly and efficient service make it a favourite with A-list celebrities, but everyone is made to feel at home. This is the perfect antidote to the hustle and bustle of the city's thriving medina, with its choice of swimming pools, many gorgeous dining areas, aromatherapy and yoga sessions, healthy food from its own organic garden, and clay tennis courts. It is the perfect place to relax.

🚩 182 C1 ⊠ Douar Abiad, La Palmeraie ☎ (024) 32 94 23; www.jnanetamsna.com

## Riad Farnatchi £££

This exotic, sumptuous "boutique hotel" has just five huge suites. Manageress Lynn adores the place claiming that it is her job to meet the wildest dreams of her guests, and from the guestbook it seems she often succeeds. Three *riads* were converted into one, so there are plenty of places to relax, as well as a small swimming pool, all this in the heart of the medina.

**182 C1** ⊠ 2 derb el Farnatchi, Kaat Benahid, medina ☎ (024) 38 49 10; www.riadfarnatchi.com

## Riad Tarabel £££

A small, friendly *riad* with seven rooms. One of the more recent arrivals on the scene, the Tarabel is in a quiet part of the medina with easy access to the chic shopping area of Mouassine and Dar el Bacha. The house with elegant and airy rooms around a simple green courtyard, is beautifully decorated in muted colours. Gorgeous local furniture is mixed with family heirlooms,

including huge 17th-century French paintings and mirrors. Breakfast is served on the grand rooftop terrace.

**182 C1** ⊠ 8 derb Sraghna, Dar el Bacha ☎ (024) 39 17 06; www.riadtarabel.com

## Riad Yima ££

Small boutique hotel owned and designed by London-based Moroccan pop-art artist, Hassan Hajjaj. Accommodation comprises charmingly colourful rooms filled with his art and furniture, and the service is very friendly. His work is on sale at the hotel's small boutique.

**182 C1** ⊠ 52 derb Arjane, Rahba Qedima ☎ (024) 39 19 87; www.riadyima.com; www.hassanhajjaj.com

## Riyad Edward ££–£££

This unusually large *riad* which once belonged to members of the royal family, has a great variety of rooms around a tiled courtyard with a swimming pool and a 100-year old cypress tree. Unlike many other minimal boutique hotels in town, the house was restored keeping

the original decorations intact. All the rooms are different, filled with pictures, books and interesting finds from the local junk market. The atmosphere is very relaxed with plenty of secluded corners to sunbathe, read or hang out. Very friendly staff and helpful owners are on hand.

**182 C1** ⊠ 10 derb Marestane, Zaouia Abbassia, Bab Taghzoute ☎ (024) 38 97 97 / (061) 25 23 28; www.riyadedward.com

## Sherazade £

You will have to book well in advance if you want to stay in this delightful budget hotel in a renovated *riad* near Djemaa el-Fna. The comfortable, and spotless rooms open onto two relaxing courtyards. The roof terrace, where breakfast is served, has great views over the medina. Rooms on the first floor are light and quiet.

**182 C1** ⊠ 3 derb Jemaa, riad Zitoun el-Kedim ☎ (024) 42 93 05; www.hotelsherazade.com

## Tchaïkana ££

Superb *riad* behind the Musée de Marrakech with five rooms around a beautiful and atmospheric courtyard. The Belgian owners make their guests feel really at home, and many of their clients return year after year. The rooms are spacious and tastefully decorated with local furniture and objects from their travels.

**182 C1** ⊠ 25 derb el Ferrane, Azbest ☎ (024) 28 45 87; www.tchaikana.com

## Tlaata wa Sitteen £

Delightful budget hotel in two connected *riads* with an authentic feel. The rooms are simple but clean and stylishly furnished with local finds. Communal bathrooms are clad in shiny *tadelakt*. It is run by young Moroccans who can prepare a good couscous or tagine for dinner, which you can eat on the roof or in the courtyard.

**182 C1** ⊠ 63 derb el Ferrane, Riad Laarous ☎ (024) 38 30 26; www.tlaatawa-sitteen.com

# Where to...
## Eat and Drink

### Prices

Expect to pay for a three-course meal per person, excluding drinks but including taxes and service

£ under 200dh    ££ 200–400dh    £££ over 400dh

Marrakech has a wide range of restaurants and bars but booking is essential in all top restaurants. From 6pm, the square of Djemaa el-Fna turns into a huge open-air restaurant and great spectacle and perfect for people-watching over a snack or casual dinner.

### Al-Fassia ££

Run by an all-female staff, this is a popular Moroccan restaurant. The lunchtime special menu is a perfect introduction to the delights of Moroccan cuisine. At night the menu is à la carte, including great

tagines, *pastilla* stuffed with pigeon, and roast lamb. Food is served in ornate Moroccan salons or in a small garden in summer.

🖂 **Résidence Taïeb, 55 boulevard Zerktouni, Guéliz** 🕾 **(024) 43 40 60** ⏱ **Daily noon–2:30, 7:30–11pm**

### Café des Épices £

Overlooking the spice market, this laid-back café is the perfect place to stop in the hectic souks. Have a fresh juice, mint tea or daily special, all at reasonable prices compared, while watching the city from one of the terraces. No alcohol.

🖂 **Place Rahba Qedima, medina** 🕾 **(024) 39 17 70; www.cafedesepices.net** ⏱ **Daily 8am–10pm**

### Café du Livre £

Delightful English language bookstore with a selection of second-hand books, and new books on Morocco, with a small but delicious menu of soups, salads, juices and daily specials to be consumed while you browse.

🖂 **44 rue Tareq ibn Ziad, Guéliz** 🕾 **(024) 43 21 49;** **www.cafedulivre.com** ⏱ **Daily 9:30–9pm**

### Catanzaro ££

This popular, French-run Italian restaurant specialises in grilled meats and pizzas baked in a wood oven, but is also renowned for its pasta. The décor is kitsch, but swift service and great food mean it's never empty.

🖂 **66 rue Tarik ibn Ziyad** 🕾 **(024) 43 37 31** ⏱ **Mon–Sat lunch and dinner**

### Chez Chegrouni £

Chez Chegrouni is an institution with cheap but well-prepared Moroccan

staples such as couscous, and excellent tagines. No alcohol.

🖂 **Djemaa el-Fna** 🕾 **(065) 47 46 15** ⏱ **Daily 7am–11pm**

### Le Comptoir £££

This dark, chic Oriental den is one of the hotspots to eat in town. The waitresses sashay tasty Moroccan and Mediterranean dishes through the crowds, while belly dancers perform. Upstairs is a cool bar area and there is a lounge bar in the garden.

🖂 **Avenue Ech Chouhada, Hivernage** 🕾 **(024) 43 77 02** ⏱ **Daily 4pm–1am, 2pm on weekends**

### Dar Marjana (House of Coral) £££

One of the original *riad* restaurants that gives diners an entire evening's programme in sumptuous surroundings. The set price includes drinks in the courtyard, a dinner of several courses and live music.

🖂 **15 derb Sidi Ali Taïr, Bab Doukkala** 🕾 **(024) 38 51 10; www.dar-marjana.com** ⏱ **Wed–Mon dinner; by reservation only**

## Grand Café de la Poste ££

Popular café-restaurant that looks like a café from colonial times with a huge terrace and high ceilings, but it is in fact one of the more recent arrivals on the Marrakchi scene. A great place for a drink, a relaxed lunch or a more formal dinner of good Mediterranean food with a few Moroccan classics.

⊠ just off avenue Mohammed V, behind the post office ☎ (024) 43 30 38 ◉ Daily 8–1am

## Le Foundouk ££–£££

This trendy restaurant is decorated with touches of bright colour, and has a gorgeous terrace with great views. The lunch menu offers light dishes such as salads, quiches, pastas and desserts, while the evening menu is more substantial.

⊠ Souk Hal Fassi, Kaat Bennahid, medina ☎ (024) 37 81 90; www.foundouk.com ◉ Tue–Sun noon–4, 7–midnight

## Kechmara ££

Very popular and trendy restaurant in the heart of Guéliz with a contemporary décor and a great

rooftop terrace. Good-looking waiters, well-chosen mix of music and excellent Moroccan-Mediterranean dishes make this a great spot for a relaxed meal while people-watching.

⊠ 3 rue de la Liberté, Guéliz ☎ (024) 43 40 60 ◉ Daily, lunch and dinner

## Le Kosybar ££–£££

Three venues in one, this bar-restaurant is a bit of a coup in the more traditional neighbourhood of the Mellah (Jewish Quarter). It has fast become the place to meet for a sundowner or to have drinks late at night. With a large selection of imported and local liquors and wines, and a cigar humidor, it has a quiet piano bar on the ground floor, a Moroccan salon on the first and a wonderful rooftop terrace. The food ranges from couscous to sushi, but is not really why you come here.

⊠ 47 place des Ferblantiers, medina ☎ (024) 38 03 24; http://kozibar.tripod.com ◉ Daily noon–1am

## Le Marrakchi ££

Here you'll find great views over the square, a glam atmosphere and a good introduction to Moroccan cuisine with a well-prepared dishes.

⊠ Corner Djemaa el-Fna and rue des Banques, medina ☎ (024) 44 33 77 ◉ Daily 11:30am–11pm

## Les Terrasses de l'Alhambra £–££

A welcome addition to the mostly mediocre restaurants in the square, this friendly French-run café-restaurant is the perfect place to relax after a hectic shopping spree in the busy souks. Delicious fresh juices, home-made ice-creams, fresh salads, pastas and pizzas are all served on the little terrace or in the cool interior.

⊠ Place Djemaa el-Fna, medina ☎ (024) 42 75 70 ◉ Daily 8am–11pm

## Terrasse des Épices £–££

From the same Moroccan/French owners as Café des Épices, this is a cool new lounge bar-restaurant

located on a rooftop in the medina. The style is simple but contemporary Moroccan chic, with a terrace under the stars for the night and shaded booths for the day. There is Wi-Fi, great music, an art gallery and an excellent menu with delicious Moroccan-Mediterranean dishes and desserts.

⊠ 15 Souk Cherifia, Dar El Bacha ☎ (024) 37 59 04; www.terrassedesepices.com ◉ Daily, lunch and dinner

## Villa Rosa £££

The city's hippest restaurateur Nourdine Fakir, who also owns Nikki Beach (▶ 70) has hit it right with his latest venture. This über-trendy bar-restaurant has dark red velvet interior is over the top but elegant. On the menu are contemporary French dishes, which are well prepared and attractively presented. The bar area is the place to meet of the moment. Book ahead.

⊠ 64 avenue Hassan II, Guéliz ☎ (024) 44 96 35 ◉ Daily dinner only

# Where to...
## Shop

With so many foreigners buying *riads* in the medina, the shops in Marrakech are going more upmarket. If you want more than just a stroll in the souks, you can book a personal shopper for a day or half-day: Laetitia Trouillet (tel: 074 217228; www.lalla. fr), a designer who speaks English and French, knows the city inside out, and can even bargain for you. She sells great handbags in her funky shop **From Marrakech with Love** in Souk Cherifia, Dar el Bacha, under the Terrasse des Épices (▶ 67).

The main drag in the medina, **Souk Smarine** has antiques dealers at the entrance, but most shops cater for tourists. **Au Fil D'Or** (10 rue Souk as-Smarrine; tel: (024) 44 59 19) is curtained off to hide the high-

quality kaftans and hand-stitched shirts in beautiful hues. Further down the street at No 82 is **Chez Brahim** with the best quality *babouches* (slippers) in the souk. The **Rahba Qedima**, an open square lined with spice and apothecary vendors, is the place for love potions and traditional toiletries, particularly at **Herboriste Avicenne** at No 172–174, which claims to have a cure for every ailment. Just off the square is **La Criée Berbère** (where slaves were sold until 1912), now a carpet market with auctions late in the afternoon. Back on the main street is the **Souk des Babouches**, with slippers in all shapes and sizes. In a narrow alley is the **Souk el Haddadine**, where blacksmiths produce inventive work. The **Souk des Teinturiers** (Wool Dyers) has roughly spun wool, and

one of the last fez makers, as well as copper and junk shops.

The Mouassine Fountain marks the heart of the **Mouassine** quarter, for those who want something slightly different. **La Maison du Kaftan** (65 rue Sidi el Yamani; tel: (024) 44 10 51) has an array of traditional and fashionable kaftans and *djellabas*. Around the corner is funky **Kulchi** (1 rue Ksour, Bab el-Ksour, Mouassine; tel: (024) 42 91 77) with a quirky collection of boho chic. **Darkoum Gallery** (8, Leksour derb Sania, Mouassine; tel: (024) 44 09 31) offers everything to give a home that *"riad* feeling", with an incredible selection of antiques. A world apart is **Ministerio del Gusto** (22 derb Azzouz, Mouassine; tel: (024) 42 64 55) where Italian designers Bizzari and Lippimi give their creativity a free run. Back at the square of Bab Ftouh, to the right is a *funduq* (merchants' inn) with, on the first floor, **Belhadj** (22–33 Fundup Ourzazi; tel: (024) 44 12 58), a tiny shop stuffed with good-quality Berber jewellery and

reliable semi-precious stones at reasonable prices. Across the square is the sumptuous **Akbar Delights** (45 place Bab Fteuh; tel: (071) 66 13 07) boutique with Moroccan shirts and dresses embroidered in Kashmir. Some of the five-star *riads* have great little boutiques too, with some of the most fashionable clothes and accessories available at the shop of **Riad Noir d'Ivoire** (33 derb Djedid, Bab Doukkala; tel: 024 380975).

For great homewares, go to **Mustapha Blaoui** (142–144 Bab Doukkala; tel: (024) 38 52 40), a huge warehouse selling furniture, lanterns, pottery and other crafts.

The southern part of the medina, near the **Mellah** is less touristy. At its centre is **place des Ferblantiers** with the gold and silver souk, as well as the haberdashery souk. In her small, shop **Aya's** (11 bis derb Jdid Bab Mellah, medina; tel: (024) 38 34 28 / (061) 46 29 16) the friendly Nawal sells handmade and made-to-order kaftans, shirts and *djellabas*, tailored to fit Europeans.

## VILLE NOUVELLE

Some say the best antiques are found in Guéliz, and **Al Badii** (54 boulevard Moulay Rachid; tel: (024) 43 16 93) is a good place to start. The shop sells high-quality, authentic pictures, furniture, jewellery, and an excellent selection of tribal carpets in the basement. This is the shop where visiting VIPs are brought.

In **l'Orientaliste** (11 and 15 rue de la Liberté; tel: (024) 43 40 74), Madame Amzallag sells a large selection of old embroideries, textiles, fine craftwork and quirky antiques, pictures and old books.

**Darkoum** (5 rue de la Liberté; tel: (024) 44 67 39) is a stunning art gallery/shop where owners of private *riads* buy their rich furnishings sourced from all over the world.

At **Intensité Nomade** (139 boulevard Mohammed V; tel: (024) 43 13 33) you'll find a good selection of leather goods on the ground floor, but the basement is worth checking out for elaborately embroidered kaftans and *djellabas*. The shop also sells amazing creations by the young Moroccan fashion designer Noureddine Amir – sculptural Moroccan-influenced clothes in fine woven linen, cotton, wool and silk.

The best place in town for shoes is **Atika** (35 rue de la Liberté; tel: (024) 43 64 09) with a great selection of well-made, reasonably priced Western-style shoes for men and women. Their other store, **Tesorucio**, on the corner of rue de la Liberté and boulevard Mohammed V, sells great kids' shoes. **Scenes de Lin** (70 rue de la Liberté; tel: (024) 43 61 08) offers locally produced, embroidered linens as well as exquisite Moroccan homeware, and candles by Amira.

## FOOD

One of the best places to stock up for a picnic is the **Marché Municipale** on rue Ibn Toumert, off avenue Mohammed V in Guéliz, or the market on the east side of Djemaa el-Fna. The supermarket **Aswak Assalam** (avenue du 11 Janvier at Bab Doukkala has everything, while the largest selection of imported foods is available from the **Marjane** megastore on the Casablanca road, 4km (2.5 miles) out of town.

**Patisserie Belkabir** at 25 rue el Houria (corner of rue Tarik ibn Ziad) sells some of the best Moroccan sweets in town. Hakima Alami at **Al-Jawda** (11 rue de la Liberté) has been making traditional cakes for the last 15 years – try the delicious gazelle horns and cream *feqqas*. **Amandine** (177 rue Mohammed el Beqal, Guéliz; tel: (024) 44 96 12) is the best place for French pastries, and also serves a great breakfast, while **Oliveri** (9 boulevard El Mansour Eddahbi; tel: (024) 44 89 13) has the best ice cream in town.

## BOOKS/NEWSPAPERS

The **Café des Livres** (44 rue Tareq ibn Ziad, Guéliz, ▶ 66) is an English-language bookshop with a café-restaurant. There is an excellent selection of second-hand books, as well as new and old books on Morocco and North Africa.

The **American Bookstore** (3 Impasse du Moulin, off boulevard Mohammed Zerktouni) stocks a good selection of English-language books, as does the kiosk in front of the Hotel La Mamounia (▶ 64). At the ACR **Librairie d'Art** in the Résidence Tayeb (55 boulevard Mohammed Zerktouni; tel: (024) 44 67 92) you'll find glossy illustrated books on Morocco, mainly in French.

The largest selection of foreign newspapers is available from the newsagents outside the **Tourist Office** on avenue Mohammed V in Guéliz.

## ENSEMBLE ARTISANAL

The government shop on avenue Mohammed V (tel: (024) 38 67 58; open daily, 8:30–7:30) has workshops where crafts are made and sold. Prices are fixed and reasonable.

# Where to...
# Be Entertained

## NIGHTLIFE

Most entertainment in the medina revolves around **Djemaa el-Fna** (▶ 50–51). Marrakech is becoming even livelier at night, with an increasing number of lounge clubs and discos attracting wealthy Moroccans as well as the European jet-set. The coolest place to hang out is the **Terraces des Épices** (▶ 67 Souk Cherifia, rue Dar el-Bacha). The most popular nightspot in town is **Pacha** (Complexe Pacha Marrakech, boulevard Mohammed VI; tel: (024) 38 84 05; www.pachamarrakech. com) with two restaurants, several bars and a huge club. **L'Abyssin** (Palais Rhoul, Dar Tounsi, Palmeraie, Route de Fès; tel: (024) 32 85 84; www.palais rhoul.com) is another crowd puller in the summer. Le

**Comptoir** (rue ech-Chouhada, Hivernage; tel: (024) 43 77 02; www. ilove-marrakesh.com/lecomptoir) is popular, with a nightly belly dancing show. The old theatre at the Hotel Saadi was converted into the fashionable nightclub **Teatro** (Hotel Saadi, Avenue el Quadissia, Hivernage; www.teatromarrakech. com), while **Jad Mahal**(10 rue Haroun er Rachid, Hivernage; tel: (024) 43 69 84) has live music. More down to earth is **Montecristo** (20 rue Ibn Aicha, Guéliz; tel: (024) 43 90 31). **Hotel El Andalous** is a tapas bar (Hivernage, tel: (024) 44 82 26).

Marrakech has two casinos, for which you need to dress up a little. The most sumptuous is in the **Hotel La Mamounia** (▶ 64). The other is **Casino de Marrakech** at the Saadi hotel (tel: (024) 44 88 11).

## CINEMA, THEATRE AND MUSIC

**Le Colisée** (boulevard Mohammed Zerktouni, Guéliz; tel: (024) 44 88 93), shows good recent films, mostly uncensored. Other cinemas show Arab or Hindi films. Try also **Cinéma Rif** (Cité Mohamedi, Daoudiate; tel: (024) 30 31 46), an old-style movie palace, or the **Institut Français de Marrakech** (route de la Targa, Jebel Guéliz, tel: (024) 44 69 30). The annual **international film festival** in December attracts movie stars.

## SPORT

The best way to relax is in a *hammam*. **Les Bains de Marrakech** (2 derb Sedra, Bab Agnaou, medina; tel: (024) 38 14 28) provides an upmarket scrub and massages with argan oil. A more traditional *hammam* is **Hammam el Bacha** (20 rue Fatima Zohra, medina).

For a more indulgent *hammam*-massage head for the **Beldi Country Club** (P59) or the **Palais Rhoul &**

Spa in the Palmeraie (tel: (024 32 94 94/95; www.palais-rhoul.com),. For poolside relaxation try the **Beldi Country Club** (▶ 59) or the **Nikki Beach** (circuit de la Palmaraie (063) 51 99 92). Those with children might opt for the waterpark **Oasiria**. **Lake Lalla Takerkoust** near Marrakech is a more natural setting for swimming.

Marrakech has three superb golf courses: **Marrakech Royal Golf Club** (tel: (024) 40 98 28); **Palmeraie Golf Club** (tel: (024) 30 10 10) and **Amelkis Golf Club** (tel: (024) 40 44 14).

Go **horse-riding** at **Les Cavaliers de l'Atlas** (tel: (061) 46 43 27; www. lescavaliersdelatlas.com) and **Club Equestre de la Palmaraie Golf Palace** (tel: (024) 30 10 10).

**Bicycle rental** is available from **Action Sports Loisirs** (flat 4, 1 avenue Yacoub el Mansour, Guéliz; tel: (024) 43 09 31), **D & O** (tel: (024) 42 19 96) and **Hotel Toulousain** (rue Tarek ibn Ziad; tel: (024) 43 00 33; www.geocities. com/hotel_toulousain).

# The Atlantic Coast

# Getting Your Bearings

The Atlantic coast is Morocco's economic and political centre. The 500km (310 miles) from Kenitra to Essaouira alone, including the cities of Rabat and Casablanca, are home to nearly 7 million people, a fifth of the country's population. Less exotic and perhaps less obvious at first as a tourist destination, the coast has more to offer than its beaches: impressive Portuguese fortresses, colonial architecture, good surf, plenty of seafood and some less-visited monuments.

Rabat, the country's charming capital, has a relaxed, provincial air and some great monuments, including a splendid kasbah. Its neighbour and former rival, Salé, is not as well preserved, except for its wonderful white medina. Casablanca, the country's economic capital, prides itself on having the largest port in North Africa and substantial industrial activities, but it also offers stately colonial architecture, busy cafés, relaxed souks, nearby beaches and excellent restaurants. Smaller cities such as Essaouira are even more laid back and have plenty of character. Agadir, the country's most popular beach resort, boasts pleasant year-round temperatures, but is also the least Moroccan of all the coastal towns. For a more authentic beach holiday try nearby Tarhazoute, the lagoon town of Oualidia or, if you are looking for good surfing waves, go to Sidi Kaouki, south of Essaouira, or Dar-Bouazza near Casablanca.

**Azemmour** 6
**El-Jadida** 7

Sidi-Smail

**Oualidia** 8

Cap Beddouza
Khèmis-des-Zememra
N7
Sidi-Bennour

**Safi** 9

N1
Tleta-Sidi-Bouguedra

R204
Chemaïa

Dar-Caïd-Hadji

Moulay-Bouzerktoun
Talmest
Tensift

**Essaouira** 3
Île de Mogador
Tleta-Henchane
Chichaoua
Sidi-Kaouki N1

Imi-n-Tanoute

Tamanar
N8

Pointe Immessouane
Jebel Touchka
3555m Jebel Aoulime

Tamri
Taghazout
**Imouzzer des Ida Outanane** 10

**Agadir** 11
Taroudannt
Souss
Inezgane N10
Biougra

Previous page:
Hassan Mosque in
Casablanca (left);
Royal Guardsman
patrols the entrance
to Mohammed V
Mausoleum (centre);
Rabat's skyline (right)

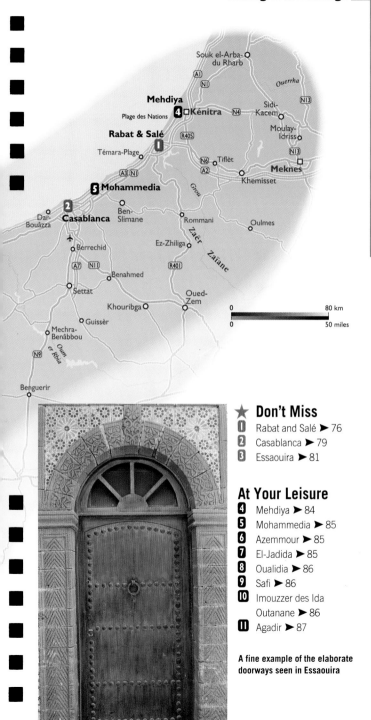

Souk el-Arba-du Rharb

*Ouerrha*

A1
N1

**Mehdiya**

Plage des Nations

**4** Kénitra

N4

Sidi-Kacem

N13

**Rabat & Salé**

R405

Moulay-Idriss

Témara-Plage

N6  Tiflèt

N13

A3  N1

A2  Khemisset

**Meknes**

Grou

**5 Mohammedia**

Dar-Bouâzza

Ben-Slimane

Rommani

Zaër

Oulmes

**Casablanca**

Ez-Zhiliga

Zaïane

Berrechid

A7  N11

Benahmed

R401

Settat

Oued-Zem

Khouribga

Guissèr

Mechra-Benâbbou

Oum er Rbia

N9

Benguerir

| 0 | | 80 km |
| 0 | | 50 miles |

## ★ Don't Miss

**1** Rabat and Salé ► 76
**2** Casablanca ► 79
**3** Essaouira ► 81

## At Your Leisure

**4** Mehdiya ► 84
**5** Mohammedia ► 85
**6** Azemmour ► 85
**7** El-Jadida ► 85
**8** Oualidia ► 86
**9** Safi ► 86
**10** Imouzzer des Ida
Outanane ► 86
**11** Agadir ► 87

**A fine example of the elaborate
doorways seen in Essaouira**

# In Five Days

If you're not quite sure where to begin your travels, this itinerary recommends a practical and enjoyable five days on the Atlantic Coast, taking in some of the best places to see using the Getting Your Bearings map on the previous page. For more information see the main entries.

## Day One

**Morning**
Start in **❶ Rabat** (➤ 76–78) with a pleasant stroll through the medina, including **rue des Consuls**, the **Kasbah des Oudaïas** and the **Oudaïa Museum**. Stop for tea in Café Maure, in the Andalucian gardens, or head to the beach for a delicious lunch at the **Restaurant de la Plage** (➤ 92).

**Afternoon and Evening**
Take a taxi to **Bab er Rouah** and then walk to the **Archaeological Museum**. Continue downtown to the **Hassan Tower**, the **Mausoleum of King Mohammed V** (right) and the **Hassan Mosque** in time for the daily changing of the guard at 5pm. As the sun sets, enjoy an apéritif at the Hotel Balima on avenue Mohammed V, then eat dinner in one of the excellent downtown restaurants such as **Le Petit Beur** (➤ 92).

## Day Two

**Morning**
Take a taxi or bus to **Salé** (➤ 77) and visit the main sights, including the **Souk el Ghezel** and the **Medeusa**. Return by grand taxi for lunch at the atmospheric **Le Grand Comptoir** (➤ 92).

**Afternoon and Evening**
Visit the picturesque Roman ruins and Muslim cemetery of **Chellah**. If you're driving, head to Témara beach (15km/ 9 miles south of Rabat) for a swim before continuing to Casablanca, otherwise take the train to Casablanca for dinner at **Le Port de Pêche** (➤ 90).

# Day Three

### Morning
Start your visit to **2 Casablanca** (➤ 79–80) with a tour of the **Mosque of Hassan II** (right), then return to the centre to explore the magnificent colonial architecture. Have lunch in a restaurant in the Marché Central.

### Afternoon and Evening
Take a taxi to the **Quartier Habous** for some shopping, a pastry from **Bennis** (➤ 93) and a mint tea in the café on the square. Head for the old medina for a more Moroccan shopping experience before dinner at **Sqala** (➤ 91).

# Day Four

### Morning
Start early for the drive to Essaouira, and in just over an hour you'll reach the Portuguese town of **7 El-Jadida** (➤ 85–86). After refreshments on place Mohammed ben Allah, continue for 80km (50 miles) to **8 Oualidia** (➤ 86) for lunch at a seafood restaurant on the beach.

### Afternoon and Evening
Have a swim in the lagoon if the tide is in, before continuing for another 65km (40 miles) to the pottery town of **9 Safi** (➤ 86). Follow the coast road through windswept villages to **4 Essaouira** (➤ 81–83), and stroll across the main square to **Le Chalet de la Plage** for dinner (➤ 91).

# Day Five

### Morning
Have breakfast in place Moulay Hassan before walking along the old walls to **Skala de la Ville**, the **woodworkers' souk**, the small **Musée Sidi Mohammed ben Allah** and through the old *mellah* (Jewish quarter). Return through the souks to the fish stalls outside the port where you can eat grilled fish fresh from the boats.

### Afternoon and Evening
Visit the galleries on avenue Mohammed Zerktouni, and go for a long walk along the beach, returning around dusk to see the fishing boats. End with dinner at **Elizir** (➤ 91).

# ❶ Rabat and Salé

Rabat is Morocco's second imperial city. With its tree-lined avenues, splendid colonial architecture, public gardens and peaceful residential areas, the city exudes an air of elegance and good living. Less dramatic than Fez, less exotic than Marrakech and less turbulent than Casablanca, it is calm and airy, with a provincial feel.

The Phoenicians, like the Romans and their successors, were attracted by Rabat's safe harbour in the estuary of the Bou Regreg. The Almohad Sultan Yacoub el Mansour made the city his capital in 1184, ringing it with 6km (4 miles) of walls with five monumental gates, expanding the kasbah and building the colossal mosque of Hassan, its minaret even taller than the grand Giralda Mosque in Seville, Spain.

Soon after his death, however, the city he called "Rabat el-Fath" (Rabat of Victory) went into decline until the 17th century and the arrival of the *mariscos* (Moors expelled from Spain). Both Rabat and neighbouring Salé then flourished from a new source of income: piracy (➤ 28–29).

## The New Town

In 1912 the French made Rabat their colonial capital. They left the medina alone, but built a **Ville Nouvelle** (new town) of broad avenues and residential quarters. This area's main artery is palm-lined **avenue Mohammed V**, between

**The Hassan Tower was to be as grand as the Koutoubia minaret in Marrakech, but it was never finished**

the royal palace and the medina, with shops, a theatre and cinemas. One of the chief sights is the surviving Almohad wall and gates running parallel to the avenue. Near the splendid Almohad gate of **Bab el Rouah** (Gate of the Winds), the **Archaeological Museum** houses excellent Roman bronzes from Volubilis (► 126–127) and Chellah. These include the fine figure of the attacking *Dog of Volubilis* and superb busts of Cato the Younger of Uttica – an orator who died for the freedom of the republic rather than live under Roman rule – and of the Berber king Juba II.

The main thoroughfare then becomes avenue Yacoub el-Mansour, leading to the romantic ruins of **Chellah**. This long-deserted Roman city became a burial ground during the 13th century under the Merenids. The entrance to the walled site is a stunning Merenid gateway flanked by two towers. The Roman ruins are to the left, while a path to the right leads to Muslim tombs and mosques in an overgrown garden of fig trees, olive branches and wild flowers.

The 17th-century Spanish immigrants responsible for the **medina** also built the **Andalucian wall** that runs along avenue Hassan II. The heart of the medina is **rue des Consuls**, lined with good crafts shops and running into **Souk el Ghezel**, the wool souk and former slave market. The **Kasbah des Oudaïas**, named after the tribe installed here by the Alaouites, was built in the 10th century.

## The Medina and the Kasbah

The entrance to the kasbah is through the splendid and well-proportioned **Porte des Oudaïas**, built in the late 12th century by Yacoub el-Mansour. In the middle of this whitewashed village, in the 17th-century palace built by Moulay Ismail (► 128), is the **Oudaïa Museum**, containing a wonderful collection of Moroccan jewellery. Equally delightful is the palace's **Andalucian garden**, filled with lemon and cypress trees, date palms and flowers.

A field of columns and an unfinished minaret is all that remains of Yacoub el-Mansour's enormous **Mosque of Hassan**. The mosque was never finished and later rulers used the stones to restore the kasbah. The 44m (144-foot) minaret, the **Tour Hassan**, has different decoration on each face. Mohammed V chose this spectacular background for his traditional **mausoleum**, where he is buried with his two sons, including the late King Hassan II.

## Salé

The estuary of the Bou Regreg river is undergoing major redevelopment, with a smart new marina and an artificial island proposed. Salé, across the river has less to show for its illustrious past, but its whitewashed medina is much more picturesque and characterful than Rabat's, and makes for a pleasant stroll. From **Bab Mrissa** walk to the **Souk el Ghezel**, the wool souk, and then towards the **Grande Mosquée**. Nearby is a beautiful 14th-century **Merenid Medersa** with superb views from the terrace over Salé and the river, and the *marabout* (tomb) of Sidi Abdallah ben Hassoun, the city's patron saint of travellers. Further on, the northwest tower houses a ceramics museum.

The entrance
gate to the
Grand Mosque
Salé

## TAKING A BREAK

The tranquil Moorish **Café Maure** (➤ 91) in the Andalucian
garden of Kasbah des Oudaïas is an enchanting place to rest

### Rabat

⊞ 183 D3
✉ Tourist Office: corner rue
Oued el Makhazine and rue Zalaka,
Agdal; ☎ (037) 674013; www.
visitrabat.com 🚌 Buses from
Casablanca, Tangier, Marrakech,
Fez and Meknès 🚆 Trains from
Tangier, Fez, Meknès, Casablanca
and Marrakech

### Archaeological Museum

✉ 23 rue el Brihi, near the es Souna
Grand Mosque
🕐 Wed–Mon 9–4:30
✋ Inexpensive

### Chellah

✉ 2km (1 mile) from centre
🕐 Daily 9–5:30
✋ Inexpensive

### Oudaïa Museum

☎ (037) 73 15 37 🕐 Wed–Mon 9–5
✋ Inexpensive

### Mohammed V Mausoleum

✉ Boulevard de la Tour Hassan
🕐 Sunrise–sunset; dress modestly
✋ Free

### Salé

⊞ 183 D4
✉ 3km (2 miles) from central Rabat
🚌 Bus 12, 13, 14, 16 or 34 (Dh4
from place Mellilla in Rabat) or
*grand taxi* from seaside end of Ave
Hassan II

### Merenid Medersa

✉ Next to the Grande Mosqueé
🕐 Daily, 9–noon, 2:30–6
✋ Inexpensive

## RABAT AND SALÉ: INSIDE INFO

**Top tips** The **view over the river from Café Maure** in the grounds of Kasbah des
Oudaïas is particularly beautiful at sunset.
■ Salé is **accessible by bus or *grand taxi*.** Otherwise, it's about 30 minutes' walk
across Pont Moulay Hassan.

# ② Casablanca

More than most Moroccan cities, Casablanca (Dar el-Beida) is modern. Most visitors inevitably pass through "Casa", as Moroccans affectionately call the city, and it is a delightful place to spend a day or two. The souks are more hassle-free than most, it is easy to get around and there is plenty of art deco and art nouveau architecture along the broad boulevards. But don't come looking for the Casablanca of Humphrey Bogart and Ingrid Bergman because the film was shot entirely in Hollywood.

**The floodlit Hassan II Mosque rises from the city like a beacon in the night**

North Africa's largest port, Casablanca was built by the French and modelled on Marseille. Casa represents Morocco on the move, and the city looks and feels very European. Women are rarely veiled and beach clubs are often throbbing with a moneyed and cosmopolitan crowd.

The most obvious and only "real" monument in town is the gigantic **Mosque of Hassan II**, finished in 1993. King Hassan II wanted to build a mosque on the water, so the French architect Michel Pinseau designed the vast complex on reclaimed land. Its 200m (650-foot) minaret, a beacon of Islam, is the tallest in the country. Up to 25,000 worshippers can pray inside, some kneeling on a glass floor that reveals the ocean below. The courtyard can hold another 80,000. More than 2,500 of Morocco's master craftsmen worked day and night on the mosque's decoration, and the enormous cost of the building, an estimated £500 million, was financed purely by donations.

Most of the grand colonial buildings, built in a French interpretation of Moorish style, are grouped around **place Mohammed V** (formerly place des Nations Unies) and **boulevard Mohammed V**, where the **Marché Central** offers the country's best selection of fruit and vegetables. At the end of boulevard Mohammed V is the current **place des Nations Unies** (confusingly, the former place Mohammed V) with café-terraces and the entrance to the **old medina** and souks. The palm-lined boulevard Félix Houphouet leads to **the port**. The French-built new medina, **Quartier Habous**, is opposite the royal palace.

### TAKING A BREAK

**Oliveri** (132 avenue Hassan II) is the most popular ice-cream parlour in town. Café terraces on **place des Nations Unies** are buzzing in the afternoon, while several reasonably priced restaurants in the **Marché Central** sell fresh fish snacks.

*The entrance gates of Hassan II Mosque surpass those of any mosque in Morocco*

🔛 182 C3
✉ Tourist Office: 98 boulevard Mohammed V  ☎ (022) 22 15 24; www.visitcasablanca.ma

**Ain Diab Beach**
✉ 3.5km (2 miles) west of the centre  🚌 9

**Hassan II Mosque**
✉ Boulevard de la Corniche
☎ (020) 22 25 63
⊕ Obligatory guided tours
Sat–Thu 9, 10, 11, 2  💰 Expensive

**Quartier Habous**
✉ 1km (0.5 mile) southwest of town
🚌 81

### CASABLANCA: INSIDE INFO

**Top tips** Parc de la Ligue Arabe is a wonderful place to relax among the palm trees and exotic flowers.
■ Locals hang out in the beach clubs on **Ain Diab** beach.

**One to miss** Avoid going to the old medina at night; it can be dangerous.

# ③ Essaouira

This charming blue-and-white city is where Arab, Berber, African and European influences merge happily. It is a place out of time, although here too foreigners are buying *riads* in the old medina. It is still relaxed, however, with the only disturbance being the frantic bustle of the fishing harbour. Essaouira's beauty has long attracted and inspired writers and artists. Add to this the *alizé*, a forceful wind blowing from the Atlantic (Sawiris, the city's inhabitants, say that it blows away the bad spirits and also crowds of tourists) but it is hard not to fall in love with Essaouira.

**Skala de la Ville viewed through a circular peephole on the port**

Formerly called Mogador, Essaouira looks older than it is. Although originally settled by Phoenicians, today's city was built in 1764 by Sultan Mohammed ben Abdallah. Designed by French architect Théodore Cornut, it was called "es Saouira", the "well drawn".

## Out to Sea

The liveliest part of town is the **fishing harbour**, especially in the late afternoon when the boats come back. The fishermen's

wives have the first pick; the rest of the incredible variety of fish is then sold by auction – a colourful spectacle. On the south side of the port is a shipyard where boats are constructed in the traditional way.

**Essaouria's great beaches are popular with surfers**

## A Dramatic Setting

The port is reached from the city through the 18th-century **Porte de la Marine**, whose stairway leading up the walls of the **Skala du Port** offers great views over the town. The American actor and director Orson Welles filmed several scenes of his acclaimed *Othello* (1952) here. The **Skala de la Ville** is an impressive sea bastion with a collection of European bronze cannons on the top, and wide views of the ocean crashing into the rocks. Underneath are the workshops of the carpenters who work mainly with *thuja* (thuya) wood from evergreen coniferous trees. Near by, the small **Musée Sidi Mohammed ben Abdallah** has pictures of old Essaouira and displays of marquetry and costumes.

## Lovingly Crafted

The souks, with some excellent crafts (► 93), spread from here to the *mellah* (Jewish quarter). The town always had a large Jewish community who acted as intermediaries between the Muslim sultan and foreign powers. Only a few members of the community still live here, a far cry from 8,500 in the 19th century.

### THE GNAOUA

Traditionally, the Gnaoua people, descendants of slaves from Mali and Senegal, were healers and musicians, whose music was reputed to exorcise evil spirits. On religious festivals they hold a *lila*, when their drums, castanets and flutes send participants into a trance. Nowadays you are more likely to see them performing on café-terraces, with strings of cowrie shells on their hats. The annual festival of Gnaoua music (www.festival-gnaoua.co.ma), held around mid-June, has put their music on the map. In Essaouira several Gnaoua draw on these traditions as subjects for their colourful, almost naive paintings.

On either side of avenue Mohammed Zerktouni is the new **Souk Djedid**, with the spice and fish market on one side and the grain and jewellery market on the other. At the harbour end of the same street, several galleries sell the work of Essaouiri artists, the best of which is **Galerie Fréderic Damgaard**, who started promoting the work of Gnaoua painters (see box and ► 93).

## A Windy City

The city's splendid beach stretches for several kilometres, but the constant wind makes it better for windsurfing than swimming or sunbathing.

Opposite town are the **Îles Purpuaires**, named after the purple dye – the colour of choice of Roman emperors – made from the shells of the native murex (a tropical marine mollusc). The largest island, Île de Mogador, has a small harbour, fort and mosque. The islands were declared a nature reserve as they are the only breeding ground of Eleonora's falcon (*Falco eleonorae*).

*The lotar, a three-string violin, is a traditional Moroccan instrument*

### TAKING A BREAK

Have a mint tea in **place Moulay el Hassan**, located 3.5km west of the centre. For lunch sit on the harbourside terrace and enjoy the many simple delights of **Taros** (► 92), or enjoy the wide views from the equally relaxing terrace of **Le Chalet de la Plage** (► 91). Or be adventurous and have a **grilled fish snack** at the stalls just outside the harbour.

🔲 182 A1
✉ Tourist office: Syndicat d'Initiative, 10 rue du Caire
☎ (024) 78 35 32; www.essaouira.com
🚌 From Marrakech, Casablanca, Agadir and Tiznit

**Musée Sidi Mohammed ben Abdallah**
✉ Rue Laalouj ☎ (024) 47 53 00
🕐 Wed–Mon 8:30–6
💰 Inexpensive

**Galerie Frederic Damgaard**
✉ Avenue Oqba ibn Nafii
☎ (024) 78 44 46
🕐 Daily 10–1, 3–7
💰 Free

---

## ESSAOUIRA: INSIDE INFO

**Top tips** The best way to get to know Essaouira is on a leisurely **stroll around** the city looking for secret passages, gorgeous gateways, picturesque alleys and amazing *riads* and houses.

■ Spend some time in **place Moulay el Hassan** watching the constant passage of Sawiris and visitors.

■ Stroll along the **windswept beach** in the late afternoon.

■ The **best surfing beach** is Sidi Kaouki, 25km (15 miles) south of town.

# At Your Leisure

## 4 Mehdiya

Despite being founded by the ancient Carthaginian civilisation, Mehdiya's only historic monument, the **kasbah**, dates from the 16th century. By then, the town had become a corsair stronghold from where pirates attacked passing ships. The kasbah, built by the Spanish to protect their interests along the coast, is fronted by an impressive gateway added by Moulay Ismail (➤ 128). Inside the kasbah are the ruins of a 17th-century mosque, the souks, the governor's palace and the northwest bastion with ship's cannons and gorgeous views over the Sebou River. During the summer, Mehdiya Plage is a busy beach resort, as is the Plage des Nations, 9km (6 miles) away. Near this beach is the **Musée Dar Belghazi**, which houses a private collection of Moroccan crafts and Islamic art gathered by the Fassi artist and antiques dealer Mohammed Abdallah Belghazi.

Near by are the delightful **Jardins Exotiques de Sidi Bouknadel**, planted in the 1950s by the French horticulturist Marcel François. The gardens are divided into three main sections: a splendid Andalucian garden, an area of indigenous plants and a park with wonderful Asian plants, including some huge bamboos to admire.

✚ 183 D4 ⊠ 40km (25 miles) north of Rabat
🚍 Buses from Rabat and Salé

**Musée Dar Belghazi**
⊠ Near Plage des Nations ☎ (037) 82 21 78; www.museebelghazi.marocoriental.com
🕐 Daily 8:30–6:30
🚍 Bus 35 from Salé 💰 Expensive

**Jardins Exotiques de Sidi Bouknadel**
⊠ 9km (6 miles) from Plage des Nations, on the west side of the Rabat road 🕐 Daily 9–5, until 7 in summer 💰 Inexpensive

The attractive medina at Azemmour
behind its well-preserved ramparts

## 5 Mohammedia

Mohammedia is Morocco's second port and the centre of its oil industry. It is also a popular summer resort with a long sandy beach. The town was a significant port and trading post in the 16th century, when the Portuguese built the kasbah. The old fortified town has been restored, and the alleys of its quiet residential quarter make for a pleasant stroll.

➕ 182 C3 ✉ 28km (17 miles) north of Casablanca 🚆 Train from Rabat and Casablanca 🚌 Bus 900 from Casa-Port

## 6 Azemmour

This picturesque village is built on a cliff over the estuary of the poetically named river Umm er Rbia (Mother of Spring) and is home to many artists. The Portuguese occupied the ancient river port of Azama for only 30 years (from 1510), but their colonial architecture has lasted much longer. A walk on the well-preserved ramparts around the 16th-century **Portuguese kasbah**, including the arsenal of **Dar al-Baroud**, is a great introduction. The medina's souks and alleys are decorated with paintings by local artists. The best views are from the bridge on the northeastern side of the medina. About 2km (1 mile) away is the beach of **Haouzia**; the sands stretch all the way to El-Jadida.

➕ 182 C3 ✉ 17km (11 miles) north of El-Jadida 🚌 Daily buses from El-Jadida and Casablanca 🚆 From Casa Voyageurs and El-Jadida

### ESTEVANICO

Also know as Stephen the Moor, Estevanico (c.1500–1539) was born in Azemmour and enslaved to the Spanish explorer Cabeza de Vaca. Consequently, he went on the 1527 expedition to the Americas, and was the first African to set foot in America. Estevanico was given his freedom, and wa one of the few surviving travellers. He went on to traverse the continent, and opened up Arizona and New Mexico. He was killed by the Zuni Indians.

The vast Portuguese cistern in El-Jadida is an amazing sight, particularly when lit by the strong midday sun

## 7 El-Jadida

El-Jadida is a summer resort popular with young Moroccans for its great sports facilities and mild climate, but the main draw is the old Portuguese quarter, following in the footsteps of Orson Welles's footsteps. The well-preserved **Portuguese garrison**, known as Mazagan, was built in 1502 and has four surviving bastions; **Bastion de l'Ange** offers fine views over the old town. The Muslims turned the area into the *mellah* in 1815, hence the large Jewish cemetery just outside the walls. On the main axis of the citadel is the **Portuguese Cistern**, a vast, spectacular, underground cellar. It so impressed Welles that he filmed part of *Othello* here in 1952. The light streams in through a small skylight in the vault, supported by 25 massive columns. The beach of Sidi Bouzid is also undergoing a major development with several hides and two more golf courses 7km (4 miles) to the south.

➕ 182 B3 ✉ 89km (55 miles) south of Casablanca ☎ Tourist office, place Mohammed V: (023) 34 47 88 🚌 Daily buses from Casablanca, Essaouira and Agadir 🚆 From Casa Voyageurs and El-Jadida

**Portuguese Cistern**
✉ Rue da Carreira ⏲ Daily 9–1, 3–6:30
💲 Inexpensive

## 8 Oualidia

Famous for its excellent Japanese oysters, Oualidia sits above a fine lagoon beach protected from the Atlantic surf by a barrier of little islands, which makes it the calmest beach along this stretch of coast. Little more than a village, it was named after the Saadian sultan El-Oualid, who built a kasbah to defend himself from the Portuguese in El-Jadida. Overlooking the vast beach is Mohammed V's picturesque, but now abandoned, royal villa. Oualidia is fast becoming a trendy resort, as Essaouira is getting more crowded, but it's still a great place to relax for a few days, and to try out some excellent fish and seafood.
➕ 182 B2 ✉ 80km (50 miles) south of El-Jadida 🚌 Bus from Casablanca, Essaouira and Safi

## 9 Safi

This industrial town is not an obvious stop, but its charming old medina and pottery industry flourish beside the phosphate factories. The Portuguese also built a fortress here in the 16th century – **Ksar el Bahar**, overlooking the port. Near by is the Kechla, another Portuguese fortress, which houses a small **Ceramics Museum**. The souks in the medina culminate with the Souk des Poteries, a showcase for work made on the nearby Colline des Potiers. The colourful plates that you'll see on sale across the country, and most of the green roof tiles of Morocco's mosques and palaces, are made here.
➕ 182 B2 ✉ 66km (40 miles) south of Oualidia ☎ Tourist office, avenue de la Liberté: (024) 62 24 96; www.safi-ville.com 🚌 Buses from Casablanca, Essaouira and Marrakech 🚆 Train from Benguerir with connection to Marrakech, Casablanca and Rabat

**Ksar el-Bahar**
✉ Place de l'Indépendance ⏲ Mon–Fri 9–noon, 2:30–6:30 💲 Inexpensive

**Ceramics Museum**
✉ Off avenue Moulay Youssef ☎ (024) 46 38 95 ⏲ Wed–Mon 8–6 💲 Inexpensive

## 10 Imouzzer des Ida Outanane

Reached via the Vallée du Paradis, this popular picnic spot offers a great escape from the beaches. The small village of white houses overlooking a palm grove lies at the foot of the High Atlas, at 1,250m (4,100 feet). This is the administrative centre of the Ida Outanane, a Berber tribe that occupies the whole area from the lower mountain slopes to the Atlantic Ocean. The Thursday souk is a popular affair, noted for its medicinal

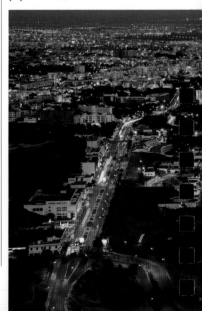

---

### FOR THE KIDS

- Bigger kids will appreciate the surf along most of the Atlantic coast, but smaller ones may prefer the calmer waters of Agadir, Tarhazoute and the lagoon in Oualidia (▶ above).
- Check out **Sindbad**, the small amusement park on the Corniche in Casablanca.
- The park at **Vallée des Oiseaux** in Agadir has a little zoo and playground.

(but illegal) mountain honey made from marjoram and marijuana. Only 2km (1 mile) away are the **Imouzzèr Falls**, with rock formations and a deep-green natural pool into which locals dive from dangerous heights.

⊞ 184 A3 ⊠ 60km (37 miles) north of Agadir
🚌 Daily bus from Agadir

## 🔟 Agadir

Agadir has two main attractions: a fine beach and a superb climate. As a modern city it offers a choice of hotels catering mainly for northern European package tourists. It is worth visiting the largest **fishing port** in the country. The ruined **kasbah**, Ancienne Talborjt, has sweeping views over the port, while the grassland below it covers what was the old medina. The **Musée du Patrimoine Amazigh** displays Berber artefacts and nearby is **Vallée des Oiseaux**, a children's park. For a quieter beach go north 19km (12 miles) to Taghazout.

⊞ 184 A3 ⊠ 225km (140 miles) southwest of Marrakech 🕿 Tourist office: Immeuble A, place Prince Héritier Sidi Mohammed: (028) 84 63 77 🚌 Buses from Marrakech, Essaouira, Casablanca, Taroudannt, Ouarzazate, Tiznit ✈ Flights from Casablanca, Marrakech and Fez

### BEST SEAFOOD RESTAURANTS

- **Chalet de la Plage**, at the beach in Essaouira (▶ 91)
- **Restaurant du Port**, fishing-boat shaped restaurant, Casablanca (▶ 91)
- **L'Hippocampe**, hotel with excellent restaurant, Oualidia (▶ 89)
- **Fish and seafood vendors** at the fishing harbour in Essaouira (▶ 83)

**Musée du Patrimoine Amazigh**
⊠ Passage Aït Souss, boulevard Hassan II
🕐 Mon–Sat 9:30–7:30 🎫 Inexpensive

**Vallée des Oiseaux**
⊠ Boulevard Hassan II
🕐 Daily 9:30–21:30, 2:30–6
🎫 Inexpensive

**New Medina**
⊠ Ben-Sergaou, 4km (2.5 miles) south of Agadir 🕿 (028) 28 02 53; www.medinapolizzi.com
🕐 Daily 8:30–6:30 🎫 Expensive

The vast stretch of beach and calm waters in Agadir lights up at night

# Where to...
# Stay

**Prices**
Expect to pay for a double room per night, including breakfast and taxes
**£** under 600dh    **££** 600–1,600dh    **£££** over 1,600dh

## AGADIR

### Hôtel Kamal £

This downtown hotel in a modernist white block is perfectly located for all the sights and is an excellent option if you're on a budget. The ensuite rooms are comfortable and clean, although the street-side ones can be noisy. The hotel also has a small pool.

➕ 184 A3 ⌖ 2 avenue Hassan II, Nouveau Talborjt ☎ (028) 84 28 17

### Ksar Massa £££

This is a fabulous place to get away from it all, on its own wild stretch of beach in the heart of the protected national park, a sanctuary for rare birds. The rooms are spacious and simply beautiful, and the *hammam* offers traditional beauty treatments.

➕ 184 A3 ⌖ Sidi R'bat in the Souss-Massa National Park, 25 miles (40km) (south of Agadir) ☎ (061) 28 03 19; www.ksarmassa.com

## AZEMMOUR

### Riad Azama £

Totally charming old *riad* converted into a hotel with grand rooms decorated in traditional style, set around a courtyard. The *riad* has a cosy dining area, where breakfast is served. There is a small library and a roof terrace with views over the town.

➕ 182 C3 ⌖ 17 impasse Ben Tahar ☎ (023) 34 75 16; www.riadazama.com

## CASABLANCA

### Hôtel Guynemer £

This welcoming family-run budget hotel in a lovely art deco building just gets better. The comfortable and incredibly good-value rooms are annually renovated and equipped with plasma TVs, Wi-Fi access, new bathroom fittings and firm beds. The hotel can also arrange a handy airport pick up, has a good Moroccan restaurant serving excellent food and two apartments that can accommodate families.

➕ 184 A4 ⌖ 2 rue Mohammed Belloul ☎ (022) 27 57 64; www.guynemerhotel.com

### Hyatt Regency £££

Excellent five-star hotel located right in the centre of Casablanca.

Guests enjoy spacious and well-appointed rooms overlooking all of the city as well as the ocean. All the rooms are comfortably appointed and decorated in an elegant contemporary style. The hotel boasts several good restaurants and bars, a discotheque and a spa.

➕ 184 A4 ⌖ 2 place des Nations Unis ☎ (022) 43 12 34; www.casablanca.hyatt.com

## EL-JADIDA

### Dar el Manar ££

The friendly French-Moroccan couple who built this gorgeous house, outside El-Jadida, but overlooking the town and ocean, fell in love with the location. Part of their house is a B&B with just a few stylish rooms decorated in a warm contemporary Moroccan style. Dinner can be ordered, and is made with produce from their organic vegetable garden.

➕ 182 B-C3 ⌖ Off the road to Casablanca, near the Phare Sidi Mesbah ☎ (023) 23 35 1645/(061) 49 54 11; www.dar-el-manar.com

## La Villa ££

This lovely early 20th-century villa is now a funky boutique hotel and is conveniently located less than five minutes walk from the beach and the market. The peaceful rooms are set around a small Zen-like courtyard. All the simple but elegantly furnished rooms, have walls finished in Moroccan *tadelakt* (polished plaster). Well-appointed ensuite bathrooms, plasma screens and a Wi-Fi connection ensure a comfortable stay. The restaurant is also excellent.

**182 B3 ☒ 4 avenue Moulay Abdelhafid ☎ (023) 344423; www.villa-david.com**

## ESSAOUIRA

### L'Heure Bleue Palais £££

The former home of the local chieftain Mbark Saïdi, brings serious luxury to the hotel scene in Essaouira. It has 36 sumptuously appointed and beautifully designed rooms, as well as a rooftop pool, solarium, *hammam*, gastronomic restaurant and cinema, and is located in the heart of the medina. More than staying in a hotel, this feels like staying as an honoured guest in the home of a noble family. Recommended.

**184 A4 ☒ 2 rue Ibn Batouta, Bab Marrakech, Essaouira ☎ (024) 47 42 22; www.heure-bleue.com**

### Madada ££

Tucked away down an alley, this grand house overlooks the sea and the harbour. The superb rooftop terrace is protected from the wind and from here all you can see is blue, from the sea and the sky. The rooms are contemporary in design, but cosy and with plenty of atmosphere, the service is young, laid-back and friendly. This is a great place to stay, or at least to stop and have a drink on the terrace.

**184 A4 ☒ 5 rue Youssef el Fassi ☎ (024) 47 55 12; www.madada.com**

### Riad Nakhla £

This popular budget option in Essaouira fills up quickly and guests tend to come back for the good value and well-appointed bedrooms, all kept immaculately and the very friendly service. Breakfast is served on the rooftop with great views over the town and the ocean.

**182 A1 ☒ 2 rue d'Agadir ☎ (024) 47 49 40; www.essaouiranet.com/riad-nakhla**

## OUALIDIA

### L'Hippocampe ££

The Hippocampe is a wonderful, reasonably priced place to relax for a few days. Its comfortable bungalows are set in a beautiful garden with swimming pool and restaurant on the beach overlooking the lagoon. Half board is compulsory, but the food is excellent. Book ahead.

**182 B2 ☒ Oualidia beach ☎ (023) 36 61 08**

## RABAT

### Le Piétri Urban ££

Excellent new boutique hotel located in the former Hôtel Oudayas, in a quiet residential part of town, near the downtown restaurants. The 36 rooms have elegant wooden floors, are decorated in beautiful hued tones and are well equipped with roomy bathrooms and plasma screens to ensure a comfortable stay. The downstairs restaurant offers delicious Moroccan and Mediterranean specialities with a contemporary twist. Recommended.

**183 D3 ☒ 4 rue Tobrouk, Rabat ☎ (037) 70 78 20; www.lepietri.com**

### Riad Dar Baraka ££

At the end of the main street of Rabat's picturesque kasbah there is just a blue door to mark this simple but stunningly located guesthouse with plunging views over the ocean and river. The two rooms, one small and one large, are both painted in white and bright blue, and have clean bathrooms. Recommended, but it is popular so book ahead.

**183 D3 ☒ 26 rue de la Mosquée, Rabat ☎ (037) 73 03 62 / (061) 78 33 61; www.darbaraka-rabat.com**

# Where to...
## Eat and Drink

### Prices

Expect to pay for a three-course meal per person, excluding drinks but including taxes and service

£ under 200dh    ££ 200–400dh    £££ over 400dh

## AGADIR

### Mezzo Mezzo £-££

A favourite with local residents, this Italian restaurant serves the best pizza and home-made pastas in town. The atmosphere is busy and buzzing, and the maître d' knows just about everyone. Expect to well-cooked food and excellent service.

🗺 184 A3 ⊠ Boulevard Hassan II
☎ (028) 84 88 19 ⓒ Daily lunch and dinner

### Yacht Club Restaurant £££

Another great fish restaurant in the harbour – they are usually the best for fresh seafood. The décor inside is nothing special but don't underestimate the quality of the food and service. The outside terrace has great views and is delightful place to eat on a warm evening.

🗺 184 A3 ⊠ Commercial port ☎ (028) 84 37 08 ⓒ Lunch and dinner

## CASABLANCA

### À Ma Bretagne £££

Reputed to be the best French restaurant in Casablanca, you'll find this in a modernist building overlooking the sea and the shrine of Sidi Abder Rahmane. The classic food, impeccably prepared by the French chef, includes duck and fish dishes, such as steamed fillet of sole. The equally impressive wine list features the best of French and Moroccan offerings. The service is attentive and the décor is delightful.

🗺 182 C3 ⊠ Boulevard de la Corniche, Aïn Diab ☎ (022) 36 21 12 ⓒ Mon–Sat dinner only

### Al Mounia ££

Al Mounia is one of the best Moroccan restaurants in town, renowned for serving delicious bstilla au pigeon (sweet pigeon pie) and delicious tagines and spiced couscous, all served in stylish surroundings with a dazzling Moorish décor. This is Moroccan cuisine at its best.

🗺 182 C3 ⊠ 95 rue du Prince Moulay Abdellah ☎ (022) 22 26 69 ⓒ Mon–Sat lunch and dinner

### Paul £

Worth going to, just to sit and admire the gorgeous art deco Villa Zevac, in which the new tearoom is set. The French chain of bakeries has arrived in Casa with its good but pricey salads and sandwiches, and lovely breakfasts and lovely patisserie. This is the place to stop for refreshments and for people-watching.

🗺 182 C3 ⊠ Corner boulevard d'Anfa and boulevard Moulay Rachid ☎ (022) 36 60 00; www.paul.ma ⓒ Daily 7am–9pm

### Le Port de Pêche ££

The name speaks for itself at this establishment for fans of fish and shellfish. This restaurant, with red-and-white gingham tablecloths and fishing nets on the walls, is a local family favourite. If you haven't booked in advance you will have to join the long queue to get a table, but the food is definitely worth the wait. The soupe de poisson is legendary, and freshly caught fish comes cooked every way possible: tagine, fried, baked and in filo pastry.

🗺 182 C3 ⊠ Casablanca harbour (turn left at customs) ☎ (022) 31 85 61 ⓒ Daily lunch and dinner

## Rick's Café £-£££

Built against the walls of the lovely old medina, Rick's Café is located in a gorgeous mansion, and was of course inspired by the film *Casablanca*. It is both glamorous and elegant: handsome waiters wear red fezes while serving exquisite cocktails to an international crowd, accompanied by delicious delicacies such as roast duck in mango sauce, seared foie gras or grilled fish. The film is continually screened in a corner upstairs. Come here just to experience the atmosphere

✚ 182 C3 ⊠ 248 boulevard Sour Jdid, Old medina ☎ (022) 27 42 07 ⓒ Daily noon–3 and 6:30pm–1am

## Sqala ££

This popular Moroccan-Mediterranean restaurant is set in an old fortress, with tables in its enchanting courtyard garden. The menu offers simple but well-prepared and beautifully presented salads, tagines and grills. A part of the complex is also the **Café Maure**

(➤ 78) with ten different kinds of mint tea from the country's regions, and Moroccan sweets, with a space for cultural events and a gallery for the contemporary photography that can also be seen on the walls of the café.

✚ 182 C3 ⊠ Boulevard des Almohades ☎ (022) 26 09 60 ⓒ Tue–Sun 8–10.30pm

## EL-JADIDA

### Restaurant du Port ££

Great views over the port of El-Jadida, and one of the best restaurants in town, this restaurant specialises, of course, in serving the freshest fish and seafood. There is a large choice of wines to accompany your meal. Highly recommended and good value for money

✚ 182 A3 ⊠ Port, El-Jadida ☎ (023) 34 25 79 ⓒ Mon–Sat lunch, dinner, Sun lunch

## ESSAOUIRA

### Le 5inQ ££

This ultra-contemporary style lounge bar and restaurant with a great terrace

overlooks the harbour. Cool punters come in for sunset cocktails and great food, especially fish and seafood, all served with a little twist by good-looking waiters.

✚ 184 A4 ⊠ 7 rue Youssef el Fassi, ☎ (024) 78 47 26 ⓒ Wed–Mon 7–11 Sat–Sun lunch and dinner

### Le Km8 £-££

A favourite of Essaouira locals who meet here at weekends to eat and socialise, this cosy restaurant serves delicious French Moroccan specialities, including a tagine with camel meat balls. Book ahead.

✚ 184 A3 ⊠ At Km8 on the road to Agadir ☎ (066) 25 21 23 ⓒ Tue–Sun lunch and dinner

### La Chalet de la Plage ££

The Chalet has a terrace on the waterfront overlooking islands and the long sweeping beach. The menu is large, including deliciously fresh *crevettes* (shrimps) and sea urchins.

✚ 184 A4 ⊠ Avenue Mohammed V ☎ (024) 47 64 19 ⓒ Daily lunch and dinner

## Océan Vagabond £

The atmosphere is relaxed in this small café restaurant that is attached to the surf club. Tasty breakfast, paninis, salads and snacks are served on the breezy white and electric-blue terrace, and the music is good too.

✚ 184 A4 ⊠ Boulevard Mohammed V on the beach ☎ (024) 78 39 34; www.oceanvagabond.com ⓒ Daily 8–8

### Elizir £-££

This delightful restaurant in an old house is located just off the main street, and is furnished with eclectic junk-market finds, iconic 20th-century furniture and fun art by young Moroccan artists. The food is great too, a mix of inventive Italian and Moroccan dishes, all well prepared. The service is swift and very friendly. Book ahead.

✚ 182 A1 ⊠ 1 rue d'Agadir ☎ (024) 47 21 03 ⓒ Daily lunch, dinner

### Taros £-££

Taros features several attractions in one big house: a terrace on the square

– a wonderful, sunny roof terrace with views over the port and the town – and several rooms inside the house which become a pleasant lounge bar in the evening. There is also an extensive library on Morocco. This is a calm place where you could easily spend an afternoon dining, browsing or relaxing with a pot of mint tea and some pastries enjoying the simple Moroccan surroundings.

☩ 184 A4 ⊠ 2 rue Skala, place Moulay Hassan ☎ (024) 47 64 07 ◷ Daily breakfast–late

## OUALIDA

### À l'Araignée Gourmand ££

Large restaurant with sea views and an old-fashioned no-frills décor. The food however is well-cooked and delicious, if you like fresh seafood, with a large selection of both. The seafood platters, in fact, are the things to choose here, served with crisp white wine. Good value set menus.

☩ 182 B2 ⊠ Near the beach ☎ (023) 36 64 47 ◷ Daily lunch and dinner

## RABAT

### Dinarjat £££

The best Moroccan food in Rabat comes at a price, but the experience will surely be a memorable one. The restaurant is set in a splendidly lit "1,001 Nights" palace and offers a superb selection of food to match the surroundings – several different couscous dishes and tagines, including a sweet one that's famous for satisfying the cravings of pregnant women. No alcohol.

☩ 183 D3 ⊠ 6 rue Belgnaoui, medina Rabat, opposite the kasbah; a caretaker can take you by candlelight from the car park on avenue el-Alou ☎ (037) 72 42 39 ◷ Daily lunch and dinner

### Le Grand Comptoir ££

This central colonial style café-brasserie, buzzing with life, is a great place to stop for a mid-morning caffè latte or tea. There is also Wi-Fi access, and it makes a chic stop for a good lunch. The menu is contemporary French with a few old brasserie classics such as veal kidneys or delicious steaks. The décor is grand with lots of wood, huge palms, candelabra and a swirling stairway to the first floor.

☩ 182 C3 ⊠ Avenue Mohammed V ☎ (037) 20 15 14; www.legrandcomptoir.ma ◷ 8am–11pm

### Le Petit Beur £

The two brothers who run this delightful Moroccan restaurant transport you to the south of the country, with the warm convivial atmosphere and the large variety of tagines, the speciality of the house. In the evening you will often hear local musicians play traditional Moroccan folk songs and quite often the owners, or even clients, break into song as well.

☩ 183 D3 ⊠ 8 rue de Damas, Ville Nouvelle ☎ (037) 73 13 22 ◷ Mon–Sat lunch and dinner

### Restaurant de la Plage ££

The menu at this excellent fish restaurant, frequented by a wealthy crowd from Rabat, includes fresh oysters from Oualida, lobster, grilled fish and squid, and several excellent meat dishes. The spacious and airy dining room is elegantly decorated in light tones and the sheltered terrace has lovely views. This is a particularly pleasant place to spend some time. Recommended.

☩ 183 D3 ⊠ On the beach below the kasbah ☎ (037) 70 75 86 ◷ Daily lunch and dinner

### Ty Potes £–££

This charming tearoom has a tiny garden to relax and soak up the atmosphere, and is run by a friendly young French woman. The place is deservedly popular with locals who come for tea or for a light lunch. On the menu are a range of tempting home-made cakes, healthy salads, sandwiches and delicious crêpes. Sunday brunch is renowned for being excellent value.

☩ 184 D4 ⊠ 11 rue Ghafsa ☎ (037) 70 79 65 ◷ Mon–Wed lunch, Thu–Sun lunch & dinner

# Where to...
## Shop

### SOUKS

In **Rabat**, the main market street is **rue Souika** and **Souk es Sebbat**. **Rue des Consuls** is the best place to shop with its carpet souk on Thursday morning. The **Ensemble Artisanal** near the Kasbah des Oudaïa is also good for crafts. A daily *joutia* (flea market) takes place in the *mellah* below Souk es Sebbat towards Bab el-Bahr, and there's a daily flower market on **place Moulay Hassan**.

**Casablanca's** medina sells more clothes than crafts, but for traditional clothing and crafts visit **Quartier Habous**, the new medina.

### ARTS AND CRAFTS

At the **Oulja** Complexe des Potiers, 2km (1 mile) from Salé, look out for master potters **Tarfaya** at stall No 9 and **Hariky** at No 10, who make some of the finest pottery in Morocco.

In **Casablanca** many craft shops are concentrated on **boulevard Felix Houphouët-Boigny**, but the relaxed **Quartier Habous** also offers reasonable prices.

**Essaouira's** pedestrianised **medina** offers some of the most interesting shopping in Morocco, as the town has long inspired artisans, and has a deep-rooted tradition of crafts. Traders are more relaxed here than elsewhere. The town is famous for its woodwork and, at the **Skala de la Ville**, craftsmen make beautiful big bowls, original furniture and picture frames in woods that include argan, which grows only in Morocco.

The best place to look for paintings in Essaouira is **Galerie Frédéric**

**Damgaard** (avenue Oqba ibn Nafiaa, tel: (024) 78 44 46), which represents the widest range of Gnaoua artists. The gallery is passionate about this genre of art and has done much to bring it to international notice (▶ 82) and promote its popularity.

### GIFTS

Argan oil from the indigenous tree contains a lot of vitamins and is used against burns and rheumatism as well as for cooking. You can buy it in Essaouira at **Produits Naturels** (rue Sidi Mohammed ben Abdallah, left of Hotel Central), which also sells natural honey. A women's co-operative produces the argan oil on sale at **Chez Aicha** (Marché aux Grains), which also stocks extremely fine Berber pottery.

Near Essaouira's fish and spices souk is a **weavers' workshop** where you can buy traditional *haïks* (veils) that also work well as throws or tablecloths. In the street off the fish market, shops sell typical Gnaoua musical instruments such as *gimbris* (long-necked lutes) and *garagabs* (metal castanets).

### JEWELLERY AND FASHION

Essaouira is also known for its raffia shoes, sold handmade to measure. The best of these is **Rafia Craft** (82 rue d'Agadir, tel: (024) 78 36 32; rafiacraft@yahoo.fr). French designer Poupa Litza (rue Mohammed el Qory, near L'Heure Bleue hotel; tel: (024) 78 35 65) makes lovely fashionable leather bags in her quirky little shop. The jewellery souk nearby has many selling everything from heavy Berber silver to gaudy gold. Several surf shops sell locally produced T-shirts.

### FOOD

While in Casablanca stop at **Patisserie Bennis** (2 rue Fquih el-Gabbas, quartier Habous) for the best sweets in town, such as honey biscuits and *cornes de gazelles*, (pastries stuffed with almond paste).

# Where to...
# Be Entertained

## NIGHTLIFE

The liveliest **nightclubs** in Casablanca are along the strip of the Corniche in Ain Diab. One of the hotspots is at No 55 **Candy Bar** in the Hotel Riad Salam (tel: (022) 79 84 40). Near by is **Armstrong Legend** (tel: (022) 79 76 56), a live music venue. Slightly calmer is the **Mystic Garden** (tel: (022) 79 88 77), a restaurant-bar. The **Villa Fadango**, rue de la Mer Égée (tel: (022) 39 85 08) is where Casablanca's trendy crowd gathers.

Agadir has a lively nightlife with clubs and hotel discos open into the early hours. The best are **So** (Sofitel Agadir, Baie des Palmiers), the hippest and most expensive club with guest DJs, and **Bar Fly** (boulevard du 20 Aoút, tel: (028) 84 01 23). Agadir's annual music festival in July, the **Festival Timatar** (www.festival-timatar.com; 028 82 03 38), attracts the best Moroccan and African musicians. The most fashionable nightclub in Rabat is **Amnesia** (18 rue Monastir, tel: (037) 78 18 60). Essaouira is quieter, but you can order cocktails at the bar in **Taros.**

## CINEMA AND THEATRE

Most cinemas in Rabat show films in French, except for the small art house **Salle du 7ième Art** (avenue Allal ben Abdallah), **Atelier** (16 rue Annaba) and **Marsam** (6 rue Usqutiah). The **Théâtre National Mohammed V** (rue du Caïro; tel: (037) 70 75 28) has concerts and films. Casablanca has several cinemas – listings are in the free magazine *7 jours à Casa* – and most films are dubbed into French.

The best ones are **Cinema Rialto** (rue Mohammed el Qori, tel: (022) 26 26 32); and **Cinema Lynx** (150 avenue Mers Sultan; tel: (022) 22 02 29).

## SPORT AND LEISURE

**Golfers** are well catered for at **Dar es Salaam Golf Club** in Rabat (tel: (037) 75 58 64; www.royalgolfdaressalam. com). Agadir has three courses: the **Royal Golf Club** (tel: (028) 83 12 78), **Dunes** (tel: (028) 83 46 90) and **Golf du Soleil** (tel: (028) 33 73 29). There's also a 9-hole course in Anfa, Casablanca (tel: (022) 36 53 55) and an 18-hole course at **Mohammedia** (tel: (023) 32 46 56).

The beaches around Essaouira – "Windy City Africa" – are popular with **windsurfers**, particularly at **Moulay Bouzertoun**, 26km (16 miles) north, and **Sidi Kaouki**, 20km (12 miles) south. Lessons and equipment rental are available at **Océan Vagabond** (Essaouira, tel: (024) 78 39 34; www. oceanvagabond.com) and **UCPA** (tel: (024) 47 65 27; www.ucpa.com).

The coast between Essaouira and Agadir has several surf camps. **Kahina** (Pointe de Immessouane, tel (028) 82 60 32; www.kahinasurfschool.com) is on a wild stretch of coast, and so is **Surf Marokko** (Tamraght, tel (068) 39 51 24; www.surfmarokko.de).

Surfers with their own gear head for Dar Bouazza, south of Casablanca.

Casablanca has two major **football** teams: RAJA and WYDAD, and **horse-racing** takes place some Sundays at the Hippodrome in Anfa.

**Horse-riding** can be organised at **Ranch REHA**, 17km (11 miles) from Agadir (tel: (028) 84 75 49) or at the **Ranch de Diabat**, in Diabat south of Essaouira (tel: (062) 29 72 03).

The latest craze in Essaouira is **quad biking** on the beach at Diabat. Rent bikes from **Cap Quad** (tel: (066) 25 21 45; www.capquad.com).

For total relaxation, the **Centre de Thalassothérapie d'Agadir** on Tikida Beach (tel: (048) 84 21 20) or the **Sofitel Mogador Thalassa** in Essaouira (tel (044) 47 90 00) offer hydro massages and algae therapy.

# The North

# Getting Your Bearings

Northern Morocco is where Europe meets Africa or, more precisely, where Andalucian culture meets Berber traditions. Between the Atlantic and the Mediterranean coast, the Hispanic-influenced cities contrast starkly with the wild landscapes of the Rif Mountains. In the towns, stylish urbanites mix in markets and squares with the more traditional Rifians who come to sell their produce.

Tangier is a place all its own, with memories of intrigue and dreams. Its stories and scandals involving bad boys and femmes fatales, lawlessness and beauty, inspired many writers, film-makers and artists. Elegant Tetouan and attractive Chefchaouen have preserved their Andalucian heritage, as have the seaside towns of Asilah and Larache. And Spain still holds five enclaves along the Rif coast: Ceuta, Melilla and three small, uninhabited islets.

The Rif Mountains form a barrier between the Mediterranean world and central Moroccan culture. The ruined settlements of many foreign powers, from Phoenicians and Romans to Arabs and Spaniards, are scattered along the coastline – but the Rif only ever belonged to the Berbers. Very few Moroccan sultans succeeded in conquering the region and even today it remains troublesome. The eastern mountains are remarkably beautiful, but something of a no-go area because of the flourishing but illegal cannabis trade. However, King Mohammed VI's has plans to develop several major tourist areas in the region.

**Previous page:** An alley in Chefchaouen (left); the ocean at Tangier (centre); on the steps of the Hotel Continental, Tangier (right)
**Right:** Carved plaster with floral motives, calligraphy and *zellij* in spectacular geometric compositions all vie to capture the attention

**Above:**
**Shopping in**
**Chefchaouen**

# In Five Days

If you're not quite sure where to begin your travels, this itinerary recommends a practical and enjoyable five days in the North, taking in some of the best places to see using the Getting Your Bearings map on the previous page. For more information see the main entries.

## Day One

### Morning
Start in ❶Tangier (opposite page, bottom, ➤ 100–103) at the **Grand Socco square**, then visit the **Mendoubia Gardens**, **La Légation des États-Unis** and the **Musée d'Art Contemporain de la Ville de Tanger**. Stop at the small market on the way to place de France, and have a drink at **Café de Paris** (➤ 103) before lunch at the **Restaurant Populaire** (➤ 114).

### Afternoon and Evening
Returning to the **Grand Socco** (below), enter the **medina** and head towards the **Petit Socco**, the **kasbah** and **Dar el-Makhzen**. Later, relax on the terrace of the **Café Hafa** (➤ 113), the Gran Café de Paris or the **Hotel Continental** (➤ 112) before a delicious dinner in the **El Minzah** hotel's Moroccan restaurant (➤ 112).

## Day Two

### Morning
Leave town along Zankat Belgika and follow signs west to **La Montagne** for grand views over Tangier and the Mediterranean, then continue to **Cap Spartel**. Walk towards the lighthouse, and then walk or drive 3km (2 miles) to the **Grottes d'Hercule** before having a drink or lunch on the nearby panoramic terrace of the **Hotel Le Mirage** (➤ 112).

### Afternoon and Evening
Drive back to Tangier and follow the road out towards Ceuta, passing **Cap Malabata** and more good views over the city. Continue on the spectacular road to Ceuta along the ❼**Rif coast** (➤ 109), then turn south and stop at one of the beaches near **Cabo Negro** for a swim before heading to Tetouan for a delicious dinner at the superb **El Reducto** (➤ 112).

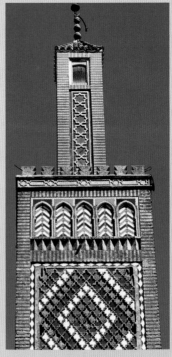

# Day Three

### Morning
Start your exploration of
**2 Tetouan** (left, ➤ 104–105)
at place Hassan II and visit the
medina and the souks. Have
lunch at **Le Restinga** (➤ 114).

### Afternoon and Evening
After a visit to the **Musée
Archéologique**, walk through
the Jewish quarter to the **Musée
d'Art Marocain** and the **École
des Métiers** craft school on the
other side of the Bab el Okla. Eat
dinner at **El Reducto** again.

# Day Four

### Morning
It's a two-hour drive to
**3 Chefchaouen** (➤ 106–107) for
a stroll round the sights of **place
Uta el-Hammam** before lunch at a
restaurant on the square.

### Afternoon and Evening
Visit the **Musée Artisanal** in the Kasbah and then stroll through the
souks, maybe stopping for a *hammam* (Turkish bath). Drive out of town
towards the Hotel Asmaa for great views over the Jebala Mountains and
Chefchaouen, and then have a
delicious dinner at **Casa Aladdin**
(➤ 113).

# Day Five

### Morning
From Chefchaouen drive 3km
(2 miles) south for a cooling
dip and a stroll at **Ras el-Maa**,
a charming river with small
pools and waterfalls. Continue
through the **Jebala Mountains** to
**8 Ouezzane**; ➤ 109) for lunch.

### Afternoon and Evening
Visit the **medina** and **souks
of Ouezzane**, stopping for a
drink at the terrace under the
vines on rue Nejjarine before
heading back to **Chefchaouen**
for dinner.

# Tangier

Tangier (also known as Tanger or Tanja) looks splendid from the sea, an amphitheatre of blue-and-white houses overlooking the bay, interspersed with minarets and palm trees. Gone are its golden days as the "International City", when it attracted millionaires and inspired artists. The Tangier-born writer Tahar ben Jelloun compares his city to " a lady who no longer dares to look at herself in the mirror". But Tangier has kept an air of individuality, if not eccentricity, and has plenty to offer, from its medina and evocative bars to the beautiful landscape around it.

Looking over the Strait of Gibraltar, controlling the entrance to the Mediterranean and the easiest crossing from Europe to Africa, Tangier was always of great strategic importance. From the 1920s until Morocco's independence in 1956, it flourished under its special designation of "International City". Its easy tax laws and free-port status attracted banks and other businesses, and in turn an influx of foreigners. These days the city is undergoing a major redevelopment as

**The best way to approach Tangier, like any port town, is undoubtedly from the sea**

part of King Mohammed VI's plans for the North and the new port of Tangier-Med.

The **Grand Socco** (place du 9 Avril 1947) links old and new Tangier. Flanking the square are the **Mendoubia Gardens** – look for the beautiful banyan tree that's said to be more than 800 years old. On nearby Zankat Salaheddine and Zankat el Oualili is a food market where Rifians sell their produce. The 19th-century **Church of St Andrew** on rue d'Angleterre reveals a blend of Moorish and English styles. The American journalist Walter Harris is buried in its cemetery alongside many other foreigners who made the city their home, including the British eccentric David Herbert whose tombstone, in contrast to his flamboyant lifestyle, reads simply "He loved Morocco". Along the same street, the small **Musée d'Art Contemporain de la Ville de Tanger** fills the former British consulate with Moroccan art.

**The Petit Socco was the centre of nightlife at the time of the "International City"**

The US created its first embassy back in 1777 in **La Légation des États-Unis** (Old American Legation), a fascinating palace containing historical exhibits of the city as well as paintings, mainly by Americans in residence. A room is dedicated to the writer Paul Bowles (► 30–31), with photographs of him and his contemporaries. The **Bab Fahs** leads from the Grand Socco into **rue des Siaghin** (silversmiths' souk) and the **Petit Socco**, once a centre of prostitution and intrigue, but now much quieter with jewellers' shops and café terraces. A stroll through picturesque alleys and streets leads to **place de la Kasbah**, offering views over the straits and the Moroccan and Spanish coasts.

The **kasbah**, an administrative area and palace since Roman times, rises to the right of the square. It had always been home to royalty, but from the 1920s it also became a playground for foreign millionaires and jet-setters attracted by Tangier's atmosphere of decadence, lawlessness, drugs and homosexuality. Among those tempted by its many delights were the writer Richard Hughes, who built an oriental palace within the kasbah, and the Woolworth heiress Barbara Hutton, who flew friends in from around the world and organised lavish parties at her palace.

Dar el-Makhzen, the 17th-century sultan's palace, houses the **Musée d'Art Marocain**. At the entrance to the main part of the museum, dedicated to Moroccan arts, is the **Beit el Mal** (the old treasury). The museum has a small collection of mosaics and objects from Volubilis (➤ 126-127), but the highlight of any visit is the definitely the superb collection of ceramics from Fez and Meknes.

From the kasbah gate, rue Asad ibn Farrat leads past stunning Moorish villas to the residential area of **Marshan** and the **Palais Mendoub**, a former home of the American publisher Malcolm Forbes (1919–90), which also housed his collection of tin soldiers. The nearby **Café Hafa** (➤ 113), where Paul Bowles (➤ 30-31) and his friends often hung out, enjoys commanding sea views.

The Bay of Tangier stretches between two capes. To the west is **Cap Spartel**, known to the Romans as "the Cape of Vines". Past the lighthouse, built in 1864, **Robinson Beach** overlooks dangerous waters where the Atlantic meets the Med. On the spit are the **Grottes d'Hercule**, natural rock formations enhanced by centuries of quarrying. To the east of Tangier is **Cap Malabata** with many old villas, as well as new hotel complexes. The **Villa Harris**, built by the flamboyant travel writer Walter Harris, can be visited through the Club Med complex. Widely travelled as the Morocco correspondent for the British newspaper *The Times*, he was one of the first foreigners to enter the sacred city of Chefchaouen (➤ 106), as described in his book *Morocco That Was* (1921).

**One of the six entrances to Tangier's kasbah quarter**

**READ ALL ABOUT IT**
Literature written about the International City will help enliven it even more. Try:
*Let It Come Down* by Paul Bowles (1952)
*Enderby* by Anthony Burgess (1968)
*Naked Lunch* by William Burroughs (1959)
*Tangier, City of the Dream* by Ian Finlayson (1992)
The movie *Casablanca* was actually based on Tangier.

## TAKING A BREAK

**Gran Café de Paris** on place de France, popular since the 1940s, is still a great place to stop. Nearby is the **El-Minzah** hotel (► 112), whose **Caïd Bar** attracts wealthy expats. For sea views head for **Café Hafa** (► 113) in the Marshan area.

---

➕ 183 E5
🚌 Regular buses from all main cities 🚆 Trains from Oujda, Meknès, Fez, Rabat and Casablanca ⛴ Boats from Sète (France) and Algeciras (Spain) ✈ Flights from Casablanca, Rabat, Fez and Marrakech

**Church of St Andrew**
📧 Zankat Angleterra 🕐 By caretaker: Mon–Fri 9:30–12, 2:30–6
💷 Donation

**Musée d'Art Contemporain de la Ville de Tanger**
📧 Rue d'Angleterre 🕐 Closed for restoration

This opening in the Caves d'Hercules resembles Africa

**La Légation des États-Unis**
📧 8 rue d'Amérique (entrance on rue du Portugal) ☎ (039) 93 53 17
🕐 Mon–Fri 10–1, 3–5, or by appointment 💷 Free, but tip the guardian

**Dar el-Makhzen**
📧 Kasbah 🕐 Mon, Wed, Thu and Sun, 9–noon, 3–5.30 Fri 9–11:30
💷 Inexpensive

**Grottes d'Hercule**
➕ 183 E5 📧 15km (9 miles) west of Tangier 🕐 Daily 9 am–sunset 🚌 17
💷 Inexpensive ℹ no public transport

**Palais Mendoub**
➕ 183 E5 📧 Rue Shakespeare Tangier
☎ (212) 93 36 06 🕐 Daily 10–4
💷 Free

---

## TANGIER: INSIDE INFO

**Top tips** Tangier can be problematic at first, with **persistent hustlers** (*faux-guides*), drug dealers and pickpockets, particularly in and around the port and train station. Otherwise, it's a relaxed and easy place to get around.

**One to miss** Avoid the beach at night (except for the beach bars) as muggings are quite common, and the water is fairly dirty.

**Hidden gem** The 1960s Café Detroit in the kasbah is where the Rolling Stones met the Master Musicians of Jajouka (traditional Moroccan music), who subsequently appeared on their 1989 album *Steel Wheels*. It's a bit shabby but still has plenty of atmosphere and a splendid view.

# 2 Tetouan

The splendid white city of Tetouan, often known as "the Andalucian" or "the daughter of Granada", covers the slopes of Jebel Dersa and overlooks the fertile Martil Valley and the dark rocky mass of the Rif Mountains. The elegant city appears Hispanic at first sight, but it is influenced equally by the traditions and culture of the Berber tribes from the surrounding Rif. Some people claim the name Tetouan comes from the Berber word *Tit'ta'ouin* (the springs), which feed the city's many gardens and fountains.

Tetouan was founded in the 15th century by the military commander Sidi el Mandari and a group of Muslims and members of the Jewish community who were fleeing Spain after the fall of Granada. Soon after his death, el-Mandari's wife Fatima became the leader of the much-feared corsairs (► 28–29), bringing great wealth to the city, and also building most of Tetouan's ramparts in the 17th century. The refugees brought the artistic traditions of el-Andalus, reflected in the fine houses in the medina. When the Spanish occupied this part of Morocco in 1912, they made Tetouan the capital of their protectorate.

The best way into the **medina** is through Bab er Rouah on place el Feddan (formerly place Hassan II), which is dominated by the royal palace. The first street to the left of this gate leads to the charming **Souk el Hots**, overlooked by the **Alcazaba fortress**, with vendors selling traditional crafts, and the square of **Guersa el Kebira**.

The souks around **Souk el Foki** and **rue de Fes** are some of the nicest in Morocco, famous for *djellabas* (woollen hooded cloaks), leatherwork and woodcarving. UNESCO declared the medina a World Heritage Site in 1997, to protect its 50 or so mosques and other monuments.

To the right of Bab er Rouah is the **mellah** though, as elsewhere in Morocco, most of Tetouan's Jewish community have emigrated. Towards Bab Okla is the **Musée d'Art Marocain**, an ethnographic museum with textiles and embroidery.

The elegant mosque of Sidi Saïdi, named after a 13th-century saint who was buried at the same time as the city was founded

**View of the picturesque medina in Tetouan**

On the other side of the gate, the **École des Métiers** is worth visiting for both the building and the Moorish craft demonstrations. Near Bab Tout is the small **Musée Archéologique** with ceramics from nearby Tamuda, and fine mosaics from Lixus (► 108).

### TAKING A BREAK

Have a drink on the delightful **place de l'Oussa** in the medina. **Patisserie Rahmouni** (10 rue Youssef ibn Tachfine) has excellent Moroccan pastries and sweets, as does **Café-Patisserie Smir** (17 avenue Mohammed V).

---

🚩 183 E5
✉ Tourist ofice: 30 avenue Mohammed V ☎ (039) 96 19 15 🚌 Buses from Tangier, Chefchaouen, Fez and Meknes 🚆 Trains from Tangier, Rabat, Fez and Meknès ✈ Flights from Casablanca and al-Hoceima

**Musée d'Art Marocain**
✉ Scala, near Bab el-Okla ☎ (039) 97 05 05 🕐 Mon–Fri 9–4
💷 Inexpensive

**École des Métiers**
✉ Opposite el-Okla ☎ (039) 97 48 42 🕐 Mon–Thu and Sat 8–12 and 2:30–5:30 💷 Inexpensive

**Musée Archéologique**
✉ 2 Rue ben Hussain, off place el-Jalaa ☎ (039) 96 73 03 🕐 Mon–Fri 1–4
💷 Inexpensive

---

### TETOUAN: INSIDE INFO

**Top tip** In the late afternoon join in traditional Spanish *paseo*, when everyone goes out for a walk or sits on the terraces of pedestrianised rue Mohammed V.
■ **Beware of *faux-guides*,** sometimes cannabis dealers from the mountains, who are notorious for being the most aggressive in the country. If you want a guide, choose an official one recommended by the tourist office.

# ❸ Chefchaouen

Chefchaouen (or Chaouen), with its whitewashed houses perched high against the mountains, is one of Morocco's most picturesque towns. The name Chaouen comes from the Berber for "horns", a reference to the shaped rock above the town. This sacred "Blue City" of tranquil alleys and friendly people exudes an air of calm and mystery.

The city was founded in the 15th century by Moulay Ali ibn Rachid (a descendant of the Prophet Mohammed) near the tomb of Moulay Abdessalam, the Djebali tribe's patron saint believed to possess strong supernatural powers. This sacred city of many mosques provided a safe haven for many Andalucian Muslims fleeing the Catholic kings of Spain, but for a long time it was closed to non-Muslims.

The road from Chaouen to al Hoceima (► 110) is spectacular but it is also wild and dangerous. It takes around five hours to cover the 220km (140-mile) route, which features hairpin bends, steep mountain cliffs and, seasonally, strolling donkeys, mud slides and thick cloud.

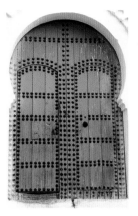

**Above: The fine light in the medina is created by reflections on the whitewash and blue houses**

**Opposite: In the maze of the medina, stumble upon beautiful doorways, sacred *marabouts* and weaving workshops**

Before the Spanish broke through in 1920 only three Christians had managed to enter and leave with their lives, including Walter Harris in 1889 (➤ 102).

The town is still traditionally divided into quarters, each with four mosques, four *hammams* and four *medersas* (Koranic schools). Elongated **place Uta el Hammam**, the central square, is dwarfed by the surrounding mountains. On one side of the square are small cafés and restaurants, with crowded cannabis smoking rooms on the upper floor. Although officially illegal, this is very much part of life here. On the other side are the imposing walls of the **kasbah**, and the **Grand Mosque** with a fine octagonal minaret. Inside the **kasbah** fortress is a wonderful **garden** with palms, fig trees and flowers, and a small museum containing old photos, musical instruments and crafts. The kasbah was built in 1672 by Moulay Ismaïl. The square is surrounded by *fondouks* (➤ 21), particularly on rue el Andalous. The Ville Nouvelle has a colourful souk on Mondays and Thursdays, where Berbers congregate from the surrounding mountain villages. The light in the medina is extraordinary, reflected on the walls of the houses that glow with a mix of whitewash, blue and ochre. The Djebala tribesmen had a strong tradition of homosexuality, and it is said that there was a boys market here until 937 when the Spanish abolished it.

On the southeast side of town is a Spanish mosque (open to non-Muslims). A path from here climbs into the mountains, beside small cannabis farms, and offers spectacular views over the town. A short walk from the medina is the small **Ras el Ma** river, a pleasant place for a dip, whose waters irrigate Chaouen's gardens.

## TAKING A BREAK

**Café-terraces** on place Uta el Hammam are the best place to rest, have a snack and watch the people go by.

➕ 182 E5
🏙 Souk: Mon, Thu 🚌 Bus from Tetouan, Fez, Meknès, Tangier and Ouezzane

**Kasbah/Musée Artisanal**
✉ Place Uta el Hammam 🕐 Daily 9–1, 3–6:30 💷 Inexpensive

---

### CHEFCHAOUEN: INSIDE INFO

**Top tip** Chefchaouen is a centre for the *kif* trade. Smoking cannabis is illegal in Morocco, so steer clear of the dealers.

**In more depth** As a location of maraboutism (➤ 12), there are a number of important *moussems* in and around Chefchaouen throughout the year, including that of Moulay Abdessalam ben Mchich in May.

# At Your Leisure

## ④ Larache

The pleasant little town of Larache
was a Spanish protectorate until
1956 and is still a good place to
eat paella and to watch the *paseo*
in the early evening. The medina
has retained plenty of character,
particularly in streets descending to
the sea. Prices in the souks are lower
than many places in Morocco, mostly
because foreign tourists have not yet
arrived in any numbers. The Spanish
fortress, the **Château de la Cicogne**,
overlooks a fine esplanade. Near
the 16th-century **Kebibat fortress**
and the lively fishing harbour is the
longer esplanade of avenue Moulay
Ismail. The French writer **Jean
Genet** is buried in a solitary tomb
in the Spanish cemetery.

Nearby is **Lixus**, one of the oldest
and almost continuously inhabited
settlements in Morocco, founded by
the Phoenicians in the 12th century
BC. The ancient town boasts a Roman
theatre and amphitheatre, baths with
a beautiful mosaic of *Neptune*, an
acropolis and temple sanctuaries.
➕ 183 E5 ✉ **96km (60 miles) south of
Tangier** 🚌 **Regular buses from Tangier,
Asilah, Rabat, Meknès and Ksar el-Kebir**

### Lixus
✉ **5km (3 miles) north of Larache** 🚌 **Bus 4
and 5 from Larache** 🕐 **Daily 8:30–5** 💵 **Free,
but tip the guard**

## ⑤ Asilah

This beautiful, whitewashed beach
resort, squeezed within ochre
ramparts and reminiscent of a village
in the Greek islands, was a Spanish
stronghold. At the end of the 19th
century Asilah was ruled by a local
bandit called Raissouli, whose palace,
between Bab Homar and the bastion,
is open during the international
music festival in August. The town
is peaceful now, and the medina –
best entered through Bab Homar
– is a pleasant and relaxed place
to stroll around. In summer sleepy
Asilah comes to life when crowds
of Moroccan families descend on its
splendid white beach.
➕ 183 E5 ✉ **45km (28 miles) south of
Tangier** 🚌 **Buses from Tangier, Larache, Fez
and Rabat** 🚆 **Trains from Tangier, Rabat and
Casablanca**

## ⑥ Ceuta

The Spanish enclave of Ceuta (Sebta)
on the peninsula of Monte Acho
faces Gibraltar across the strait, with
mountains on both sides forming
the so-called Pillars of Hercules.
Ceuta has a long history but little
to show for it. The baroque church
of Nuestra Señora de Africa and the
baroque cathedral flanks the Plaza de

**The Roman remains of Lixus are located
near by Larache**

The spectacular blue and white houses in Asilah on the Moroccan coast

Africa. The nearby Muséo de Ceuta has a small display of archaeological finds from prehistoric times to the Islamic period. The small **Museo de la Legión** offers a glimpse into the town's Spanish-African military history. The town's duty-free shops are a major attraction, but land border crossings are slow.

🚹 183 E5 🖂 40km (25 miles) northeast of Tangier. Tourist office opposite Ceuta Port Authority ☎ (056) 52 81 46; www.ceuta.es 🚌 Buses from Tangier, Casablanca, Tetouan and al-Hoceima

**Museo de la Legión**
🖂 Paseo de Colón 🕐 Mon–Sat 10–1:30 💲 Free

**Muséo de Ceuta**
🖂 Paseo del Revellin 🕐 Mon–Fri 10–2, 5–8, Sat 10–2 💲 Free

## 🛛 Rif Coast

The vast, wild and beautiful Rif Mountains, more than 300km (185 miles) long and 2,500m (8,200 feet) high, form the border between Europe and Africa, and Morocco and North Africa. The mountain scenery is spectacular, but best enjoyed from the safety of a bus, as passengers in foreign and rented vehicles have been robbed at knifepoint or forced to buy drugs, particularly around Ketama.

Shortly after ascending the throne in 1999 King Mohammed VI earmarked the whole Rif for development. However, progress has been hampered by limited access, as the mountains are often very close to the shore. Despite this, several tourist resorts have emerged along the coastline between Ceuta and Tetouan – **Smir-Restinga**, **Cabo Negro** and **Martil**. Southeast of Tetouan, the coast road climbs into the mountains and, although the beaches – such as **Oued Laou** and **Kaaseras** – are not as pretty and developed as those further north, they are almost deserted. The attractive road from al-Hoceima (► 110) to Cala Iris is dotted with tranquil little fishing villages.

🚹 186 A4 🚌 Regular buses from Tetouan to al-Hoceima and Fnideq; *grand taxi* to Oued Laou, Martil and Cabo Negro

## 🛛 Ouezzane

The town of Ouezzane, on the edge of the Rif Mountains, is twice sacred. It was founded in 1727 and developed around the Zaouia of Moulay Abdallah ben Brahim Cherif – a *sherif* (descendant of the Prophet Mohammed) and founder of the Tabiya Sufi brotherhood. The Sufi influence spread all over North Africa, and the *zaouia* (tomb), with its octagonal minaret, is still an important pilgrimage centre. The brotherhood is now based

**The heart of Ouezzane's medina is home to workshops of craftsmen and artisans**

elsewhere but the founder's *moussem* is still held at his *zaouia* (closed to non-Muslims). The tomb of the pious Rabbi Amrane, renowned for his miracles, also attracts Jewish pilgrims. The old town has much charm, while the souks are famous for woven rugs and iron work.

➕ 183 E4　✉ 60km (37 miles) southwest of Chefchaouen　🚌 Buses from Meknès, Fez, Chefchaouen and Rabat

### 9 Al Hoceima

Tiny and relaxed, this is one of best of the Rif coast beach resorts and a pleasant hang-out for a few days. It tends to get overrun by holiday-makers in midsummer, but is very sleepy for the rest of the year. The main attractions is the view over the Spanish islands of Peñon de Alhucemas and the chance to swim at the beach, **plage Quemado**, or nearby **Asfiha beach**. The road between al Hoceima and Chefchaouen is dramatic but can be dangerous.

➕ 186 A5　✉ 325km (202 miles) east of Tangier　🚌 Buses from Chefchaouen, Tetouan, Fez and Nador　✈ Flights from Tangier and Casablanca

### 10 Oujda

Oujda is important as one of only two border posts between Algeria and Morocco. The country's sixth city has considerable and valuable industry and mineral mines and is also a major agricultural centre. The **medina's** entrance is from the Bab Sidi Abd el Ouahab, where the heads of criminals were once hung. Place el-Attarine is the heart of the medina, with the Grand Mosque nearby.

At **Kissaria** traditional Moroccan clothing, jewellery and hand-woven cloth are for sale. Oujda is the perfect base to explore the spectacular **Beni Snassen Mountains (Monts de Beni Snassèn)**, with the **Gorges du Zegzel** and the **Grotte du Chameau**.

➕ 186 C4　🚌 Buses from main towns　🚆 Trains from Casablanca, Rabat, Fez and Meknès　✈ Flights from Casablanca

### 11 Moulay Bousselham

This small village on the Atlantic Ocean is the perfect base for walking or boat trips on the **Merdja Zerga (Blue Lagoon) National Park**.

The national park spreads over 7300ha (18,031 acres), with more than half of that taken in by the lagoon, and the rest with marshes. It is one of Morocco's prime birding spots, as it attracts thousands of migrant birds, including wildfowl, waders and flamingos. The lagoon is between 50cm (20 inches) and 4m (13 feet) deep depending on the tide, as most of the water comes from the sea, and only a fraction is fed by the Oued Dredr south of the lagoon.

The largest flocks of birds can be seen from December to January, but there are birds at any time of the year. You don't have to be an avid birder to enjoy this wonderful place. It is a forgotten corner of Morocco, overlooking the ocean and on the edge of a gorgeous lagoon. The fishermen around the lake are usually happy to take tourists on the lagoon, and there is a professional bird guide,who knows all the habitats Hassan Dalil (tel: (068) 43 41 10).

➕ 183 D4　✉ 325km (202 miles) east of Tangier　🚌 Regular trains from Tangier or Rabat to Souk el-Arba du Rharb, then bus or *grand taxi*　✈ Flights from Tangier and Casablanca

# Where to...
## Stay

**Prices**

Expect to pay for a double room per night, including breakfast and taxes

£ under 600dh    ££ 600–1,600dh    £££ over 1,600dh

Tangier has numerous hotels but, in summer, they get crowded with Moroccan families, so you will need to book in advance. Tetouan, however, has very few facilities, restaurants and hotels.

## ASILAH

### Hôtel Azayla £

Modern hotel in a quiet back street near the main street, the medina and the beach. The rooms are immaculate, some have partial sea view and all have large windows. The owner is a photographer and his black and white pictures hang throughout the hotel. Friendly service with a warm atmosphere.

➕ 183 E5 ✉ 20 rue ibn Rochd
☎ (039) 41 67 17

### Patio de la Luna £

This welcoming hotel is run by a Sevillian who fell in love with the place. Although right in the middle of the action, opposite the walls of the old city, the eight rooms decorated in traditional Moroccan style are surprisingly peaceful. There are terraces and a courtyard and a fireplace for winter.

➕ 183 E5 ✉ 12 place Zellaka
☎ (039) 41 60 74

## LARACHE

### La Maison Haute £

Wonderfully restored Hispano-Moorish house in the medina, with six charming and colourful rooms decorated in traditional style, but with modern bathrooms. Breakfast is served at a large central table or on the rooftop terrace with sweeping views over the souks and the ocean.

➕ 183 E5 ✉ 6 derb ben Tham
☎ (065) 34 48 88; www.lamaisonhaute

## CHEFCHAOUEN

### Dar Terrae ££

Moorish-Andalucian *riad* converted into a lovely hotel with a roof terrace overlooking the town.

➕ 183 E5 ✉ Avenue Hassan II
☎ (070) 98 75 98/46 53 70

### Hotel-Restaurant Tissemlal £

Decorated with local antiques, the first-floor rooms in this delightful, individual hotel are spotless. They do, however, overlook the courtyard restaurant and can be noisy during the evening. There is a large covered roof terrace, and a small gallery, which adds to the hotel's charm.

➕ 183 E5 ✉ 22 rue Targhi, next to the Parador Hotel ☎ (039) 98 61 53

### Parador ££

On the edge of Chefchaouen's medina you'll find this luxury hotel with small but beautifully decorated rooms. The terrace is a great place to relax with a small pool and great views over the mountains.

➕ 183 E5 ✉ place el-Makhzen
☎ (039) 98 61 36

## TANGIER

### Dar Nour £–££

Perched high up in the kasbah, this is a most charming hotel with a roof terrace with sweeping views. The rooms and suites are decorated with furniture from local flea markets and, although they have featured in several fashion and style magazines, feel homely. The breakfast is served in the rooms or on the terrace.

⊞ 183 E5 ☒ 20 rue Gourna, Kasbah ☎ (062) 11 27 24; www.darnour.com

### El-Minzah £££

This former villa of an English aristocrat is now an interesting luxury hotel. As Tangier's most stylish place to stay, it has seen its fair share of celebrities, including Sir Winston Churchill, King Juan Carlos of Spain and American actors Rita Hayworth and Dustin Hoffman. The swimming pool is shaded by majestic palm trees and surrounded by a garden filled with flowers and bougainvillea. The excellent restaurant serves the sophisticated Fez-style cuisine, while Caïd's Bar, with its list of cocktails and champagnes, is great for a relaxed drink while you're people-watching.

⊞ 183 E5 ☒ 85 rue de la Liberté ☎ (039) 93 58 85; www.elminzah.com

### Hotel Continental £

Tangier's most characterful hotel is set in a colonial and Moorish-style building commanding great views over the medina and the harbour. The refurbished rooms have retained their old-world atmosphere and gained some contemporary touches such as modern artworks and comforts. Many artists and writers have stayed here, including the French painter Edgar Degas (1834–1917). The former British prime minister Sir Winston Churchill (1874–1965) is reputed to have stayed in No 108, a large room with a four-poster bed and old-fashioned furniture.

⊞ 183 E5 ☒ 36 rue Dar el-Baroud, medina ☎ (039) 93 10 24/37 58 51

### Hotel Le Mirage £££

A great hotel, built on terraces, with sweeping sea views and surrounded by well-maintained gardens, the Mirage consists of luxurious, very stylish bungalows with flower-filled balconies. Extras include satellite TV, air-conditioning and room service. The restaurant is well worth a visit for its views alone, but the food is also extremely good. Specialities include lobster and fish cooked in a crust of sea salt, but the varied menu ranges from ordinary sardines to more exotic shark and sophisticated sea bass. Leave room for dessert.

⊞ 183 E5 ☒ Above the Grottes d'Hercules, Cap Spartel ☎ (039) 33 33 32; www.lemirage-tangier.com

### Riad Tanja £££

This is arguably the best, and one of the most popular, places to stay in Tangier, the Riad Tanja is centrally located near the American steps, the beautiful townhouse has six lovely and spacious rooms with traditional tiling and satellite TV. The *riad's* tiny but atmospheric restaurant boasts Moroccan-style nouveau cuisine, light and delicious, but expensive. ⊞ 183 E5 ☒ 2 Rue Amar Aïllech, off Rue de Portugal near the American Legation ☎ (039) 33 35 38; www.riadtanja.com

### La Tangerina £-££

A gorgeous guest house in a painstakingly restored *riad*, run by a friendly Moroccan-German couple who offer a warm welcome, and are very helpful in suggesting to guests how to make the best of their time in Tangier. The house is bright and tastefully decorated and the rooms are well-appointed. The rooftop terrace commands views over the bay.

⊞ 183 E5 ☒ 19, Riad Sultan, Kasbah ☎ (039) 94 77 31; www.latangerina.com

## TETOUAN

### Riad El Reducto ££

This traditional 18th-century mansion, the former home of the Spanish Governor, has been entirely renovated while keeping many of its original features: great Andalucian mosaic tiles, a wonderfully sculpted wooden courtyard and four splendid bedrooms sumptuously furnished in Moroccan style. Definitely the nicest place to stay in Tetouan.

⊞ 183 E5 ☒ Mechouar Essaid, 38 Zanqat Zawouia Qadiriya, Tetouan ☎ (039) 96 81 20; www.riadtetouan.com

# Where to...
# Eat and Drink

**Prices**

Expect to pay for a three-course meal per person, excluding drinks but including taxes and service

£ under 200dh  ££ 200–400dh  £££ over 400dh

In Tangier the cheapest places to eat are in the medina, but the food tends to be fairly basic. For more stylish restaurants, head for the Ville Nouvelle near place de France or the seafront.

## ASILAH

### Casa Garcia £–££

Spanish-style fish dishes and tapas are the specialities at this small restaurant opposite the beach. Go for succulent paella, grilled fish or octopus, eel, shrimp and barnacles, served with a glass of crisp and refreshing Moroccan rosé wine on the large and breezy terrace. This is the perfect place to relax and drink in the atmosphere.

➕ 183 E5 ⊠ 51 Rue Moulay Hassan ben el-Mehdi ☎ (039) 41 74 65 ◉ Daily 11:30am–11pm

### El-Oceano (Casa Pepe) £–££

The outdoor terrace, just beyond the ramparts, is a great place to eat Spanish-style fried fish or paella. The fish is always cooked to perfection. Recommended.

➕ 183 E5 ⊠ Rue Zellaka ☎ (039) 91 73 95 ◉ Daily lunch and dinner

## CEUTA

### Club Nautico ££

This very pleasant dining spot has views of the port and the Hacho fortress serves good and reasonably priced freshly caught fish dishes.

➕ 183 E5 ⊠ Calle Edrissis, in front of the yacht harbour ☎ (956) 51 44 40 ◉ Daily lunch and dinner

## CHEFCHAOUEN

### Casa Aladdin £

Good Moroccan food served in a traditional Moroccan-style restaurant on the second floor on a panoramic roof terrace. Specialities include tagines and grilled squid.

➕ 183 E5 ⊠ Rue ibn Askar ☎ (039) 98 90 71 ◉ Daily 10am–11pm

## LARACHE

### Restaurant du Port ££

A little out of the centre, near the harbour, this excellent fish restaurant is worth the trip as it serves the best fish and seafood in town. It is also the most upmarket place in Larache.

➕ 183 E5 ⊠ Larache Harbour ☎ (039) 41 74 63 ◉ Daily 11–5pm & 7–11pm

## TANGIER

### Café Hafa £

*Hafa* means "cliff", and this large café built on the cliff is worth visiting for its sea views. With tables set among flowerpots and plants, and with cats strolling around, the ambience makes it easy to linger here. This is where the Rolling Stones smoked *kif* and it's easy to understand why this was Paul Bowles's (➤ 32) favourite spot.

➕ 183 E5 ⊠ Behind the sports stadium in Quartier Marshan ◉ Daily 8am–10pm; closed in the day during Ramadan

### El Baraka (Chez Didi) £

Sweet little restaurant serving simple but tasty Moroccan dishes like tagine, couscous and *pastilla* (sweet pigeon pie). Excellent food and very good value.

183 E5 Near Hotel Andaluz, Rue Sidi Salem, Tangier (039) 98 69 88 Daily 11:30am–11pm

## El Korsan £££

Superb Moroccan specialities in an elegant, traditional décor. Some of the choices are pastilla and couscous with seafood. Service is excellent, with a floor show on weekends of local music and a belly dancer. This is a fun place to spend the evening.

183 F5 Hotel El Minzah, 85 rue de la Liberté (039) 93 58 85 Tue–Sun dinner only

## Laachiri £–££

This charming roadside restaurant, boasts a large terrace with great views overlooking the river, sea and the old fortress, is always popular with Moroccan families. Many come to enjoy the large portions of well-cooked fresh fish, available at reasonable prices.

183 E5 Ksar es Seghir, 33km (20 miles) from Tangier on the road to Ceuta and Tetouan Daily

## Restaurant Populaire Saveur de la Méditerranée £

This authentic restaurant is decorated with crafts, fishing nets and herbs, is a great place to enjoy simple fish dishes. There's no menu, but the friendly owner offers his suggestions and always has a pot of delicious fish soup on the stove. The sardines stuffed with chermoula (onion, spices, chilli and lemon), and the shark marinated in saffron are heavenly.

183 F5 2 escalier Woller, from place de France take the first stairway right into rue de la Liberté (039) 33 63 26 Sat–Thu lunch and dinner; closed during Ramadan

## Salon de thé Porte £

The swishest tea room in town, popular with local writers including Mohammed Choukri, has leather seats and tall columns. Delicious ice creams, fresh juices, coffee and pastries, are served.

183 E5 12 rue ibn Noussair (039) 93 34 33 Daily 8am–11pm

## Aux Vitamines £–££

This excellent fish restaurant is tiny – just seven tables. The owner, Ahmed, is a former racing driver who goes to the fish market every morning for fresh supplies, and does the cooking.

183 E5 Rue Walli al Hahd, Martil, Tangier Daily noon–3:30, 6:30–10:30

## Raîhani ££

This is an excellent Moroccan restaurant with colourful décor and wonderful ambience. It is justly famous for its couscous and pastilla with pigeon. Alternatively, there is also a French-Mediterranean menu.

183 E5 10 rue Ahmed Chaouki, Tangier (039) 93 48 64 Daily lunch and dinner

## Villa Joséphine £££

Built by Walter Harris, the famous Times journalist and the final summer residence of the Glaoui family of Marrakech, the Villa Joséphine is one of the most luxurious hotels in Morocco, with a restaurant overlooking the sea, serving the most sophisticated French cuisine in Tangier. This is the place for a special celebration. Book ahead.

183 E5 231 route de la Vieille Montagne, Cap Malabata (039) 33 45 35; www.villajosephine-tanger.com Lunch and dinner

## TETOUAN

## El Reducto ££

This riad hotel offers by far the best food and service in town, including tagines and excellent couscous, in a traditional Moroccan room.

183 E5 Mechouar Essaid, 38 Zanqat Zawouia Qadiriya (039) 96 81 20; www.riadtetouan.com

## Le Restinga £–££

The service is efficient and friendly at this old-fashioned restaurant, which serves excellent budget Moroccan meals, including tagines, couscous, and fried fish. Sit either inside or in the pleasant courtyard.

183 E5 21 rue Mohammed V (039) 96 35 76 Daily 11:30–11:30

# Where to...
## Shop

Although Tangier has an excellent range of shops to browse, there are no real bargains to be had. However, check out the antiques and junk shop opposite el-Minzah hotel, **Bazar Tindouf** (64 rue de la Liberté, tel: (039) 93 15 25), which has lanterns, carpets, copper and other objets d'art. The **Ensemble Artisanal** in the kasbah and on rue de Belgique (tel: (039) 93 31 00) sells Moroccan crafts.

Tangier has some interesting art galleries including the leading commercial art gallery in town, the **Lawrence-Arnott Art Gallery** (68 rue Amr Ibn Ass; tel: (039) 33 34 82; www.arnott-lawrence.com). The British directors are the North African representatives for the British auction house, Bonhams. They also sell engravings, books and antiques.

At **Volubilis** (6 rue Sidi Boukoiya, near the kasbah) you'll find a range of fine crafts, as well as clothes.

The **Ensemble Artisanal** on avenue Hassan 1 in Tetouan has a good if rather dusty selection of local crafts. For a better choice head for the souks in the medina. Stalls in **Souk el-Hots** sell traditional *foutas* – hand-woven cloth in red, white and black stripes or in plain brown – while at the weavers' co-operative you can buy fine woollen cloth normally used for *djellabas*. The **Souk el Foki** is a good place to look for traditional crafts. Chefchaouen has a good souk (Mon and Thu), and the **Galerie Hassan** at the Hotel-Restaurant Tissemlal (▶ 111) has local crafts

for sale, as well as works by local and Spanish painters. Shops in the souks sell the beautiful hand-woven cloth for which the town is famous.

Ouezzane is known as a good place to buy carpets, especially in the **weavers' souk**, where you'll need to bargain fiercely, or at the fixed-price **Ensemble Artisanal** on place de l'Independance, where the Thursday souk takes place. Colourful painted **furniture**, in the souk, is also a local speciality.

### ANTIQUES AND JEWELLERY

Tangier's **rue Touahin**, the first road off rue Siaghin from Grand Socco, has a line of eye-catching jewellery stalls selling Berber jewellery, but don't expect to find any real antiques.

**Boutique Majid** (66 rue Les Almohades; tel: (039) 93 88 92; www.boutiquemajid.com) has a long-standing reputation for its vast collection of rare Moroccan antiques, including textiles, woodwork, carpets, jewellery and ceramics.

### PERFUME

The Madini family has been making **essential oils** and **perfumes** for 14 generations. At their shop at 14 rue Sebou in Tangier's medina, they explain the processes involved in making different essences. They can match any perfume at a fraction of the original price. They also have a shop (5 boulevard Pasteur).

### FOOD

The **Marché Remla Kebira** (rue de Fez, Tangier; open 7am–9pm) is a good place to go food shopping for spices and dried fruits.

### BOOKS

The **Librairie des Colonnes** (54 boulevard Pasteur, Tangier; tel: (039) 93 69 55) has an excellent collection of French books, as well as a small range of English books on Morocco, and also Moroccan novels translated by Paul Bowles (▶ 30–31).

# Where to...
# Be Entertained

Listings for cultural and other events in and around Tangier can be found in the weekly *Les Nouvelles du Nord*, published on Friday and available free in most restaurants and hotels.

## NIGHTLIFE

The nightlife of Tangier is not what it was, though in summer the **beach bars** attract quite a crowd. Tourists should stick to the bars and avoid strolling on the beach at night as it can be dangerous. Many of the city's **discos** are in the streets off place de France. The liveliest is the **Morocco Palace** (13 avenue du Prince Abdallah Tangier), where the locals come for a night out with live Oriental music and the wonderfully kitsch décor. The

Mondial (opposite Hotel Solazure on avenue des FAR) is popular with affluent Moroccans and European residents. **The Tanger Inn** (16 rue Magellan, Tangier) is a great bar decorated with pictures of William Burroughs, Allen Ginsberg and Jack Kerouac, who lived above. **Dean's** (rue d'Amérique du Sud, Tangier) was another haunt of writers and artists. Much of Tetouan's nightlife takes place near the beach. Most nightclubs are in hotels in Cabo Negro, Mdiq and Restinga Smir.

## MUSIC, CINEMA AND THEATRE

The Spanish **bullring** in Tangier's Ville Nouvelle has been converted into a rock concert venue, but it rarely stages large gigs. Information on venues and dates for musical

performances is available from the tourist office (tel: (039) 94 80 50). **Institut Français de Tanger** (86 rue de la Liberté, tel: (039) 93 21 34) and **La Légation des États-Unis** (▶101) have regular films, theatre, dance and exhibitions.

Tangier's best cinema complex is **Dawliz**, in the Istiraha Tourist Complex on rue d'Hollande. In Tetouan try the **Ciné-Théâtre Espanyol** behind place el Jalal and the **Avenida** on place el Agdal, off avenue 10 May, which show mainly American or French movies. Every May, the Tanjazz Festival (www.tanjazz.com) attracts more than 100 international musicians to Tangier.

## SPORTS

The **Tangier Royal Golf Club** (tel: (039) 94 44 84) in the suburb of Boubana has a good course, as does the **Cabo Negro Royal Golf Club** just outside Cabo Negro (tel: (039) 97 83 03).

**Horse-riders** can hire excellent mounts for trips into the surrounding countryside at the **Club Équestre de l'Étrier**, on the road to Boubana (tel: (039) 93 48 84).

Stylish beach hotels and clubs in Tangier, Tetouan, Cabo Negro, Mdiq and Restinga Smir provide **watersports** such as waterskiing, jetsking and windsurfing.

## BIRDING

Birders can discover habitats in the wetlands and flatlands around Larache, and on the road from Larache to Tangier. Try the beautiful **Loukos** wetlands, southeast of Larache on the Ksar el-Kebir road. About 175km (110 miles) south of Tangier at **Moulay Bousselham** is the protected **Merdja Zerga** (Blue Lagoon), attracting a diversity of birds, including flamingos, bustards, crested larks and cranes. Hassan Dalil (068 43 41 10), a professional bird guide, is excellent and takes clients on fishing or walking tours.

# Imperial Cities
# and Middle Atlas

# Getting Your Bearings

The plain of Saïss and the Imperial cities of Fez (Fes) and Meknes are Morocco's heartland, and their history was for a long time also the country's history. Protected from the Mediterranean by the Rif Mountains and from the Sahara Desert by the Middle Atlas range, the fertile plain amply provided for the cities. Outside the grand urban centres the region's gentle natural attractions include the cedar woods near Azrou, picturesque landscapes, romantic lakes and the splendid Cascades d'Ouzoud.

The highlight of the Middle Atlas is undoubtedly Fez, the country's ancient political and administrative capital, and still its religious and intellectual centre. The city's medina – a UNESCO World Heritage Site – has a wealth of medieval monuments, some of them outstanding jewels of Islamic architecture. Its people, the Fassi – a mixture of Andalucian, Tunisian and Berber – have always had an independent identity and are often intellectuals and political leaders.

In the 17th century Moulay Ismail turned his back on Fez and moved the capital to Meknès, but over the years his megalomaniac building projects have fallen into spectacular ruin.

The Romans had already appreciated the area, and built Volubilis, the most important Roman ruins in Morocco. Not far from Volubilis is the shrine of the kingdom's most venerated Muslim saint, Moulay Idriss, the founder of Fez.

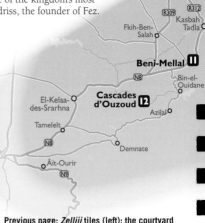

Previous page: *Zelliji* tiles (left); the courtyard of the Kairouine mosque at Fez el-Bali (centre); Fez medina
Left: A tour of the walls of Fez is a perfect introduction to the city. Right: Fez is the most complete medieval city in the Muslim world

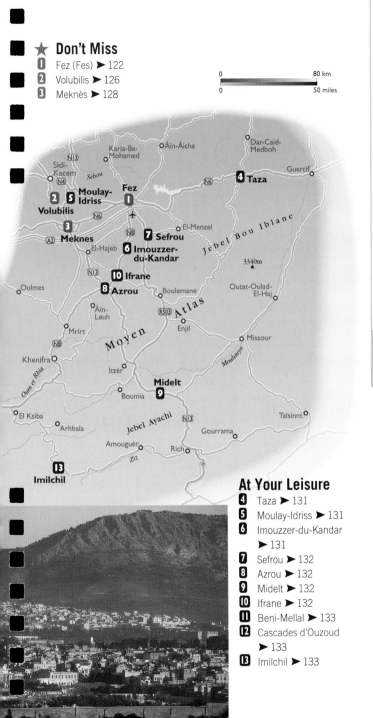

0            80 km
0            50 miles

# In Five Days

If you're not quite sure where to begin your travels, this itinerary recommends a practical and enjoyable five days in the Imperial Cities and Middle Atlas, taking in some of the best places to see using the Getting Your Bearings map on the previous page. For more information see the main entries.

## Day One

### Morning
Hop in a taxi and begin **❶Fez** (➤ 122–125) by viewing the city from a height, such as the terrace near the Merenid tombs. Drive to Bab Boujeloud at the entrance to the medina, then walk to the **Dar Batha Museum**. Follow rue Talaa Kebira to the **Medersa Bou Inania** and on to the **Medersa Mesbahiya** and the **Medersa Attarine**. Have lunch at the **Palais des Mérinides** (rue des Cherabliyin).

### Afternoon
Walk to the **Kairaouine Mosque** and the **Nejjarine complex**, then stop for tea in the lovely café of the **Nejjarine Museum**. Stroll around the **souks** and return to Bab Boujeloud.

### Evening
Have a romantic dinner in the Fassia restaurant of the **Sofitel Palais Jamaï** (➤ 135), on the terrace overlooking the medina (book in advance).

## Day Two

### Morning
From **Bab Jamaï** walk to **Bab Guissa**, then follow rue Hormis to place Sagha for refreshments before continuing through the **jewellers' souk** to the Medersa Attarin. South of the Seffarine Medersa is the **dyers' souk**, and nearby the **tanneries** (right). Continue to the **Andalous quarter**, then take a taxi to Bab Boujeloud for lunch at the Noria café in the Boujeloud Gardens.

### Afternoon and Evening
Stroll through **Fez el-Jedid** and the **mellah**, then tour the city walls by taxi before dinner in one of the *riads* in the medina.

# Day Three

**Morning**
Take a *grand taxi* to **5 Moulay-Idriss** (➤ 131) 65km (40 miles) away,
then walk the 4km (2.5 miles) to **2 Volubilis** (➤ 126–127). Have lunch
at the Corbeille Fleurie, next to the archaelogical site entrance.

**Afternoon and Evening**
Return to the sacred village of **Moulay-Idriss** for a wander around and a
drink at a café on the square before returning to your hotel.

# Day Four

**Morning**
Starting again from Moulay-Idriss, take a *grand taxi* 30km (19 miles) to
**3 Meknès** (➤ 128–130) for a stroll around sights such as the **Tomb of
Moulay Ismail, Bab Mansour** and **Heri es Souani**.

**Afternoon and Evening**
Have lunch at the Riad Bahia (P136) before visiting the **Dar Jamaï
Museum**, the **Bou Inania Medersa** and the **souks**. Stroll around the lively
Ville Nouvelle before dinner at **Le Riad** (➤ 135).

# Day Five

**Morning**
Buy a picnic in Meknès market and drive 55km (34 miles) south to the
market town of **8 Azrou** (➤ 132). Continue south on the Midelt (above)
road and after 8km (5 miles) take the gorgeous forest **Route Touristique
des Cèdres**. At Ain Leuh turn left on the S303 to the waterfalls of **Oum
er Rbia**, the source of Morocco's largest river, and a popular picnic spot.

**Afternoon and Evening**
After lunch and a swim, drive north to the beautiful Berber village of
**6 Imouzzer-du-Kandar** (➤ 131), then continue to the ancient walled
town of **7 Sefrou** (➤ 132) before heading back to Fez.

# ❶ Fez (Fes)

The oldest of Morocco's imperial capitals is not only the most complete Islamic city in the Arab world, it also has two medinas, Fez el-Bali and Fez el-Jedid. Fez el-Bali is the ultimate medina, designated a Unesco World Heritage Site in 1981. The maze of streets and alleys, some less than 60cm (2 feet) wide, is confusing at first, but it's a great place to get lost, and there are magnificent sights around every corner.

Moulay Idriss I founded Madinat Fez in the 790s, but it was his son Idriss II who developed it into a grand Arab city, with Muslims from Cordoba in the Andalucian quarter, and Tunisian Arabs in the Kairouanese, and a Jewish community. Without these foreigners' urban culture and artistic traditions, Fez may never have developed such grandeur.

At the end of the 11th century, the Almoravid prince Youssef ben Tachfine united the two parts of the city within walls. The city flourished further under the Almohades and enjoyed its golden age in the 13th and 14th centuries under the Merenids.

## Fez el-Bali

To understand the city's complicated layout it's best to start with a panoramic overview, especially from the terrace near the crumbling **Merenid Tombs** or from the **Borj Nord** fortress, both on a hill just outside the medina. The fortress also houses a small armoury museum. The main entrance to the old medina of Fez el-Bali is **Bab Boujeloud**, a gate built in 1913. Near by is **Dar Batha**, a beautiful Moorish building with a tranquil courtyard, where you can see one of Morocco's most interesting collections of popular arts, including carpets, *zellij* work, outstanding ceramics and calligraphy. Two main lanes lead from the gate to the **Souk el Attarine**, the **Talaa es Seghira** and the more interesting **Talâa el Kebira**. Here you'll find one of the country's most magnificent monuments: the grand **Medersa Bou Inania**, built in the 14th century by Merenid sultan Abou Inan, who had a reputation for being more interested in sex and murder than religion. Legend says that the religious leaders of the Qairaouine Mosque (see opposite) wanted Abou Inan to build his *medersa* on a rubbish dump if he wanted to build one at all. The sultan was then determined that his *medersa* would be more beautiful and more important than the Qairaouine Mosque. And his wish came true, at least for a short time, when his simple yet ornate construction became Fez's most important religious building. The skillful stucco, *zellig* and carving remain well preserved.

Opposite the *medersa* is Bou Inania's amazing **waterclock** (under restoration), which kept perfect time, but no one ever discovering exactly how. Further along the street are several *fondouks* (caravanserais), of which the city was supposed to

**Housewares stall in a souk in Fez**

A street vendor selling tempting desserts at Patisserie Dounia in Fez souk

have more than 200. Along rue Cherabliyin, several vendors sell reputedly the best *babouches* (slippers) in Morocco. The **Souk el Attarine** (spice market), the focus of the old medina, is where the most precious goods were sold, such as fine cloth, silk thread and jewellery.

## The Qairaouine Mosque

This grand mosque, founded in the 9th century by Fatima el-Fihriya, the pious daughter of a wealthy Fez merchant, was the largest in Morocco until the opening of **Casablanca's Hassan II Mosque** in the early 1990s. It also claims to be the oldest university in the world and still plays a leading role in the country's religious life. For non-Muslims it is hard to see the mosque, its exterior hidden behind surrounding buildings, the fine interior off limits. Also closed to non-Muslims is one of the city's holiest shrines, the **Zaouia and Tomb of Moulay Idriss II**. Nearby **place en Nejjarine** has the most beautiful of the city's fountains. The square is dominated by the 18th-century **Nejjarine** *fondouk*, with its small **woodwork museum** that houses well-displayed, beautifully made traditional objects, carvings and tools. The 14th-century **Medersa el Attarine** approaches the Bou Inania in its refined decoration and also has great views from the rooftop.

Near place Seffarine is the colourful **Souk Sebbaghin** (dyers' souk), and on the other side are the pungent but fascinating tanneries, best seen from the rooftops.

## Andalous Quarter

Although the residential Andalucian Quarter has no souks or major sights, being away from the tourist area, it's somehow more authentically Fassi. Highlights here include the **Andalucian Mosque** with its elegant courtyard. It was built in the 9th century by Myriem, the sister of Fatima el-Fihriya (founder of the Qairaouine Mosque), but was largely rebuilt by the Almohads in the 13th century. The 14th-century **Medersa es Sahrij**, a crumbling jewel of the Merenid period, is still partly used to accommodate Islamic students.

## Fez el-Jedid

New Fez is not new at all, but was built by the Merenids in the 13th century. Like Djemaa el-Fna in Marrakech, **Petit Méchouar** square was the playground for assorted performers until it was closed for repairs in the 1970s. These were never really finished, so it has not reopened. It is flanked on one side by the **royal palace** (closed to the public), one of the most sumptuous in Morocco.

The **Grande Rue des Mérénides** cuts through the *mellah* (Jewish quarter) of synagogues, cemeteries, abandoned 18th- and 19th-century houses, and a few less touristy souks. Most of Morocco's Jewish population left for Israel after its creation in 1948, and particularly after the Suez Crisis in 1956 when there were strong anti-Jewish feelings throughout the Arab world. The French-built **Ville Nouvelle** has hotels and restaurants but otherwise little of interest

### TAKING A BREAK

Enjoy the superb views from the beautiful garden of the hilltop **Sofitel Palais Jamaï** hotel (➤ 135). The café-terrace of the **Musée Nejjarine** is another great place, as is the cultural centre **Fez Hadara** (24 Oued Sourafine, Douh in Fez el-Bali; tel: (035) 74 02 92) with its large garden.

The huge, ornate entrance gates to the King's palace in Fez el-Jedid

The Zaouia of Moulay Idriss II is a site of pilgrimage, particularly for pregnant women, and for boys who are to be circumcised

🔲 183 F4

✉ Tourist office: place de la Resistance, Ville Nouvelle ☎ (035) 62 34 60
🚌 Buses from all main cities 🚆 Trains from Casablanca, Tangier, Rabat, Marrakech and Meknès

**Borj Nord Armour Museum**
✉ Near Hotel des Mérénides ⏰ Wed–Mon 8:30–noon, 2:30–6 🚌 Bus 20 from place de Florence 💰 Inexpensive

**Medersa Bou Inania and other medersas**
✉ Talaa Kebira, Fez el-Bali ⏰ Daily 8:30–noon; closed Fri prayer times 💰 Inexpensive

**Musée Nejjarine**
✉ Place en Nejjarine ☎ (035) 74 05 80 ⏰ Daily 10–5 💰 Inexpensive

**Dar Batha**
✉ Place de l'Istiqlal ☎ (035) 63 41 16 ⏰ Wed–Mon, 8:30–4:30 closed Tue 💰 Inexpensive

## FEZ: INSIDE INFO

**Top tips** If the medina looks overwhelming, **walk around it first with an official guide** from the tourist office and then return alone to stumble upon its secrets.
- See the medina from Borj Sud in the early hours or from Borj Nord or Sofitel Palais Jamaï at night, when it is lit by **thousands of small lights**.
- Sample some famous **Fassi gastronomy**, such as *choua* (steamed mutton with cumin), mutton stuffed with almonds, semolina and raisins, or tagine with wild artichoke hearts. These dishes usually require hours of preparation, so you need to order them 24 hours in advance.

# 2 Volubilis

The well-preserved Roman town of Volubilis, surrounded by lush countryside at the foot of Jebel Zerhoun, is one of the finest and most romantic archaeological sites in the country. The Berbers call it "Oualili" after the oleander flowers covering the nearby, and usually dry, riverbed. A guided tour of the highlights usually takes about an hour, but it's certainly worth spending a few hours strolling among the monuments.

The complex straddles the Fertassa River, with the entrance on one side and most of the ancient sights on the other. There are several Roman villas to explore, all divided into public and private rooms and now named after the mosaics found in them. The largest is the **House of Orpheus**, with fine mosaics of Orpheus with his lyre, of dolphins and of Amphitrite, wife of Neptune and goddess of the sea. Next door are the **Gallienus Baths**, which extended more than 1,000sq m (10,750sq feet).

The **Forum** is dominated by the impressive arcaded wall of the 3rd-century courthouse and the raised **Capitoline temple**, with elegant Corinthian columns, dedicated to Jupiter, his wife Juno and the goddess Minerva. North of the Forum is the **House of the Athlete** and the city's

**View of the residential area of Volubilis, still set in the countryside**

The impressive Triumphal Arch is built in local Zerhoun stone

## THROUGH THE AGES

The original Berber settlement was taken by Caligula in AD 45. As the Roman Empire's most remote outpost, the city flourished during the 2nd and 3rd centuries. But the Berbers returned at the end of the 3rd century and by the time the Arabs arrived in the 7th century there was a mixed population of Latin-speaking Berbers, Syrians and a Jewish community. Volubilis declined after 786 when Moulay Idriss (► 122) founded his capital in Fez, but it remained in good repair until Moulay Ismail (► 128) plundered the city's marble for his new settlement at Meknès. The ruins suffered more damage as a result of the 1755 Lisbon earthquake.

largest **public baths**, probably built by the Emperor Hadrian, covering more than 1,500sq m (16,000sq feet). The **Triumphal Arch** was built in AD 217 in honour of the Emperor Caracalla and his Syrian mother Julia Domna. It was once topped with a six-horse chariot and water would cascade from carved nymphs into marble basins below. More villas line the **Decumanus Maximus** road, at the end of which is the **Gordian Palace** and the **House of Venus** with splendid mosaics, where the beautiful busts of the Berber king Juba II and Cato were found (► 77).

### TAKING A BREAK

Corbeille Fleurie (tel: (035) 45 25 08), a small cafeteria-restaurant, offers cool drinks and good tagines. Out of summer the site and surrounding countryside are perfect for a **picnic**.

➕ 183 F4
✉ 31km (19 miles) north of Meknès 🕐 Daily 8–5:30, 6 in summer 🚌 From Meknès to Moulay-Idriss, then *grand taxi* to Volubilis (agree a return time)
🎫 Moderate

# ❸ Meknès

**Once the pride of the Morocco's most fearsome ruler, Meknès is now a thriving provincial town surrounded by farmland and vineyards. It boasts a fascinating medina and the remains of Moulay Ismail's grand plans to rival the capital cities of Europe, his legacy of marble and blood.**

Meknès was founded in the 10th century by the nomadic Meknassa tribe, who were drawn to this fertile area of abundant water.

The Almohades and Merenids embellished the city with mosques and *medersas*, but it remained small until 1672, when the new king Moulay Ismail made it his capital. Moulay Ismail greatly admired the French sun King Louis XIV and was keen to encourage co-operation between Morocco and France. Architecture was his passion and in Meknès he built huge palaces, mosques and walls, sometimes with marble plundered from Volubilis (► 126–127) and Marrakech's Palais el-Badi (► 62). Soon after his death in 1727 his dream city fell into ruins, looted by his successors and damaged by the effects of the 1755 Lisbon earthquake. Since the city became a UNESCO World Heritage Site in 1996, a lot of restoration work has been undertaken.

**The walled medina of Meknès**

**Place el Hedim** is where the imperial city and the medina meet. The monumental **Bab Mansour** has fine *zellig* decoration and ancient columns from Volubilis. Just past the gate the large, central square of **Lalla Aouda** is a popular meeting place for families. This was the processional square of **Dar el Kebira**, Moulay Ismail's palace with 24 separate compounds, secluded gardens and mosques, most of which were destroyed by his son. A gate in the southwest corner of the square leads to the lovely pavilion of **Koubbet el Khiyatin**, which was used by Ismail to receive foreign dignitaries.

Through the left-hand arch is the sumptuous **Tomb of Moulay Ismail**, which attracts pilgrims from all over the country. Only the courtyard can be visited, however, but the decoration, restored by King Mohammed V, is rich and exquisite. On the opposite side is **Dar el Makhzen**, a "small" royal palace. Another impressive sight is

**A CRUEL SULTAN**
Morocco's most brutal ruler was Moulay Ismail, who reigned from 1672 to 1727. He reputedly had a harem of more than 500 women, with whom he fathered 700 sons and countless daughters, all ruled by the heavy hand and heavier whip of his legitimate wife, Sultana Zidana. His plans for the new capital required the labour of some 50,000 captives. It's said that if the sultan was not happy with a work, he would crush the worker's head with a brick, decapitate him or slit his throat. Their blood was mixed with the cement.

**The lavish tomb of Moulay Ismail**

**Heri es Souani** (or Dar el Ma), the vast imperial granary. Next to it the **Aguedal Tank**, a huge basin that once supplied water to the fine palaces and gardens, is now a popular picnic spot.

On the other side of place el-Hedim is the **Dar Jamaï Museum**, a 19th-century palace, which has fine Moroccan arts and a tranquil Andalucian garden. The main street of the souk is **Souk es Sebat**, leading to the 14th-century **Bou Inania Medersa**, one of the country's finest. Outside Bab el-Berdain, the *marabout* of Sidi ben Aissa (closed to non-Muslims) is the centre of one of Morocco 's largest *moussems* on the eve of Mouloud – the Prophet Mohammed's birthday.

**TAKING A BREAK**

The rooftop café of the **Heri es Souani** has great views. Try the **Restaurant Zitouna** (44 Jamaa Zitouna near Bab Tizimi; tel: (035) 53 02 81) for lunch, or for a salad and a fruit juice try the courtyard of **Snack Bounania** (rue es-Sebbat, next to the Medersa Bounania). In the late afternoon or evening head for the buzzing Ville Nouvelle and try the fashionable café **Glacier Le Rex** (1 place de la Mauretanie; tel: 035 52 14 40), where young Meknassis come for fresh fruit juices and pastries.

➕ 183 E3
🚌 Buses from Fez, Tangier, Rabat, Ouezzane and Chefchaouen 🚆 Trains from Fez, Tangier, Rabat, Oujda and Taza

**Tourist Office**
✉️ Place Administrative; www.meknes.net.com ☎️ (035) 51 60 22
**Dar el Ma** ✉️ Imperial City 🕐 Daily 8:30–noon, 3–9 💵 Inexpensive

**Koubbet el Khiyatin**
✉️ Bab Fillala, off place Lalla Aouda 🕐 Daily 9–noon, 3–6:30 💵 Free

**Tomb of Moulay Ismail**
✉️ Imperial City 🕐 Daily 9–noon, 3–6; closed Fri morning 💵 Free

**Dar Jamaï Museum**
✉️ Place el-Hedime ☎️ (035) 53 08 63 🕐 Wed–Mon 9–5 💵 Inexpensive

**Medersa Bou Inania**
✉️ Rue Sebat, medina 🕐 Daily 9–noon, 2–6 💵 Inexpensive

**Haras Stud Farm**
✉️ South of Agdal, on the road to Azrou ☎️ (035) 53 07 53 🕐 Mon–Fri 9–11, 3–4 🚌 14, 15, 16 from Ville Nouvelle 💵 Free

The vast old granaries of the Heri es Souani are the most impressive sight of the Imperial City

---

## MEKNES: INSIDE INFO

**Top tip** Official guides wait near Bab Mansour, but both the city and medina are fairly **easy to get around**.

**Hidden gems** Check out the *kissarias* in the souks, with shops selling textiles, as they are better preserved than those of Marrakech.
■ Just outside town you'll find the amazing **Haras stud farm**, home to some of the world's most valuable Arab horses and mules (► 138).

# At Your Leisure

## 4 Taza

Perched impressively on the edge of a plateau, the medina of Taza overlooks the strategic pass between the Rif and the Middle Atlas, the origin of numerous invasions. It was said that whoever ruled Taza would eventually conquer Fez. A tour of the Almohad walls offers great views, while a walk in the charming medina leads through partly covered souks and past grand houses with beautiful, heavy, wooden doors and ornate window grilles.

➕ 186 A4 ✉ 120km (75 miles) east of Fez
🚌 Buses from Fez, Oujda and Nador 🚆 Trains from Fez, Oujda and Meknès, Casablanca

## 5 Moulay-Idriss

Morocco's most sacred village, hugging Jebel Zerhoun, is arguably also one of the most picturesque. Although its main attraction – the tomb of its eponymous founder – is closed to non-Muslims (who are only allowed to stay overnight in one of the few very cosy bed and breakfasts that have recently opened in the village), its beautiful alleys and narrow streets are well worth a visit, particularly combined with nearby Volubilis (➤ 126–127). Moulay Idriss I, a *sherif* (descendant of the Prophet Mohammed), founded the first Muslim kingdom in Morocco in the 8th century when he came from Mecca and converted the Berbers in Oualili to Islam.

A year later he founded Fez, and is considered the "Father of Morocco". Every August, the country's largest *moussem* attracts pilgrims from all over Morocco for several weeks. It is generally believed that five pilgrimages to the shrine here equals one hajj (pilgrimage) to Mecca.

➕ 183 E4 ✉ 30km (19 miles) north of Meknes 🚌 Bus from Fez and Meknes

## 6 Imouzzer-du-Kandar

In summer, Fassis come to this Berber village and mountain resort to enjoy the cooler air, the parks, the tree-shaded avenues and a swimming

**The hilltop village of Moulay-Idriss takes its name from the "Father of Morocco"**

pool filled with spring water. A souk is held every Monday in the ruined kasbah of the Aït Seghrouchen, which features the Seghrouchen tribe's unusual underground habitations. These offer increased security and protection from heat and cold. A track east out of town leads to the watchtower on Jebel Abad, from where it's a short walk to the summit for spectacular views.

➕ 183 F3 ✉ 40km (25 miles) south of Fez
🚌 Bus from Fez and Marrakech

## 7 Sefrou

This ancient walled city, nestled in the foothills of the Middle Atlas, features a small, picturesque and charming medina. Sefrou was strongly influenced by its once-thriving Jewish community, though Moulay Idriss I (➤ 122) passed through on his way from Mecca and converted many of its Berber and Jewish inhabitants to Islam. In the hills, within easy walking distance of the medina and the Mellah, are several springs and waterfalls.

➕ 183 F3 ✉ 28km (17 miles) south of Fez
🚌 Bus from Fez

## 8 Azrou

The charm of this small town of whitewashed houses with green-tiled roofs perhaps lies in its tranquillity. Built on the crossroads of two important routes (Meknès to Tafilalt and Fez to Marrakech) it's the main market for the semi-nomadic Beni Mguild Berber tribe, who cultivate lands in the mountains. In winter they descend to the plains with their herds and in summer they climb to the higher forests. Azrou is famous for its Berber carpets and cedarwood carving, on sale at the **Ensemble Artisanal** or the Tuesday souk. It is a perfect base for hiking the cedar forests nearby.

➕ 183 E3 ✉ 80km (50 miles) south of Fez
🚌 Buses from Meknès, Fez, Midelt, Ifrane and Casablanca

### Ensemble Artisanal

✉ Boulevard Mohammed V  ☎ (035) 56 24 30
🕐 Mon–Fri 8:30–noon, 2:30–6:30

## 9 Midelt

Midelt, a friendly town of red-tiled, French colonial chalets at the foot of Jebel Ayachi, makes a pleasant stop on the road between the Middle and the High Atlas. It's also an excellent base for hiking in summer or skiing in winter. Berbers in the surrounding villages make carpets and embroideries, which are sold in the kasbah at the **Atelier de Tissage**. About 25km (16 miles) out of town on Road 3419 there's a beautiful gorge along the Oued Moulouya.

➕ 183 F2 ✉ 125km (78 miles) southeast of Azrou

### Atelier de Tissage

✉ Kasbah Miriem, on the road to Tataouine (Rd. 3418)  ☎ (064) 44 73 75  🕐 Daily, except Fri, Sun and Aug

## 10 Ifrane

The French-built Ifrane in the 1930s as a ski-resort. It is almost surreal, an idealised alpine-style resort, with quaint red-roofed and well-tended parks, where the wealthy Fassis come skiing during winter weekends. From Ifrane it makes for a pleasant daytrip, if you have your own transport, to take a picnic and do the lake circuit around Dayet Aoua.

➕ 183 F3 ✉ Buses from Rabat, Casa, Meknès, Fez and Beni Mellal, 85km (53 miles) south of Fez

**The lovely old town of Midelt among the snow-capped Middle Atlas mountains**

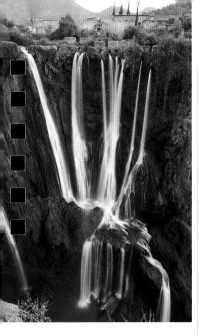

The multiple falls of Cascades d'Ouzoud are a popular day trip for locals

### ⓫ Beni-Mellal

On the road from Fez to Marrakech, Beni-Mellal is a green and pleasant town whose lushness is due to its many springs and its location near the Bin el-Ouidane dam. The town is surrounded by olive groves and citrus plantations, and its oranges are claimed to be the best in Morocco. The oldest and most pleasant part of town lies within the Kasbah Bel Kush, built by Moulay Ismail in the 17th century, but almost entirely rebuilt in the 19th. The **Aïn Asserdoun** ("Source of the Mule") is a powerful spring 3.5km (2 miles) south of town that feeds the orchards and the adjacent modern public garden. The restored stone fortress of **Borj Ras el Ain** (about 1km/0.5 mile further on) has views over the town.
✚ 183 D2 ✉ 190km (118 miles) south of Marrakech 🚌 Buses from Fez, Marrakech, Rabat and Azilal

### ⓬ Cascades d'Ouzoud

This is a popular excursion from Beni-Mellal. These 110m (360-foot) waterfalls are one of Morocco's most beautiful natural sights. Don't be tempted to dive into the shallow pools at their base; instead admire the falls from the promontory near Café Immouzzer, where you can see the water cascade through a glorious permanent rainbow. The striking surroundings include red cliffs, oleanders and wildlife such as turtles, crabs and monkeys. The falls are spectacular, but the site can get overcrowded, particularly at weekends or during the summer when Moroccan students camp in the area.
✚ 183 D2 ✉ 120km (75 miles) southwest of Beni-Mellal 🚌 *Grands taxis* and buses from Beni-Mellal

### ⓭ Imilchil

Nestled remotely amid stunning scenery in the heart of the High Atlas is this pleasant and authentic town. Although it's only accessible by four-wheel drive, it's definitely worth the effort for the famous Wedding Festival. The Berber Aït Haddidou tribe meets here every late August, or early September to celebrate the feast of the local saint. But this festival is now better known as an occasion for young Berber men and girls to meet the partner of their dreams, to get married (or sometimes divorced). It is a spectacular event with dancing, singing and romance. The event has been so overrun by tour groups that the tribe now holds one event for tourists, and one for themselves, only announcing the date of the latter at the last minute. Check with the Moroccan Tourist Office (➤ 174) for exact dates.
✚ 183 E2 ✉ 45km (28 miles) northwest of Agoudal 🚌 Four-wheel drive from Fez, Meknès and Marrakech (expensive), *grand taxi* from El Ksiba or organised tours

---

**FIVE GREAT PICNIC SPOTS**
■ **Cascades d'Ouzoud** (➤ below)
■ **Volubilis** (➤ 126–127)
■ The pools near **Immouzzer-du-Kandar** (➤ 131)
■ **Heri es Souani** and **Aguedal Tank**, **Meknes** (➤ 129)
■ The hills outside **Sefrou** (➤ 132)

# Where to... Stay

## Prices

Expect to pay for a double room per night, including breakfast and taxes

**£** under 600dh   **££** 600–1,600dh   **£££** over 1,600dh

When in Fez, the place to stay is on or near the Medina, close to the major sights and monuments. The *riads* are the most obvious places to stay and a further selection can be found on the website (www.Fesriad.com).

## AZROU

### Amros ££

This mountain hotel is surrounded by superb scenery and its location makes it a great base for hikers exploring the Middle Atlas. The rooms are cosy and comfortable, but the food isn't great.

The roof and chimneys of the hotel are covered in storks' nests.

**⊞ 183 E3  ⊠ 6km (4 miles) south of Azrou, on the road to Meknès  ☎ (035) 56 36 63**

## CASCADES D'OUZOUD

### Riad Cascades d'Ouzoud £–££

There are just seven rooms in this charming *pisé riad*, all restful and decorated in Berber style. The terrace and salon are great places to relax with views over the mountains. At night you fall asleep to the sound of the waterfalls. Breakfast is included, the Moroccan cuisine is excellent.

**⊞ 185 D4  ⊠ Next to the car park at Cascades d'Ouzoud  ☎ (023) 42 91 73; www.ouzoud.com**

## FEZ

### Dar Seffarine ££

Conveniently located in the middle of Fez el-Bali, this magnificent *riad* is superbly decorated with ancient *zellij* and sculpted wood, and many contemporary touches have been added by the current architect owners. The six bright rooms are restful and comfortable, offering excellent value for money.

**⊞ 183 F4  ⊠ 14 derb Shaa Louyate, Seffarine, medina  ☎ Tel: (071) 11 35 28/ (035) 63 52 05; www.darseffarine.com**

### La Maison Bleue £££

The entrance to this early 20th-century *riad* is through a gateway from a busy square, but inside the accommodation is calm and peaceful. Its six individual suites, all stylishly furnished with local antiques, overlook a blue-and-white tiled courtyard or the medina. The salon-style restaurant serves *pastillas*, tagines and couscous on the family silver. The house is known for its elegant Fassi evenings, when a set menu of salads, tagines, dessert and wine is accompanied by live classical *oud* or Gnaoua music. The owners also run a less expensive and livelier bed-and-breakfast with use of a swimming pool near the Riad Bleue.

**⊞ 183 F4  ⊠ 2 place de l'Istiqlal  ☎ (035) 74 18 43; www.maisonbleue.com**

### Riad al-Bartal ££

A French couple run this small, charming hotel of six suites in a 1930s trader's house. The ordinary façade hides a splendid interior – the rooms have blue-and-white tiled walls and are stuccoed in traditional Fez style. The rest of the décor is more eclectic, a mixture of local finds and old French furniture, and the bathrooms are decorated in mosaics. Children welcome.

**⊞ 183 F4  ⊠ 21 derb Sournas, Ziat  ☎ (035) 63 70 53; www.riadalbartal.com**

## Riad Fes £££

This is the grandest *riad* and the most sumptuous boutique hotel in town. The Riad Fes offers luxurious rooms and suites, elegantly decorated and well appointed, and set around two peaceful inner courtyards. The service is excellent, of course, and the hotel boasts an attractive bar, a good restaurant serving delicious cuisine and a small relaxing pool in the garden. Recommended.

☐ 183 F4 ☒ Derb ben Slimane, Zerbtana ☏ (035) 94 76 10; www.riadfes.com

## Riad Louna Bab Boujeloud ££

This charming *riad* has a fine courtyard filled with orange and apricot trees to admire. The rooms are simple but very comfortable, and the French owners are welcoming and knowledgeable about the city and how to have fun in it. They also organise cookery classes.

☐ 183 F2 ☒ 21 derb Serraj, Talaa Sghira, Bab Boujeloud, Fez medina ☏ (035) 74 19 85; www.riadlouna.com

## Sofitel Palais Jamaï £££

Set in a grand 18th-century pavilion built by a major Fassi family, this is *the* place to stay, if you can afford it. Some of the rooms overlook the ramparts, or have great views over the medina and the gorgeous Andalucian garden. The views are particularly spectacular at night, with the medina's lights and the floodlit mosque at the centre. Non-residents can enjoy dinner at al-Fassia restaurant (▶ 136) or a drink on the relaxing terrace.

☐ 183 F4 ☒ Bab Guissa, medina ☏ (035) 63 43 31; www.sofitel.com

## IMMOUZZÈR-DU-KANDAR

### Hotel des Truites £

At the entrance of Immouzzer you will find this old-fashioned hotel. It's worth seeking out just for its view over the valley. The comfortable rooms have high ceilings, wooden beds and central heating. The restaurant serves excellent food including their own wild boar ham and rabbit stew.

☐ 183 F3 ☒ Route de Fez, just outside Imouzzer-du-Kandar ☏ (035) 66 30 02

## MEKNÈS

### Palais Didi ££

The 11 sumptuous double rooms and lounges are arranged around a courtyard with a fountain. This palace was restored in purest Moroccan style, and it offers stylish accommodation. From the terrace there are spectacular views over the medina and the Royal Golf of Meknès. The service is friendly, in true Moroccan style, and the location is perfect for exploring the local sights.

☐ 183 E3 ☒ 7 Dar Lakbira, off avenue Moulay Ismail ☏ (035) 55 85 90; www.palaisdidi.com

### Le Riad

Surrounded by the walls of the Imperial city, La Riad is part of the grand 17th-century palace of Moulay Ismail. The six spacious and well-appointed rooms surround a flower-filled courtyard. The rooms are decorated with local textiles, pottery and sculpted woodwork.

☐ 183 E3 ☒ 79 Ksar Chaacha, Dar al Kabir ☏ (035) 53 05 42; www.riadmeknes.com

### Ryad Bahia ££

This tiny but very pleasant *riad* has just eight rooms, and feels more like being at home than a hotel. It is centrally located near the main square in the old city, and the rooms have been carefully restored by the owners. The décor is very Moroccan but with added colour. Friendly service.

☐ 183 E3 ☒ derb Sekkaya, Tiberbarine ☏ (035) 55 45 41; www.ryad-bahia.com

## VOLUBILIS

### Hotel Volubilis Inn ££

Set in a well-maintained garden, with views over the valley and Volubilis, this is an upmarket hotel. There is a swimming pool, and good food is served in the restaurant.

☐ 183 E4 ☒ 1km (0.5 mile) north of Volubilis, Moulay Idriss Zerhoun ☏ (035) 54 44 05

# Where to...
# Eat and Drink

**Prices**
Expect to pay for a three-course meal per person, excluding drinks but including taxes and service

£ under 200dh   ££ 200–400dh   £££ over 400dh

## FEZ

### Al Fassia £££

The Sofitel Palais Jamaï restaurant offers attentive service and good food in a romantic setting. If you want to try the Fassi specialities, such as roast lamb or sea bass with *chermoula*, order them the night before.

✚ 183 F4 ☒ Sofitel Palais Jamaï hotel, Bab Jamaï, Fez medina ☎ (035) 63 43 31 ⏰ Daily 8–11 pm

### La Kasbah £

Excellent budget option serving well-prepared Moroccan dishes, including tagines, couscous and grilled meats on two terraces with good views over the crowds at the bab Boujeloud, or in the Moroccan salon with low tables. No alcohol.

✚ 183 F4 ☒ Near the bab Boujeloud, Fez el-Bali ☎ No phone ⏰ Daily 9am–11pm

### Palais de Fès ££

This traditional Fassi restaurant is set in a sumptuous 19th-century palace. The terrace offers spectacular views over the medina. Only fixed menus are available, with delicious Moroccan salads, tagines and sweets, cooked by a women-only crew in the kitchen. There is a free taxi service available, otherwise call for directions.

✚ 183 F4 ☒ 15 Makhfia er-Cif, Fez el-Bali ☎ (035) 76 15 90 ⏰ Daily lunch and dinner

### Zagora ££

This trendy restaurant serves more sophisticated Moroccan and international cuisine than most, in colourful, contemporary surroundings. The set menu, which includes *harira* soup, *pastilla*, tagine and dessert, is good value, while the à la carte menu offers well-prepared dishes. The service is friendly.

✚ 183 F4 ☒ 5 boulevard Mohammed V, Ville Nouvelle ☎ (035) 94 06 86 ⏰ Daily lunch and dinner

## IMMOUZZER DU KANDAR

### Les Truites £

This is a very pleasant family restaurant with good views over the Fez plain, making it a relaxing place for a meal. It is equally known for the delicious French-Moroccan cuisine that is served here.

✚ 183 F3 ☒ Route de Fez ☎ (035) 66 30 02 ⏰ Daily lunch and dinner

## MEKNÈS

### Le Collier de la Colombe ££

This Moroccan restaurant serves traditional dishes in charming Moroccan rooms or on a terrace overlooking the medina. There is also a selection of international dishes including local trout with almonds. No alcohol.

✚ 183 E3 ☒ 67 rue Driba, near the place Lalla Aouda ☎ (035) 55 50 41 ⏰ Daily lunch and dinner

### Le Riad ££

Tucked quietly into the walls of the Imperial city is this beautiful *riad*, with its lovely gardens – perfect for a post-dinner wander – and terraces, where excellent Moroccan cuisine is served. The service is excellent.

✚ 183 E3 ☒ 79 Ksar Chaahcha, dar Lakhina, signs from place Lalla Aouda, ☎ (035) 53 05 42 ⏰ Sat–Thu lunch and dinner, Fri dinner only

# Where to... Shop

## ARTS AND CRAFTS

The **souks** in the medina in **Fez** are open Mon–Sat 9–8. Some also open on Sunday, while others close for Friday prayers around lunchtime. You'll find a large concentration of shops selling leather, ceramics, carpets, metalwork and musical instruments. Another good place in the city is the **Complexe Artisanal-Marocain** on avenue Allal ben Abdallah (tel: (035) 62 10 07), which has workshops and a large shop selling reasonably priced local crafts. **Fez** reputedly produces the best *babouches* (leather slippers). The most expensive are made from *ziouani* goatskin with no visible stitching. You'll find the main **leather souk** on rue ech Cherabliyin, the continuation

of rue Talla Kebira from the Medersa Bou Inania to the Medersa el Attarin (▶ 123). Fez is also famous for its blue-and-white **pottery**, found in the Potters' Quarter at the edge of the city on the road to Taza, and particularly the shop of **Fakhkhari Hamida**.

**Souk Joutiya ez Zerabi** (closed Sun), in an arcade off the textile souk in **Meknès** medina, sells good-quality carpets at a price, but it's worth bargaining. Near Bab el-Jedid is a small **flea market** (closed Sun) and a **souk** where you can buy handmade traditional musical instruments such as *ouds* (classical Arab lutes), *lotars* (Berber lutes), *rababs* (fiddles) and *tabls* (drums). The **Souk es Sebbat** (behind Dar Jamai) and the *kissarias* sell more tourist-orientated items such as jewellery, *kelims* and carpets.

The **Artisanat Moderne** (6 avenue Allal ben Abdallah, Ville Nouvelle) sells traditional and contemporary crafts. Near by is **Dal al Kitab al Watani**, a well-stocked bookshop. **Azrou** has a long tradition of producing carpets and blankets, and some good examples are sold in the Tuesday souk on the Khenifra road. Alternatively, the **Ensemble Artisanal** sells work from the weaving school, founded to preserve traditional patterns and to create new designs.

The Saturday market in **Souk Sebt des Oulad Nemaa** (22 miles) southwest of **Beni-Mellal**, is the largest in the Middle Atlas, where Berbers from all over the region sell their excellent carpets at reasonable prices. A good selection of Berber blankets, carpets and embroideries are also available from the shop at **Kasbah Miriem** run by Franciscan nuns, 500m (550 yards) from central **Midelt** on the 3418 road (tel: (064) 44 73 75; ▶ 132). The prices may be slightly higher than elsewhere, but the quality is superior. Carpets are also

sold in the small daily souk in the centre of Midelt and at the Thursday souk in **Sefrou's** small medina.

## JEWELLERY AND ANTIQUES

**Berrada**, at 40 boulevard Mohammed V in Fes, runs the most famous silver shop in Morocco, producing jewellery and other objects for the king. **La Maison Berbere** (4 Riaad Jouha, next to Medessa Attarine) sells a good selection of antiques and objets d'art. The jewellery souk in the medina at **Sefrou** has silver items inspired by the town's Jewish heritage.

## GIFTS

Spices, essential oils and traditional herbal potions and remedies are on sale in the **Souk el Henna**, just off place en Nejjarine in Fes. To the left of place el Hedim in Meknes is a beautiful covered market (Mon–Sat 9am–7pm, but some outlets close 2–5pm) selling fresh produce, spices and dried fruits.

# Where to...
# Be Entertained

## SPORT AND LEISURE

The mountains of the Middle Atlas are gorgeous and the region is perfect for **hiking**, particularly around Sefrou, Taza, Midelt and south of Azrou. From December to March there's often enough snow for **skiing**, but don't count on it. **Mischliffen**, the crater of an old volcano 12km (7 miles) from Ifrane (50km/31 miles south of Fez), has some old but functional ski-lifts and equally old-fashioned rental equipment. About 35km (22 miles) southeast of Fez is also **Jebel Bou Iblane** (3,190m/10,465 feet) with just one ski-lift.

**Anglers** will find the lakes and rivers well stocked with fish, including trout, bass and pike. You'll need your own kit and a permit from the Water and Forest Department (11 rue du Devoir in Rabat). The organisation also provides **hunting** permits, contact the **Royal Moroccan Hunting Federation** (rue al Kali, Rabat; tel (037) 70 78 35) for information.

**Horse-riders** can visit the largest stud farm in Morocco at the **Haras of Meknès** (tel: (035) 53 07 53), on the road to Azrou (bus 14 or 16 from the Ville Nouvelle). You can also take out temporary membership to exercise or ride the horses. Riding is also possible at the **Club Equestre** in Moulay Idriss at the racecourse (tel: (035) 62 34 38).

In Fez, play golf at **Royal Golf de Fes** (tel: (035) 66 52 10). Meknès has **Royal Golf** in the city centre, where you can also play at night (tel: (035) 53 07 53).

If your hotel in Fez lacks a **swimming pool** the best is at the **Transatlantique** hotel, where non-residents can swim for a fee. There are a few *hammams* in Fez, mainly used by locals, the **Hammam Bou Souifa** (Talaa Kebira; women 9am–9pm, men 9pm–8am) and **Hammam Sidi Azouz** (by Cinéma Boujeloud, women 1–10pm 10pm–noon men).

Moroccans go to two important **spa** villages near Fez. **Sidi Harazem** (15km/9 miles southeast) is the source of one of Morocco's most popular bottled waters and has age-old thermal baths and a swimming pool, but tends to be crowded. **Moulay Yaqoub** (20km/12 miles northwest) also has thermal baths used for medical treatments.

## MUSIC, THEATRE AND CINEMA

There is a good **Son et Lumière** (tel: (035) 76 36 52) where 12 centuries of history are told with lights on the medina and images.

In June each year, Fez holds the **Festival of Sacred Music**, when international artists perform at **Dar Batha** (▶ 122) and other venues in the medina (tel: (035) 63 48 24; www.fesfestival.com).

In Meknès, as elsewhere in Morocco, the **Institut Français in Zenkat Farhat Hached** (avenue Hassan II; tel: (035) 52 40 71) organises concerts, films and exhibitions (call for details). The Fez branch is at 33 rue Loukili, Ville Nouvelle; tel: (055) 62 39 21. Meknès also holds an international theatre festival during the first ten days of July in the Jardins Haboul.

## NIGHTLIFE

The bars in Fez can be seedy, but you can try the **nightclub** at the **Hotel Volubilis** (42 boulevard Abdellah, Cheïchaouni; tel: (035) 62 04 63), or at the **Jnan Palace** (avenue A. Chaouki; tel: (035) 65 22 30) or the **Hotel des Mérénides** (Borj Nord, tel: (035) 64 52 26).

# Atlas Mountains and the South

# Getting Your Bearings

Tourism has arrived since Edith Wharton wrote of southern Morocco's feudal chiefs and heat and savagery in her book *In Morocco* (1929). But the south is still exotic, and the chance of adventure remains. The tourist images of Morocco are often of the south: endless ripples of immaculate sand dunes, grand kasbahs, oases with thousands of palm trees, Berber villages hugging the mountains, and the blue men, nomadic Tuaregs who epitomize adventure and harsh desert life. But perhaps most evocative elements of the region are the majestic peaks of the High Atlas, where Africa really begins.

Tamelelt

Tensift  N7  N9  N8

Demnate

R207  Marrakech

Chichaoua

Vallée d'Ourika **7**

Telouet **10**

Imi-n-Tanoute

Amizmiz  Asni

Oukaïmeden **9**

4167m Jebel Toubkal ▲ **2**

Aït Benhaddou **4**

N8

Tizi n'Test **1**

Parc National de Toubkal

Ouarzazate **11**

Imouzzer des Ida Outanane

Aoulouz

Berhil

Souss

Haut Atlas

Tazenakht

Agadir

Taroudannt **6**

Talouine

N10

Inezgane

Biougra

Igherm

2531m ▲ Adrar-n-Aklim

Foum-Zguid

Tiferhal

Aglou Plage  N1

Tiznit **5**

Tafraoute

Anti Atlas

Tata

Mirleft (Mirhleft) **8**

Travelling has become easier here and almost every road offers spectacular vistas. Tourist facilities may be less luxurious than elsewhere, but there are plenty of other delights. The region has kept its authenticity and many of its traditions – the isolation of its villages gave rise to many reformist movements, including Ibn Toumert's Almohads. Life is hard in these extreme landscapes, but it's also simple and often joyous, and the people, mostly Berbers, are friendly and welcoming.

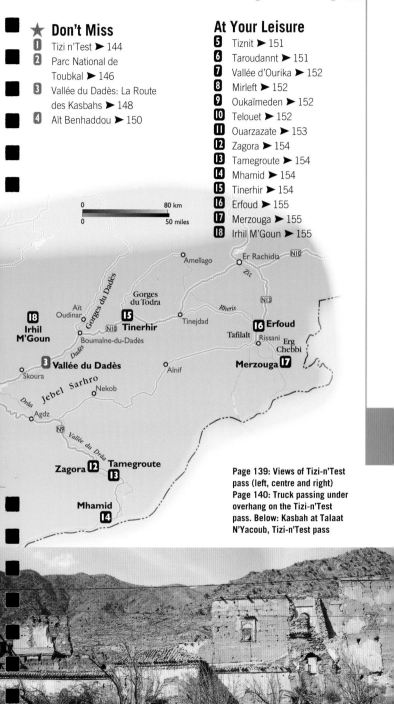

0     80 km
0     50 miles

Amellago    Er Rachidia  N10

Gorges du Dadès

Gorges du Todra

Zit

Rheris    N13

18 Irhil M'Goun

Aït Oudinar

N10  15 Tinerhir    Tinejdad    16 Erfoud

Boumalne-du-Dadès    Tafilalt    Rissani

Dadès    Erg Chebbi

3 Vallée du Dadès    Merzouga 17

Skoura    Alnif

Jebel Sarhro    Nekob

Drâa

Agdz

N9  Vallée du Drâa

Zagora 12  Tamegroute 13

Mhamid 14

**Page 139: Views of Tizi-n'Test pass (left, centre and right)**
**Page 140: Truck passing under overhang on the Tizi-n'Test pass. Below: Kasbah at Talaat N'Yacoub, Tizi-n'Test pass**

# In Six Days

If you're not quite sure where to begin your travels, this itinerary recommends a practical and enjoyable six days in the Atlas Mountains and the South, taking in some of the best places to see using the Getting Your Bearings map on the previous page. For more information see the main entries.

## Day One

**Morning**
From **6 Taroudannt** (➤ 151) take the P32 to Oved Bekhil (39km/24 miles). Stop for a drink at Riad Heda, a former palace (tel: (028) 53 10 44) then take the S201 to the **1 Tizi n'Test pass** (below ➤ 144–145), and the **Mosque of Tin Mal**. Have lunch at **Hotel La Roseraie** at Ouirgane (➤ 157).

**Afternoon**
Go for a walk or a horse ride in **2 Parc National de Toubkal** (below, ➤ 146–147) around Ouirgane, especially the **Gorges Nfiss**, a popular picnic spot. Stay at Chez Momo or continue to the **Kasbah du Toubkal** (➤ 156).

## Day Two

**Morning**
Drive towards Marrakech, then to Ouarzazate via the **Tizi n'Tichka** mountain road (➤ 170–172). Turn left after the highest point for the fascinating kasbah of **10 Telouet** (➤ 153). Have lunch opposite **Glaoui kasbah** (➤ 153, 171).

**Afternoon**
Return to the main road and turn left before Ouarzazate to explore the ksar of **4 Aït Benhaddou** (left; ➤ 150), then continue to Ouarzazate.

## Day Three

**Morning**
Explore **11 Ouarzazate** (➤ 153), then continue to the **Atlas film studios** and have a lunch at the **Kasbah Tiffoultoute** (tel: (024) 88 22 42), 8km (5 miles) west of town on the P31E to Zagora.

**Afternoon and evening**
Take the **3** **Vallée du Dadès: Route des Kasbahs,** ➤ 148–149) to Skoura for a stroll through the palms and the kasbahs of **Dar Aït Sidi el-Mati** and **Amerdihil**. Drive on to visit **Kelaa M'Gouna** and its rose gardens, before heading for **Boumalne du Dadès** and a night in the Kasbah Tizzarouine.

# Day Four

**Morning**
Take the 6901 towards **Msemrir**, following the Dadès Valley (above). After Aït Oudinar cross the bridge to reach the **Dadès** (above) and **Todra Gorges**, after which the road becomes a piste. Lunch at **Auberge Chez Pierre** (➤ 159–160).

**Afternoon and evening**
The auberge offers four-wheel drive excursions to isolated Berber villages, but you need to book in advance (tel: (024) 83 02 67). Alternatively, walk in the gorges before returning to Chez Pierre for the night.

# Day Five

**Morning**
Start early for the 75km (47 miles) drive to **15** **Tinerhir** (➤ 154–155) and enjoy views over the palmeraie from the Hotel Saghro, north of town. Explore the palmeraie by bicycle, which can be rented at **Ali VTT** (tel: (024) 83 43 59). Have lunch at **Hotel Oasis** (Avenue Mohammed V, tel: (024) 83 36 70).

**Afternoon and evening**
Drive north following the Todra River to the Hotel Yasmina at the entrance to the **Todra Gorges**. Admire the gorges on foot, then return for the night.

# Day Six

**Morning**
Return to Tinerhir early and take the 3451 – lined with kasbahs, palmeraies and oases – east towards Erfoud. About 2km (1 mile) from town stop for lunch at the **Kasbah Tizme** (tel: (035) 57 61 79).

**Afternoon and evening**
Continue to **16** **Erfoud** (➤ 155), a good base for exploring the region. Book a four-wheel-drive with guide in advance from the Kasbah Xaluca Maadid (tel: (035) 57 67 93; www.xalucamaadid.ma, ➤ 156) to visit the sand dunes in **17** **Merzouga** (➤ 155). Return to the Erfoud for the night.

# ❶ Tizi n'Test

The Tizi n'Test pass lies on a road that cuts through the
High Atlas between Asni and Taroudannt. As well as being an
amazing feat of engineering, the road is also one of the most
spectacular in Morocco.

As a main access to the south of the country, the highway
has played a significant role in Morocco's history. Before the
road was built, the mountain Berbers could easily close the
pass and block the passage to the south. But since the French
opened the Tizi n'Test in November 1928, the south and the
mountains have become much more accessible.

The Tizi n'Test starts at **Asni**, a pleasant little town in a
fruit-growing area and with an interesting Saturday souk.
This is the turn-off point for Imlil and hikes in the High Atlas.
After Asni the landscape gets increasingly dramatic – the
mountains become wilder and more barren as you climb, and
there is often snow on the peaks. **Ouirgane**, a peaceful village
16km (10 miles) away with a few comfortable hotels serving
good food, makes an excellent hiking base. The road follows
the Nfiss River, which is full of trout in spring.

At the beginning of the 20th century the Tizi n'Test was
controlled by the powerful Goundafa family, who built several
kasbahs along the way. These include the privately owned one
at **Agadir n'Gouj**, just before the Almohad **Great Mosque**

*A different
view is
around every
bend of this
spectacular
highway.*

### IBN TOUMERT

After studying in the Orient, the 12th-century Berber Mohammed ibn Toumert returned to Morocco convinced that the country's Islamic faith needed purifying. When he forced the king's sister off her horse because she was not veiled, he was banished from Marrakech and set up a base in Tin Mal, where he declared himself the Mahdi or "Chosen One". In exile he and his lieutenant Abd el-Moumen preached to the Berbers, formed a religious and military force – the Almohad or "Unitarian" movement – and went on to conquer Morocco and southern Spain.

**Fossils for sale on the Tizi n'Test pass**

of **Tin Mal** that rises high up above the Tizi n'Test on a mountain slope. Looking more like a fortress than a mosque, it was built by Abd el-Moumen in around 1153 as a cult centre for his leader Ibn Toumert (see box).

About 8km (5 miles) further south is the 19th-century kasbah of **Tagoundaft** perched on a steep rock. Another 22km (14 miles) from here is the actual col (pass) of the Tizi n'Test which, at 2,092m (6,863 feet), offers panoramic views over Toubkal (➤ 146–147) and the Sous Valley. Once past the col the road descends steeply, dropping about 1,600m (5,000 feet) in less than 30km (20 miles). Along the road, picturesque hamlets overlook cultivated terraces.

### TAKING A BREAK

**Café La Belle Vue** (past the col) really does have a great view and serves good tea and snacks. For something more elaborate try **Hotel La Roseraie** (➤ 157).

➕ 184 C3
✉ Between Asni and Taroudannt    🚌 Buses from Marrakech and Taroudannt

**Great Mosque of Tin Mal**
✉ 40km (25 miles) from Ouirgane    🕐 Sat–Thu; ask caretaker
💶 Inexpensive (plus tip)

---

## TIZI N'TEST: INSIDE INFO

**Top tips** From November to April the road can be blocked by snow. Signs in Asni, Marrakech and Tahanoute usually announce **road closures**, but check with tourist offices in Marrakech or Taroudannt beforehand.

- The best way to see it is by **driving yourself**, but experience of handling mountain roads is essential.
- **Avoid driving around midday** in summer as cars can overheat.
- Fill up with petrol before you leave as there are **no filling stations** between Asni and Oved Bekhil.

# ② Parc National de Toubkal

On a clear day, the snow-capped peaks of Jebel Toubkal, the highest mountain in North Africa, are visible from both Taroudannt and Marrakech. Hiking in the mountains is becoming increasingly popular, which isn't surprising given the majestic landscapes, where lush garden terraces and little rivers contrast with the harsh, rocky wilderness. The reserved but friendly Berbers still maintain a fascinating and relatively traditional lifestyle in their picturesque villages.

Jebel Toubkal rises to 4,167m (13,671 feet), but even the surrounding mountains are all above 3,000m (9,800 feet). The main paths are well trodden, particularly from Imlil to Jebel Toubkal, and are suitable for walkers of all levels (► 167–169). The full hike can be completed in about 16 hours, though going too fast may cause altitude sickness. Despite its popularity, the area is so vast that it is easy to escape the "crowds" which, in reality and away from Toubkal itself, seldom comprise more than a few other walkers. The paths are generally well kept and there is a good network of refuges and *gîtes*; some villagers also rent out basic rooms for the night.

The small town of **Imlil**, at 1,740m (5,709 feet), is the most obvious starting point for walks and hikes up Jebel Toubkal and around the area. It has shops selling or renting out equipment and provisions, and numerous mountain guides and muleteers on hand; mules can be rented by the day to carry luggage.

An hour's walk away is **Aremd**, a gorgeous Berber village perched on a rock overlooking the surrounding plain. Most people sleep at the Neltner hut (3,207m/10,522 feet) of the Club Alpin Français, four hours from Imlil, before climbing to Toubkal's summit, from where there are fantastic views. From Imlil, other paths lead to the main ski resort of **Oukaïmeden** (► 162) in about seven hours, the Berber village of Tachedirt (8km/5 miles east of Imlil, about three to four hours) or to **Ouirgane**, a day away on the Tizi n'Test road.

The mountains provide a unique habitat for a variety of wildlife including several species of butterfly, squirrels, vultures, larks and golden eagles, and the local Berbers raise their large herds of Barbary sheep and goats on the mountainsides.

**USEFUL ADDRESSES**
For information on hiking in the Jebel Toubkal area, contact:
- **Kasbah du Toubkal, Imlil**
  ☎ (024) 48 56 11;
  www.kasbahdutoubkal.com
- **Royal Moroccan Ski and Mountaineering Federation**
  ☎ (022) 20 37 98
- **Club Alpin Français (CAF)**
  ☎ (022) 27 00 90;
  www.cafmaroc.co.ma
- **Bureau des Guides (Imlil)**
  ☎ (024) 48 56 26

A Berber, in traditional dress, rides through the Toubkal Mountains

## TAKING A BREAK

**Berber-run kiosks** at popular stops sell tea, cold drinks and, occasionally, simple, traditional food and snacks. There are also **small restaurants** in Aremd and Imlil, or book lunch at the **Kasbah du Toubkal** (➤ 158).

🔲 184 C3
✉ 65km (40 miles) south of Marrakech
🚌 Buses from Marrakech and Taroudannt to Asni, then regular trucks to Imlil

### PARC NATIONAL DE TOUBKAL: INSIDE INFO

**Top tips** The **best time to visit the mountains** is in September and October or May and June; in summer visibility may be poor and thunderstorms or flash floods can occur. Between April and November, reasonably fit and determined walkers can also tackle the route. From December to March, snow, ice and short days make climbing to the top dangerous, even for experienced hikers.

■ There are also other beautiful, **less demanding walks** on the lower slopes starting from Imlil, Aremd or Ouirgane (➤ 167–169).
■ Take decent walking boots, hat, sun cream, sunglasses and plenty of water.
■ Spend a night or two at the award-winning **Kasbah du Toubkal** (➤ 157). in Imlil, or the new **Toubkal Lodge**.

**In more depth** For more detailed information on the great trails across the Atlas read Richard Knight's *Trekking in the Moroccan Atlas* and Michael Peyron's *Great Atlas Traverse* or other guidebooks available in Imlil.

# ③ Vallée du Dadès: La Route des Kasbahs

The Dadès River drains off the peaks of the High Atlas and cuts a deep and dramatic gorge before it flows, more gently, into the Draa River. Most visitors follow the river upstream, from Ouarzazate to Tinerhir, taking in Berber settlements, surprising oases and, best of all, the spectacular gorges of Dadès and Todra.

The Dadès Valley (Vallée du Dadès) is often exaggeratedly described as the "road of a thousand kasbahs"; however, several kasbahs along the route are both beautiful and intriguing. Along most of the route the river is hardly visible above the ground and the P32 road follows the plain, which is flanked dramatically by the High Atlas and Jebel Sarhro on either side. Oases appear like mirages in this harsh and desolate landscape. This is certainly true for **Skoura** (30km/19 miles east of Ouarzazate), one of the most beautiful oases, with lush vegetation and kasbahs appearing through the trees. At the entrance to this 17th-century oasis is the Kasbah de Ben Moro, now a fine hotel. Behind this you'll find

**The Dadès River meanders slowly past kasbahs in the broad valley at the foot of the High Atlas**

**Amerdihil** – this is the most extravagant and impressive of all the Glaoui kasbahs. Directly across the river is the grand kasbah of **Dar Aït Sidi el Mati**.

Another 50km (31 miles) on is the town of **el Kelaa M'Gouna**, famous for its fields of pink *Rosa damascina*. About 4,000 tonnes are collected annually and distilled into rose water for cooking or essential oils for perfume. A rose festival is held each year in May or June. The town has a souk on Wednesday, but rose water is always on sale in local shops and at the kasbah-like factory.

About 15km (9 miles) further along the main road is the hilltop town of **Boumalne du Dadès**. This makes a perfect base for exploring the **Jebel Sarhro** region of volcanic peaks, gorges and picturesque Berber villages, and the **Vallée des Oiseaux** – a birders' paradise offering a wealth of species that include desert larks, eagle owls and sand grouse. The town is also the gateway to the **Gorges du Dadès**.

The route to the gorge, which veers off the main road, is spectacular in itself, lined with kasbahs and *ksour* amid luxuriant gardens. But the gorge, with its high limestone cliffs

and strange rock formations, is definitely worth a detour. The kasbahs, many of which are still inhabited, come in all colours from chalk-white and earthy-reds to dark green.

The area of **Tamnalt**, 3km (2 miles) from Boumalne en route to the gorges, is also called the "Hill of Human Bodies" because of its bizarre rock formations. Further on, the river forms deep canyons past the bridge of **Aït Oudinar**. From here it's possible to cross over to the Todra Gorge only by four-wheel-drive. Otherwise you have to return to Boumalne du Dadès and continue to **Tinerhir** (➤ 160) to visit the palmeraies and the **Todra Gorge**.

### TAKING A BREAK

The **Kasbah Tizzarouine** (tel: (024) 83 06 90) at Boumalne du Dadès serves good Moroccan food. The **Auberge Chez Pierre** (➤ 159–160) in a *pisé* building near pont d'Aït Oudinar offers exceptional food.

---

## THE DADÈS VALLEY: INSIDE INFO

**Top tips** You'll need a **rented car** (preferably four-wheel-drive) if you want to try out a few pistes. An ordinary car will do for the main sights. You can rent vehicles from the local hotels, which also organise guides for the more difficult treks in the area.

- In **palmeraies** such as Skoura you need to walk and the gardens are vast: to save time and effort it may be useful to engage a local guide.
- The best way to visit the valley around the Dadès Gorges is by simply **walking along the river**.

# 4 Aït Benhaddou

**One of the best-preserved and most photogenic *ksour* in the Moroccan south features a cluster of deep-red houses and intricately decorated kasbahs on a steep rock towering over a shallow river.**

Aït Benhaddou was an important caravan stop between Ouarzazate and Marrakech, and the fortress commanded views over the entire area. It lost its importance when the French built the Tizi n'Tichka road in 1928 (➤ 170–172). However, a few families still live in the old village, some of whose buildings are said to be more than 500 years old. As the *pisé* (mud-clay) from the riverbed used in the buildings threatens the *ksar*, UNESCO has declared it a World Heritage Site and is slowly repairing the erosion to the amazing buildings.

The kasbah was so well protected that the way in is not always obvious, especially after the main entrance was apparently boarded up during a film shoot. Strangely, entry is now through a kitchen, which gives way to a small square from where you can easily explore the narrow streets, the Berber houses and the fortress at the top of a steep hill. Film buffs may recognise certain areas, as the *ksar* is a popular film location, seen in the movies *Lawrence of Arabia, Alexander the Great* and *Gladiator*.

**Hollywood can't top this spectacular setting**

### TAKING A BREAK

Visit **Dar Mouna** (➤ 156), a short walk across the river from the kasbah, for a cooling mint tea, a set lunch and perhaps a dip in the pool. Stay overnight at the auberge or in one of several simple little hotels and see the changing colours of the ksar at sunset or by moonlight.

➕ 185 D3  ✉ 30km (19 miles) northwest of Ouarzazate  🕐 Daily 8–6  🚌 *Grands taxis* from Ouarzazate  💰 Free; tip for visiting private houses

# At Your Leisure

## ⑤ Tiznit

Standing on the arid Sous plains, the salmon-pink houses of Tiznit are enclosed by 6km (4 miles) of red-mud ramparts. The town was founded at the end of the 19th century by Sultan Moulay Hassan, who brought in the Jewish craftsmen and made Tiznit famous for its fine silver jewellery that can still be found in the old **jewellers' souk**.

The minaret of the **Grand Mosque** is strewn with little perches, jutting out of the brickwork to provide resting places for the souls of the dead as they ascend to paradise. The style is more common south of the Sahara. Near the mosque is the **tomb of Lalla Tiznit**, a prostitute who reformed and became extremely pious. Legend has it that when she was martyred, God created the pool across the street, optimistically known as the Source Bleue. Northwest of Tiznit is Aglou Plage, a huge beach which is dangerous for swimming but has a good surf.

🚻 184 A2 ✉ 90km (55 miles) south of Agadir
🚌 Buses from Tata, Ifni, Agadir, Guelmim and Taroudammt

### BERBER JEWELLERY

Tiznit is famous for its Berber jewellery, always silver as gold is still believed to attract the evil eye. More than adornment, jewellery is worn to protect from evil, and to identify the status and tribe of the wearer. The necklaces, rings and bracelets include charms, such as hand of Fatma (protection),fish (fertility), the moon and stars and amulets bought from holy men or herbalists. Amber is worn as a symbol of wealth but offers strong protection against evil, while coral promotes fertility, as do shells. Large and ornate fibulas or brooches are used to hold the women's garments together.

## ⑥ Taroudannt

At the heart of the fertile Sous Valley, this is the main market town in the area, renowned for its crafts – Berber jewellery, marble animal carvings and other sculpture, and heavy woollen cloaks and *djellabas*. Taroudannt's two souks, the **Souk Arabe Artisanal** and the **Marché Berbère**, are among the most relaxed in Morocco (Thursday and Sunday), with fewer touts and less pressure to buy. The town flourished during the 16th century when the Saadian kings made it their first capital before moving to Marrakech. They built the well-preserved, ochre city ramparts around the **kasbah**, but the rest of the walls and bastions date from the 18th century. The most pleasant way to admire them is cycling or by *caleche*, particularly at dusk. The **kasbah**, a village within the town, contains the winter palace of the Saadians, the ruins of a fortress built by Moulay Ismail and the attractive Melia Palais Salam hotel.

🚻 184 B3 ✉ 80km (50 miles) east of Agadir
🚌 Buses from Agadir, Tata, Ouarzazate, Marrakech and Essaouira

Taroudannt has a more African feel than the other cities in Morocco

A typical Monday morning Souk scene in Tnine l'Ourika village

### 7 Vallée d'Ourika (Ourika Valley)

Do as the Marrakchis and escape the city heat in the gorgeous and lush Ourika Valley. You'll find country houses, small hotels, and numerous café-terraces, from where you can admire the views and enjoy the cooler climate. At the km34 marker on the S513 road from Marrakech is **Tnine l'Ourika village**, which has an excellent Monday souk.

The Ourika River curves through a deep-cut valley dotted with small mudbrick *douar* (villages). The road has superb viewpoints and follows the river up to Setti Fatma, ideal for a walk, a picnic and a dip in one of its waterfalls.

184 C4  Tourist office: Tnine village, km33 on the road from Marrakech  (068) 46 55 45  Buses, minibuses, *grands taxis* from Marrakech

### 8 Mirleft

This town has become a favourite hang out for those in search of gorgeous empty beaches and a relaxed atmosphere; in the way Essaouira (see ➤ 81) once was. The town has one very sandy dusty main road, with a few small hotels and cafe-terraces. Mornings here are usually spent choosing one of the several fantastic beaches, with Plage Marabout being the most dramatic one with a saint's tomb among the rocks. The hotels organise surfing, fishing trips or desert drives. The town seems to attract artists, surfers and backpackers, and is blessed with some charming guesthouses and fish restaurants.

184 A2  40km (25 miles) southwest of Tiznit

### 9 Oukaïmeden

On the slopes of Jebel Oukaïmeden, at 2,650m (1,650 feet) Morocco's premier ski resort. The snow varies annually, but there can be good piste and off-piste skiing from January to

---

**ON LOCATION AT ATLAS STUDIOS**

*Alexander the Great* (2004): Oliver Stone movie starring Colin Farrell and Angelina Jolie.

*Gladiator* (2000): Ridley Scott, starring Russell Crowe and some great effects.

*Kingdom of Heaven* (2005): Another Ridley Scott movie with Orlando Bloom and Eva Green, about the 12th-century Crusades.

March. A ski-lift runs to the top of the mountain (3,273m/2,034 feet) and guides are available for cross-country trips and skiing on other slopes. "Ouka" is also a summer resort, providing respite from the heat in Marrakech, or as a base for trekking in the surrounding area and Toubkal National Park (➤ 146–147).

🔲 184 C4  ⊠ 74km (46 miles) south of Marrakech  ☎ Club Alpin Français (024) 31 90 36  🚗 Private car or taxi

### 🔟 Telouet

The sleepy village of Telouet is overlooked by its magnificent crumbling **Glaoui kasbah**, built in the early 20th century. This remote spot now seems an unlikely place to built a fortress, but before the construction of the Tizi n'Tichka in 1928 (➤ 170–172) it was an important caravan stop between Ouarzazate and Marrakech. For three years, 300 workers sculpted the walls and the ceilings of the headquarters of the powerful Glaoui brothers, but they were abandoned in 1956. The labyrinthine buildings are now fast melting back into the red earth.

🔲 185 D4  ⊠ 21km (13 miles) east off the Tizi n'Tichka  🕐 Glaoui kasbah: no opening hours, but the caretaker is usually around  🚌 Bus from Marrakech  💷 Free (tip the caretaker)

### 🔢 Ouarzazate

At the foot of the High Atlas, this is a good base for exploring the Sahara, the kasbahs and river valleys. This modern town, developed in the 1920s as a French garrison and administrative centre, is less picturesque than other Moroccan cities. However, the town's only sight – the **Taourirt kasbah** – is one of the most beautiful in Morocco. This sumptuous residence of the Glaoui family, built entirely in *pisé*, has remarkable decoration, but neglect means that only the courtyard and some very ornate rooms in the harem can be visited. There are great views over the kasbah from the terrace, and the **Centre Artisanal** opposite sells good-quality crafts. The **Atlas Studios** on the other side of town have earned Ouarzazate a reputation as the Hollywood of the desert. A rather surreal sight is the grand film sets in a wilderness, but the studios can usually be visited via the Oscar Salam Hotel inside the compound.

🔲 185 D3  ⊠ 204km (128 miles) southeast of Marrakech

#### Tourist Office

⊠ Avenue Mohammed V, opposite the post office  ☎ (024) 88 24 85

#### Taourirt Kasbah

⊠ Avenue Mohammed V, 1.5km (1 mile) from the centre  🕐 Daily 8–6:30  💷 Inexpensive

The charm of Zagora is its location; it makes a superb base for expeditions into the dunes near M'Hamid

**Centre Artisanal**

✉ Opposite Taourirt kasbah ◷ Mon–Fri
9–noon, 3–6:30

**Atlas Studios**

✉ 6.5km (4 miles) out of town on the
Marrakech road ☎ (024) 88 71 71;
www.atlasstudios.com ◷ Daily 8:30–11:50,
2:30–5:50

## 12 Zagora

The town has become famous for
a signpost that reads "Tombouctou
52 jours" or 52 days by camel to
Timbuctou in Mali. It was from here
that the Saadians from Arabia began
their conquest of Morocco in the
16th century. And it was from here
that they later began the adventure
that led them to conquer Timbuctou
and control the Saharan gold trade.
The large administrative town has
little charm, but it does have a good
souk on Wednesday and Sunday.
It also makes an excellent base for
venturing into the magnificent red
sand dunes near M'Hamid, about
30km (19 miles) south, and Jebel
Zagora commands spectacular views
over the Draa Valley, the Amazrou
palmeraies and the dunes.

➕ 185 E3 ✉ 168km (104 miles) southeast
of Ouarzazate 🚌 Buses from Ouarzazate
and Mhamid

## 13 Tamegroute

This intriguing village is an old
religious centre famous for its **Zaouia
Naciriya**, a Koranic school founded
by Mohammed ben Nassir in the
17th century. Its important library of
Islamic manuscripts includes Korans
written on gazelle skin. The school
and library are open to visitors, but
the sanctuary containing ben Nacir's
tomb is closed to non-Muslims.
Pilgrims suffering from mental
problems and hypertension stay at
the *zaouia* hoping for a miraculous
cure. The village is interesting in
itself, and its kasbahs and ksour
connected by dark passages are well
worth exploring. The **potters' co-
operative** has some archaic kilns and
produces wonderfully simple green
and brown pottery, colours obtained
from local manganese and copper.
There is a Saturday souk.

➕ 185 E3 ✉ 22km (14 miles) south of
Zagora 🚌 Bus from Zagora, Mhamid

**Zaouia Naciri**

✉ Off the main road ◷ Daily 9–noon, 3–4
💷 Donations welcome

**Potters' Co-operative**

✉ Off the main road ◷ Daily 9–7

## 14 Mhamid

That Mhamid was once an important
stop on trans-Saharan caravan routes
is best illustrated by its population of
Berbers, Saharan Arabs and people
thought to originate from Sudan.
The modern town is small, with a
colourful Monday souk. The real
interest lies in the surrounding sand
dunes, which should be visited only
by four-wheel drive and with a guide,
or by camel. It is best to ignore
the travel agents in Zagora and go
straight to Mhamid where one of the
best and most experienced travel
agents is Sahara Services (tel: (061)
77 67 66; www.saharaservices.info).

➕ 185 E2 ✉ 40km (25 miles) from the
Algerian border 🚌 Daily bus from Tinfou and
Zagora (94km/58 miles)

## 15 Tinerhir

Charming Tinerhir overlooks
magnificent palm groves, some of
the largest and most beautiful in
Morocco, alongside the Todra River.
The palmeraies belong to the Aït Atta
tribe, many of whom live in small
kasbahs scattered around the palm
groves and orchards. The centre
is dominated by a ruined but still
impressive Glaoui kasbah (officially

---

**MARATHON DES SABLES**

Every year a run is held in the arid
desert around Merzouga and Foum
Zguid, when hundreds of runners
attempt to cover 229km (142 miles)
in just six days. Not surprisingly,
this competition is considered to
be the toughest run of its kind
(www.saharamarathon.co.uk).

closed). The town is noted for its ironwork and has a lively souk on Tuesday. The dramatic **Todra Gorge** is only 15km (9 miles) away.

➕ 185 E4 ✉ 70km (44 miles) northeast of Ouarzazate 🚌 Buses from Ouarzazate, Marrakech, Casablanca and er Rachidia

## 🔟 Erfoud

This small settlement on the edge of the Ziz Valley was built in the 1930s by the French Foreign Legion. It is the departure point for excursions to the **Tafilalt** region of vast palmeraies, remote Berber *ksar* and the sand dunes of Merzouga. Every October many visitors and several Berber tribes gather in Erfoud for the **Date Festival**, which features a large souk, camel races, folk dancing and the election of the Date Queen. Nearby **Rissani** is the birthplace of **Moulay Ali Cherif**, founder of the Alaouite dynasty, and is an important pilgrimage site.

➕ 186 A1 🚌 Buses from er Rachidia, Ouarzazate, Marrakech, Meknès and Rissani

## 🔟 Merzouga

The road from Erfoud to Merzouga requires a four-wheel-drive vehicle and shouldn't be attempted during a

**"Blue Men" have an almost mythical status as nomads who inhabit the desert.**

sandstorm, which can happen at any time, all year round. The attraction here is the desert, and the nearby **Erg Chebbi** dunes are breathtaking. At 150m (500 feet) high, the dune outside the Hotel Merzouga is the tallest in Morocco. It is an interesting place: Berbers swear by a sand bath, being buried up to the neck in sand in midsummer (➤ 162). Many hotels organise desert activities.

➕ 186 A1 ✉ 50km (31 miles) from Erfoud 🚌 Bus from Erfoud

## 🔟 Irhil M'Goun

The M'Goun massif is at 4,068m (13,346 feet), Morocco's second largest peak after Toubkal (➤ 146). The area, particularly the Aït Bougmez Valley, is of exceptional beauty as the sedimentary rock forms marvellous gorges and escarpments, and the Berber villages seem untouched by time, except for the satellite dishes.

➕ 185 D4 ✉ Bureau des Guides, Azilal ☎ (023) 45 94 30 🚌 Bus Marrakech–Azilal, then minibus to the Aït Bougmez Valley

# Where to... Stay

## Prices
Expect to pay for a double room per night, including breakfast and taxes
**£** under 600dh    **££** 600–1,600dh    **£££** over 1,600dh

## AÏT BENHADDOU

### Dar Mouna £–££
Friendly guesthouse overlooking the picturesque kasbah. Definitively the most pleasant place to stay in this area, with great views at night.

✚ 185 D3  ⊠ Aït Benhaddou
☎ (028) 84 30 54; www.darmouna.com

## ERFOUD

### Auberge Kasbah Derkaoua £–££
This French-run auberge in the desert, has a few simple but tasteful rooms and bungalows. Taking the evening meal is obligatory but the food, served in the olive grove or in the grand salon at night, is excellent. The owner can advise on local excursions, and the hotel has its own camels, horses and mules for exploring the desert.

✚ 186 A1  ⊠ Km23, between Erfoud and Merzouga  ☎ (035) 57 71 40; www.aubergederkaoua.com

### Kasbah Xaluca Maadid ££
A wildly extravagant new kasbah that mixes Spanish and Moroccan décor in 140 rooms built around a swimming pool. The hotel has bikes and quad bikes, and organises excursions.

✚ 186 A1  ⊠ 5km north of Erfoud
☎ (035) 57 84 50; www.xalucamaadid.com

## IGHREM N'OUDAL

### I Rocha £–££
A delightful guesthouse run by Ahmed, a geologist who was born in the village, and Catherine, who is a great cook. The rooms are simple and set around a courtyard filled with plants. It is a great base to stay while hiking in the wild scenery of the High Atlas or the Flint Oasis.

✚ 185 D3  ⊠ Tisseldi, on the Tizi n'Tichka road  ☎ (067) 73 70 02; www.irocha.com

## IMLIL

### Kasbah du Toubkal ££
An award-winning eco-friendly mountain retreat overlooking North Africa's highest peak, Mount Toubkal, and set in the picturesque village of Imlil, this is the perfect base for hikers. The 15 rooms are decorated in traditional Moroccan style and the terraces and communal salons are peaceful places to relax. The hotel has a plunge pool and a *hammam*, as well as a great restaurant, where no alcohol is served, but you can bring your own. Also a great excursion from Marrakech, so come for a walk and book lunch at this hotel.

✚ 184 C4  ⊠ Imlil, Asni  ☎ (024) 48 56 11; www.kasbahdutoubkal.com

## KELAA M'GOUNA

### Kasbah Itran £
This small kasbah overlooking the M'Goun river is a perfect base for those wanting to hike in the area.

✚ 185 E4  ⊠ On the outskirts of Kelaa M'Gouna  ☎ (024) 83 71 03/(062) 62 22 03; www.kasbahitran.com

## M'HAMID

### Dar Azawad £–£££
This comfortable hotel is located in a palm grove amongst the sand dunes south of Zagora. It has 13 air-conditioned rooms, decorated in Marrakchi style with local crafts, and

eight nomad tents in the garden with private bathrooms. When you're not admiring the desert you can relax by the pool. The restaurant is excellent.

**+ 185 E2 ⊠ Doular Ouled Driss ☎ (024) 84 87 30/(061) 24 70 18; www.darazawad.com**

### OUARZAZATE

#### Dar Daif £-££

Zineb and Jean-Pierre Datcharry's hotel, in a restored pisé kasbah, has views over the lake and the snowy Atlas peaks. The hotel has 11 well-appointed rooms, a *hammam*, swimming pool and a garden. The owners run the Désert et Montagne travel agency (tel: (024) 85 49 49; www.desert-montagne.ma), which specialises in treks into the desert.

**+ 183 D3 ⊠ Douar Talmasla, 5km (3 miles) of track after Hotel La Vallée ☎ (024) 85 42 32; www.dardaif.ma**

### OUIRGANE

#### La Roseraie £££-£££££

Splendid old-fashioned hotel at the heart of a 22ha (54-acre) park and mature gardens. The luxurious bungalows overlook the beautiful gardens and the surrounding Atlas Mountains. The hotel has a swimming pool (for residents only), stables and a terrace restaurant with good food, although not very inspired, and views over the mountains and the river below.

**+ 184 C4 ⊠ 60km Route de Taroudannt ☎ (024) 48 56 94; www.laroseraiehotel.com**

### SKOURA

#### Dar Ahlam £££

If money is no object, then Dar Ahlam offers ultimate luxury tucked away in the Skoura palmeraie. The hotel has just nine suites and three villas with private, heated pool, a large spa and a gourmet restaurant with French chefs. The hotel also has five tents in the desert, and offers 4X4 vehicle tours.

**+ 185 D3 ⊠ Northeast side of Skoura ☎ (024) 85 22 39; www.relaischateaux.com**

### TAROUDANNT

#### Dar Zitoune ££

A luxurious hotel with comfortable rooms in new bungalows set in a perfumed garden with fruit trees and a large heated swimming pool and a *hammam*. The large rooms are furnished in a simple but attractive local style with working fireplaces. The restaurant is one of the best in town, offering a mixture of Moroccan and Italian cuisine.

**+ 184 B3 ⊠ Boutarialt el Berrania, 1,5km from the centre of Taroudannt ☎ (028) 55 11 41; www.darzitoune.com**

#### Kasabat Annour ££

This newcomer right up against the kasbah walls, offers six bright and elegant rooms, a splendid swimming pool, a spa and hammam and two cheaper rooms built into the thick kasbah walls, which have separate bathrooms.

**+ 184 B3 ⊠ Kasbah ☎ (028) 85 45 76; www.kasabatannour.com**

### ZAGORA

#### Kasbah Asmaa ££

Within the pisé walls is a kasbah and with traditional rooms surrounding a courtyard. Rooms in the new building are more comfortable but those in the towers have splendid views. The lush garden has a belvedere overlooking the large palmeraie and a pool. Romantic andlelit dinners are served in the garden or in the elegant Moroccan salon.

**+ 185 E3 ⊠ 2km (1 mile) from Zagora ☎ (024) 84 72 41**

#### Villa Zagora £-££

Wonderful small villa with five lovely rooms decorated in local traditional style, and with friendly and helpful staff. In the winter you can sit and relax with a book or enjoy a delicious dinner by the warm fireplace; in summer, there is a roof terrace with views over the stunning mountain range. Very friendly service.

**+ 185 E3 ⊠ Amezrou ☎ (024) 84 60 93; www.mavillaausahara.free.fr**

# Where to...
## Eat and Drink

### Prices
Expect to pay for a three-course meal per person, excluding drinks but including taxes and service

£ under 200dh    ££ 200–400dh    £££ over 400dh

Many of the places to eat in the south of Morocco are often either in hotels or in *gîtes*. Some of the nicest restaurants are often booked by tour groups at lunchtime, which sometimes means that individual travellers are set aside and overlooked.

on a terrace, where travellers and locals like to hang out and relax.

➕ 185 F4 ✉ 103 Avenue Mohammed V
☎ (035) 577958 ⏱ Daily, lunch and dinner

### GOULMIMA

## Les Palmiers ££
This tranquil guesthouse on the edge of the palmeraie is surrounded by a large well-kept garden, and is run by a friendly French-Moroccan couple. The food served here is very good

➕ 185 F4 ✉ Goulmina, at the edge of the palmeraie ☎ (035) 78 40 04
⏱ Dinner only, by reservation

### ERFOUD

## Cafe Dadani £
Pleasant cafe-restaurant with a laidback atmosphere where the well-prepared traditional Moroccan dishes, such as tagines, are served

### IMLIL

## Kasbah du Toubkal ££
This is a great place to eat; the food is excellent and served on the terrace, or in one of the salons. Book ahead.

➕ 184 C3 ✉ Imlil ☎ (024) 48 56 11/
(061) 34 33 37; www.kasbahdutoubkal.com
⏱ Daily lunch and dinner

### MERZOUGA

## Ksar Sania £
Ksar Sania is well worth the short walk from Mezouga, both for its location and the delicious Moroccan-French food. Guests eat outside in the garden overlooking the sand dunes and oasis in summer, or in the large dining room in winter. The mainly Moroccan menu includes an couscous with lamb, salads and tagines, but the French owners offer a few classic French dishes as well.

➕ 186 A1 ✉ Ksar Sania Hotel, 1.5km (1 mile) outside Merzouga, on the piste to Taouz ☎ (035) 57 74 14 ⏱ Daily breakfast, lunch and dinner

### OUARZAZATE

## Chez Dimitri ££
This typical French-Moroccan restaurant has lots of old-fashioned charm and character. Founded in 1928 – at the same time as Ouarzazate – it served as a post and telephone office, bar and ballroom for the legionnaires stationed here. Now the high-ceilinged room is decorated with signed black-and-white pictures of visiting movie stars and other celebrities. The menu includes French and Moroccan dishes, pastas and salads, and there is an extensive wine list.

➕ 185 D3 ✉ 22 avenue Mohammed V
☎ (024) 88 73 46 ⏱ Daily lunch and dinner

## La Kasbah £–££
A pleasant restaurant, La Kasbah has several ambient terraces overlooking the kasbah, and more intimate dining rooms inside. This place serves good Moroccan food. No alcohol is served.

➕ 185 D3 ✉ Opposite the Taourirt kasbah
☎ (024) 88 20 33 ⏱ Daily 7am–11pm

## Le Relais St Exupéry ££

This is charming, nostalgic, French-themed restaurant is a treat – both aesthetically and for its delicious food. It features a beautiful dining room fitted with atmospheric, slow-moving fans and with walls adorned with interesting old photographs, including some of the French aviator and writer Antoine de Saint-Exupéry (1900–44), whose popular and touching novel *Le Petit Prince* was published the year before he was declared missing during a flight. The excellent food includes French and Moroccan specialities, or a mixture of both, such as pigeons stuffed with almonds and served with fine crêpes or Atlas trout.

🚹 185 D3 ⊠ 13 avenue Moulay Abdallah, on road to Tinerhir ☎ (024) 88 77 79 ⏰ Daily 10am–11pm. Closed Wed in Jul

### SKOURA

## Chez Talout ££

This small pension serves Moroccan food on its lovely terrace overlooking the palmeraie and mountains.

🚹 185 D3 ⊠ 7km (4 miles) before Skoura, on the Ouarzazate road ☎ (062) 49 82 83; www.talout.com ⏰ Daily lunch and dinner

### TALIAOUINE

## Auberge Souktana £

On the menu are classical Moroccan dishes from tagine of meatballs with eggs to excellent *briouats* (little stuffed pastries). Meals, including a delicious breakfast. All served in the covered central courtyard. No alcohol is served but bring your own.

🚹 184 C3 ⊠ 2km (1 mile) outside Taliouine, on road to Ouarzazate ☎ (028) 53 40 75 ⏰ Daily 7am–11pm

### TAROUDANNT

## Chez Nada £

Taroudannt's reputation for good food is well maintained by this simple but very popular Moroccan restaurant. Delicious couscous, tagines and salads are served in a pleasant dining room on the first floor, or else under a romantic moonlit sky and stars on the terrace. Specialities such as the pigeon *pastilla* need to be ordered in advance.

🚹 184 B3 ⊠ Rue Ferk Lahbab, near Hotel Les Saadiens ☎ (028) 85 17 26 ⏰ Daily 8am–11pm

## Taroudannt Hotel-Restaurant £–££

Located on the busiest square in town, this hotel restaurant serves good, old-fashioned French and Moroccan dishes in a superb colonial-style restaurant with high ceilings and plenty of romantic ambience. Service can be erratic, but that's part of the charm, and the four-course menu is excellent value for money.

🚹 184 B3 ⊠ Place al Alaouyine (Assarag) ☎ (028) 85 24 16 ⏰ Daily lunch and dinner

### TINERHIR

## Tomboctoo Hotel-Restaurant ££

Like the hotel, this excellent restaurant shows much charm and inventiveness, offering Spanish dishes as well as Moroccan food. Specialities such as *mechoui* (roast lamb) need to be ordered in advance. No alcohol but bring your own.

🚹 185 E4 ⊠ Avenue Anzarane ☎ (024) 83 46 04 ⏰ Daily lunch and dinner

### TIZNIT

## Restaurant Idou Tiznit ££

This is stylish restaurant in a large Moorish dining room in the smartest hotel in town serving fine Moroccan food, but catering mainly for tourists. The bar near the pool is a much livelier place, popular with the locals and tourists alike, and serves international and Moroccan snacks.

🚹 184 A2 ⊠ Hotel Idou Tiznit, avenue Hassam II ☎ (028) 60 03 33; www.idoutiznit.com ⏰ Daily 5am–1am

### TODRA GORGE

## Auberge Chez Pierre ££

Besides the eight tastefully decorated rooms here, there is an excellent restaurant with food, based on local produce. Specialities include delicious quiches with seasonal vegetables and spices, roast chicken with herbs and mouthwatering home-made goats' cheese with local honey. In fact, everything from the bread to ice cream is home-made. Advance booking is essential, because this is place is a treat.

🔖 185 E4 ⊠ 22km (14 miles) from Boulmane, 3km (2 miles) past the Aït Oudinar bridge, Gorges du Dadès ☎ (024) 83 02 67/(068) 24 83 75; www.chezpierre.ifrance.com 🕐 Daily lunch and dinner. Closed 10 Jan–10 Feb; 15 Jun–15 Jul; 10 Nov–20 Dec

### Les Roches £-££

This hotel-restaurant superbly located right in the Todra Gorge and is understandably a popular stop for tour buses at lunchtime, when diners can eat outdoors in the shade of Berber tents. At night the place calms down, offering romantic candlelit dinners with excellent Moroccan food, bags of ambience and friendly service. No alcohol but bring your own.

🔖 185 E4 ⊠ Todra Gorge ☎ (024) 89 51 34; be www.les-roches.mezgarne.com 🕐 Daily lunch and dinner

## VALLÉE D'OURIKA

### Auberge Le Maquis £-££

The restaurant at this small hotel is well worth a visit for its superb views and excellent French-Moroccan cuisine. It is popular with Marrakchi families at the weekends, so book ahead. The owner also organises treks in the Yaggour plateau.

🔖 184 C4 ⊠ 45km (28 miles) from Aghbalou ☎ (024) 48 45 31; www.le-maquis.com 🕐 Daily 7am–11pm

## ZAGORA

### Chez Ali £

This small inn with only four well-appointed rooms is a great place to stay, and also serves simple but excellent, well-cooked Moroccan food. Delicious sweets and snacks are served all day long in a pleasant garden filled with flowers and strutting peacocks. This is a great place to relax and eat, or stay. Recommended.

🔖 185 E3 ⊠ avenue Mohammed V ☎ (024) 84 62 58 🕐 Daily 8am–10pm

### Jnane Dar (Chez Abdessadek Naciri) ££

Freshly prepared, traditional Moroccan food is served in tents in an ambient setting. Eat in the pleasant garden or in the cosy dining room. There's always a friendly welcome and the restaurant often hosts sessions with local musicians in the evening. The perfect place to spend the evening.

🔖 185 E3 ⊠ Opposite the Naciri Medersa, Tamegroute, 18km (11 miles) south of Zagora ☎ (024) 84 06 22; www.jnanedar.ch 🕐 Daily breakfast, lunch and dinner

### Kasbah Asmaa ££

Excellent Moroccan meals are served in the relaxing pool side garden or in sumptuous Moroccan salons. The service is friendly and the food is delicious and prepared with local ingredients. The house speciality of *mechoui* (roast lamb) is worth savouring but needs to be ordered a day in advance, and alcohol is available only at mealtimes.

🔖 185 E3 ⊠ 2km (1 mile) from Zagora, on road to Mhamid ☎ (024) 84 75 99; www.asmaa-zagora.com 🕐 Daily lunch and dinner

### Kasbah Tifawte £

The restaurant of this small but charming hotel is located in a palm grove comes highly recommended because it offers some of the best food in town. Relax in comfortable surroundings and enjoy succulent couscous and steaming tajines, which are served on Moroccan-style low tables and sofas covered in brocades. A haven of tranquillity, away from the centre of town. Call ahead for a reservation. Recommended.

🔖 185 E3 ⊠ Avenue el-Mansour ed-Dahabi ☎ (024) 84 88 43/(067) 59 62 41; www.tifawte.com 🕐 Daily 8am–11pm

# Where to...
## Shop

### SOUKS AND MARKETS

**Erfoud** has a daily market near place des FAR, and a larger weekly souk on Sunday in the same place on Saturday. There's a large souk on Sunday at the entrance to **Ouarzazate** coming from Marrakech, and smaller souks are held in **Sidi Daoud** on Tuesday and in **Tabounte** on Saturday.

**Taroudannt** is known for its craftspeople, and the town's two souks are less touristy than in Marrakech, and have a more authentic feel. The Arab souk has a great spice market, and there's an excellent jewellery souk with lots of Berber jewellery and local sculpture. The Marché Berbère is aimed at locals and sells good, inexpensive Berber pottery, clothes and food.

**Tiznit** is famous for its silver

Berber jewellery on sale in the little alleys of the jewellery souk. The town's new souk, place du Méchouar, offers a wide choice, but the old souk is more authentic. There's a Thursday souk on the road to **Tafraoute**.

The covered souk in Zagora is open daily, but gets busier on Wednesday and Saturday when Berbers from the region come to sell their produce.

### JEWELLERY AND ANTIQUES

**Ait Benhaddou** has several shops within its lower kasbah that sell local "antiques", carpets and Tuareg jewellery, but you won't find many bargains. Tuareg jewellery is also on sale opposite the Tinsouline hotel in Zagora, at **Maison Berbère**, which also sells the best crafts in

town. The **Centre Artisanal** on avenue Mohammed V in Tiznit also has jewellery on sale, as well as other crafts. For a selection of good antiques and carpets try **Lichir el-Houssaine** in souk Smata, Taroudannt (tel: (048) 85 16 80).

### ARTS AND CRAFTS

The **Ensemble Artisanal** opposite the kasbah in **Ouarzazate** is the place for Berber pottery, wood and alabaster, carpets and silver jewellery. Near by is the **carpet weavers' co-operative** with a good selection of carpets, particularly the loosely woven ones made by the Ouzquita tribe. The **Centre Horizon Artisanat** on avenue de la Victoire (tel: (024) 88 24 15) sells crafts, made in their workshops with the help of local youngsters with disabilities.

**Le Paon de l'Arganier** (5 boulevard Laayoune, opposite Berbère Palace Hotel, tel: (024) 88 41 97) sells beauty products, all produced by female cooperatives

in Morocco. **Tamegroute** has several small pottery factories that still produce the local rough green glazed pottery. **Dar Azawad** in Mhamid has a shop selling upmarket crafts, while there are several other crafts shops in town selling embroidered clothes and bells, and Tuareg leatherwork.

**Erfoud** is famous for its dark **marble**, which is exported all over the world. Here it is used to make souvenirs to supply the craft shops and bazaars along avenues Mohammed V and Moulay Ismail.

A more unusual souvenir would be one of Madeleine Laurent's gorgeous **watercolours**, whose studio is at 68 rue el Wâhda, near the Salam hotel.

### DATES

Dates from **Zagora** are considered the best in Morocco and make delicious gifts to take home to friends and families. Traders will usually let you sample the varieties before you buy.

# Where to...
# Be Entertained

## DESERT EXCURSIONS

The entertainment in **Merzouga** focuses on the desert, and various sightseeing trips are on offer at most hotels. **Camel trips** are also big in **Zagora**, where travel agents offer similar trips at the same prices – for an hour, half a day or full day, including meals. They can be booked through the hotel **La Fibule du Draa** or **Caravane Désert et Montagne** (tel: (024) 84 68 98).

Ouarzazate has many companies offering desert excursions. **Sahara Services** (tel: (061) 77 67 66; www. saharaservices.info) organises great desert trips from 1 night to 14 days in the desert. **Wilderness Wheels** (44 Hay al Qods, tel: (024) 88 81 28; www.wildernesswheels.com) does guided motorbike tours. The ultimate desert trip is without doubt the **Marathon des Sables** (www. saharamarathon.co.uk; March/April), a seven-day foot race through the desert that starts/ends in Ouazarzate.

## SAND BATHS

Merzouga is the place where Berbers come for a sand bath. It involves being buried up to the neck in the sand under the hot sun. Ask for information at local hotels.

## SPORT AND LEISURE

Oukaïmeden has a ski-lift at 3,273m (10,738 feet), and offers the best **skiing** in Morocco, including off-piste, between December and March, but is being updated at the time of writing. **Hiking** is possible on the lower slopes for most of the year; contact the **Refuge du Club Alpin** (tel: (024) 31 90 36; www. cafmaroc.co.ma). The **Kasbah du Toubkal** (▶ 157) is good for hiking in the Atlas mountains. **Golfers** should head for the **Golf Royal** course in Ouarzazate (tel: (024) 88 26 53). The area of the Atlas and the south is a paradise for hikers. Most hikers head for the well-trodden **Toubkal Mountain** (▶ 146–147), but the scenery is just as spectacular elsewhere, including **Jebel Sarhro** (▶ 149) and the stunning Aït Bou Guemez Valley in **Irhil M'Goun** (▶ 155) If you prefer a desert hike near Mhamid or Merzouga, contact **Sahara Services** (Mhamid, tel: (061) 77 67 66; www.saharaservices.info).

For those feeling energetic, the attractive municipal gardens near the Palais Salam in Taroudannt have six **tennis** courts, with balls and racket rental available. A **cycle** ride around the town walls is also recommended; bikes can be rented from a stall on avenue Mohammed V.

**Horse-riders** can try **Chez Habib** (368 rue Mansour ed Dahabi) near Bab Zorgane in Taroudannt. The Proust family's **North Africa Horse** (Km20 Route de Skoura, tel:(024) 88 68 89/(061) 16 84 72) arranges stunts with horses and camels for the film industry. There is a show, and camel and horse trips can be arranged.

**Cinema Atlas** on rue de la Poste in Ouarzazate shows mostly French, Indian and Arab films.

## BIRDING

The **Oued Souss** between Taroudannt and Taliaouine is a rich bird habitat in winter and spring. Keen birders can check out **Aoulouz Gorge**, 90km (56 miles) from Taroudannt.

## DATE FESTIVAL

Every October, Erfoud holds a **Date Festival** – a mixture of religious celebration and worldly entertainment – not to be missed.

# Walks and Tours

# 1 *CALÈCHE* RIDE IN MARRAKECH

*Tour*

**DISTANCE** 4–5km (2½–3 miles) **TIME** 3–4 hours, including visits
**START POINT** *Calèche* stand behind the Koutoubia Mosque on avenue Houmane el Fetouaki (bus No 1 from the main squares in Guéliz) ✚ 182 C1 **END POINT** Djemaa el-Fna ✚ 182 C1

This relaxed horse-drawn cab ride takes you through the southern quarters of the medina, where you can see some of the city's greatest sights as well as people going about their daily business regardless of passing tourists.

The fixed rates per person are advertised on the seats of the *calèche*, but it is worth negotiating a fee for the whole tour in advance, including stops to visit sights en route. Either start the tour at 9am or, if it's not too hot, at 2pm, as many of the attractions close at lunchtime.

## 1–2

Take a good look at the minaret of the **Koutoubia Mosque (Mosquée de la Koutoubia)**, one of Marrakech's main landmarks. Turn right on to rue Sidi Mimoun, with the Koubba de Youssef

ben Tachfine on the right-hand side. This leads to two gates, **Bab Agnaou** and **Bab er Rob** (▶ 57). Bab Agnaou, a contemporary of the Koutoubia and a beautiful example of an

*Calèches* are one of the best ways to explore the medina

elegant Almohad gateway, led from the medina to the imperial city. Enter the city walls via the passage

Mosquée de la Koutoubia ①

Koubba de Youssef ben Tachfine

AVE HOUMANE EL FETOUAKI

RUE SIDI MIMOUN

Djemaa el-Fna ⑤

Dar Si Said

Maison ④ Tiskiwin

Palais de la Bahia

③

RUE RIAD ZITOUN EL JDID

PLACE DES FERBLANTIERS

### THE MELLAH

In 1558, considerably later than in most other Moroccan cities, the Saadians moved the Jewish community into a district known as the *mellah*. Located near the sultan's palace, this was a safe quarter with only two entrance gates. Most sultans valued the importance of the Jewish community, recognising its skills as bankers, traders and craftsmen. A council of rabbis controlled the community, which had its own cemeteries, gardens and markets. Until the 1940s, the population was more than 16,000 but after 1948 most emigrated to the new State of Israel, leaving only a few today.

next to Bab Agnaou. Straight ahead is the **Mosquée de la Kasbah** (Kasbah Mosque), also known as the Mosque of el-Mansour as it was built in 1190 by the sultan Yaqoub el-Mansour. An explosion destroyed part of it in 1569, but it was carefully restored by successive kings, including Hassan II (1929–99). A narrow corridor to the right of the mosque leads to the entrance to the splendid **Tombeaux Saadiens** (Saadian Tombs), ▲ 62), one of the city's not-to-be-missed highlights.

**2–3**

Continue on rue de la Kasbah and, at the end, turn left into rue du Méchouar. At the end of this, to the right, is a gateway in the ramparts leading to a large square. Take the left route through the Porte de l'Aguedal leading to the **Méchouar** where, in the 18th and 19th centuries, the sultan gave audiences and received European ambassadors. Go across the Méchouar (the Royal Palace, on the left, is closed to the public) and through the gate. Take the next gate immediately to the left, leading into rue Berrima with

the *mellah* (Jewish quarter) beyond on the right. At the end of the street, at Bab Berrima, a corridor between

**Ahmed el-Mansour is buried in the Saadian cemetery with his son and successor Zaidan, and his grandson Mohammed esh Sheikh II**

0 ────── 250 metres
0 ────── 250 yards

MELLAH

Bab Agnaou
Bab er Rob

RUE DE LA KASBAH

Mosquée de la Kasbah
Tombeaux Saadiens
2

KASBAH

RUE DU MÉCHOUAR

RUE BERRIMA

Palais el-Badi

MÉCHOUAR

Palais Royal

**3–4**
After visiting el Bahia, continue north along rue Riad Zitoun el Jdid until you reach a square with a public garden. Walk through a narrow passage called rue de la Bahia to the right, then take the first alley to the left to visit the **Dar Si Said Museum** of Moroccan arts (▶ 63). Return to rue de la Bahia where, on the left at No 8, you'll find **Maison Tiskiwin** (▶ 63), a beautiful Moorish mansion named after a Berber dance from the High Atlas.

**4–5**
Return to rue Riad ez Zitoun el-Jdid and turn right. Where the road forks, turn left, towards Café de France on **Djemaa el-Fna** (▶ 50–51).

**The Palais el-Badi has been robbed of all its former splendour**

two walls leads to the marvellous16th-century **Palais el-Badi** (Badi Palace, ▶ 62). Go back through Bab Berrima to place des Ferblantiers, a large, rectangular *fondouk* (caravanserai) of metal workshops, where many of the lanterns on sale in the souks are made. Turn right on to avenue Houmman el Fetouaki, with the cemetery on your left and the *mellah* on the right. At the corner with rue Riad ez Zitoun el-Jdid is the entrance to the late-19th century **Palais de la Bahia** (Bahia Palace and Museum), ▶ 62).

**DISTANCE** 12km (7½ miles) **TIME** 1 day **START/END POINT** Le Soleil Hotel, Imlil (minibus, truck or taxi from Asni) ✚ 184 C3 **INFORMATION** For qualified guides from the mountain refuge of Club Alpin Français (Oukaïmeden; tel: (024) 31 90 36); or from Kasbah du Toubkal; tel: (024) 48 56 11)

# 2 THE TOUBKAL REGION
*Walk*

**This hike takes you through spectacular mountains and beautiful Berber villages. It's the first and easiest part of the most popular ascent of Jebel Toubkal, but for Berbers it is also a pilgrimage route to the shrine of Sidi Chamarouch.**

Although long, this is an easy walk for most fit people, but if you're in any doubt, consider going by mule, which can be rented by the day or half day from Imlil or Aremd (ask in the cafés or restaurants). Rates are about 150dh a day, plus a tip for the muleteer. You shouldn't need a guide on this well-trodden path, especially if you have a muleteer, but if you do decide to take one, expect to pay him about 200dh a day. Imlil and Aremd have several simple hotels where you can spend the night. The hotel Kasbah du Toubkal also offers dormitory-style rooms to hikers (▶ 156; www.kasbahdutoubkal.com) or book through its Marrakech office, tel: (024) 48 56 11.

## 1–2

Start at around 8 or 9am from the Hotel du Soleil, following the mule track past the Hotel de l'Etoile and several small shops. Take the first track to the right at Laiterie Toubkal and follow the well-defined path, zigzagging up to the right of the **Mizane River**. The path goes past several houses and the **Hotel Kasbah du Toubkal**, an old Glaoui kasbah with great views. Soon the path climbs above the walnut

**Hikers rest beside the blessed waters of Sidi Chamarouch**

trees and the landscape opens out. After about 45 minutes (2km/1 mile) turn left along a trail wide enough for cars. Across the river is the picturesque village of Aremd, which is built on a large spur.

### 2–3

**Aremd** is the largest village in the Mizane Valley and has benefited from tourists climbing Jebel Toubkal. It's an authentic place where you can meet Berbers and see how they live and work. Cross the river (there is a bridge but the river is usually pretty dry) and climb through the winding streets to the top of the village. Retrace your steps back across the river and walk 100m (110 yards) to the left, towards a cluster of houses opposite the village, to stop for refreshments at the **Hotel Aremd.**

### 3–4

Take the path opposite the hotel, through the flood plain and orchards towards the mountains on the other side of the valley. After about 15 minutes, at the foot of the slopes a well-worn path to the right climbs

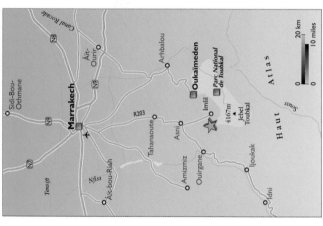

**View of Mount Toubkal and the High Atlas Mountain range, near Asni, on the Tizi n'Test road**

## PRACTICAL ADVICE

■ You'll need **sturdy shoes**, preferably walking boots, and sun protection.

■ This area is under snow from November until spring, but it is usually possible to complete the walk **all year round**. The best time to go is late spring to early autumn. Afternoons are often cloudy.

■ Although well trodden, the path is not signed so **a map would be handy** to help you navigate. You can sometimes buy a map in Imlil or Marrakech, but it is better to purchase one before you go to Morocco. If you get lost, ask a local.

into the mountains, through the hard grey rocks overlooking the river. After another 15 minutes you reach a spring, but continue along the path, which now looks down over apple orchards. After another hour's walk the boulders become larger, the river forming pools and small waterfalls around them. Suddenly you can see a white *koubba*, the **shrine of Sidi Chamarouche**, a Muslim saint associated with the traditional Berber spirits of the mountains. His tomb is closed to non-Muslims, who are requested not even to cross the bridge to the shrine. He is known as the "King of Jinns" and many pilgrims possessed by a *djinn* (that is, those with psychological problems) come to the shrine so that Sidi Chamarouche can take control of their *djinn* and thus cure them. Some serious cases stay for several years in the cells near the shrine, but most come for a few days and bathe in the sacred pool near the *koubba*.

### 4–5

The trail continues the steep climb from here to Jebel Toubkal, but this is a perfect place to stop for a picnic or a meal in the small **hamlet of Sidi Chamarouche**, which surrounds the tomb and is mostly inhabited by the saint's

descendants. The pools behind and below the shrine are not sacred and can be seriously inviting on a hot day. It's usually possible for visitors to take a dip, but be careful not to offend the locals – women should wear bathing suits at least, and go a little further on upstream.

### 5–6

The walk goes back along the same path, past the fossil and mineral shops of Sidi Chamarouche hamlet, whose owners sometimes adopt quite aggressive sales tactics at this stage. You will almost certainly not be alone here, especially at weekends when entire families from Marrakech take to the trail, often barefoot or wearing slippers. Continue back to Aremd or Imlil for the night.

### TAKING A BREAK

Drinks and snacks are available all along the route. You can get a good, simple lunch at the **Hotel Aremd** just below Aremd itself, or in the hamlet of Sidi Chamarouche. Alternatively, **bring a picnic** to enjoy at the top, followed by a dip in the pools of the little river.

# 3 ALONG THE TIZI N'TICHKA

*Tour*

**Together with the Tizi n'Test (▶ 144–145), at more than 2,000m (6,500 feet) the Tizi n'Tichka is one of the highest and most spectacular roads in the High Atlas. It also offers the chance to visit some of Morocco's most impressive kasbahs.**

This tour is possible by public transport – there are frequent buses across the mountains from Marrakech to Ouarzazate – but it would be difficult to include everything in one day,

**DISTANCE** 273km (170 miles) **TIME** 1 day **START POINT** Bab Doukkala, Marrakech ✚ 184 C4
**END POINT** Ouarzazate (daily buses and *grands taxis* from Marrakech via Telouet) ✚ 185 D3

as the kasbahs of Telouet (▶ 153) and Aït Benhaddou (▶ 150) are off the road. It's therefore easier either to hire a car or a *grand taxi* for the day. The road is good and relatively fast, but if you have a four-wheel-drive you can take the more adventurous piste from Telouet to Aït Benhaddou. A tarmac road from Telouet leads east to Anemiter, 11km (7 miles) away. From there a rough, unsurfaced track (piste) leads for 30km (19 miles) through barren landscape to Tamdaght, just north of Aït Benhaddou.

## 1–2

From Bab Doukkala follow the signs out of town for Fez –Ouarzazate. After about 7.5km (5 miles) when the road

**Rocks and minerals that are for sale along the Tizi n'Tichka road**

forks, take the N9 to the right towards Ouarzazate, through a eucalyptus plantation dotted with the occasional large villa. After 36km (22 miles) you'll see the first big village along the road, **Aït-Ourir**, with the attractive Hotel le Coq Hardi and the ruins of a crenellated kasbah. Beyond this, the road

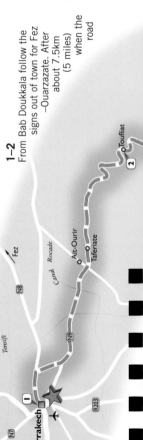

becomes more beautiful as it follows the River Oued Zate, and all along the route are clusters of villages dramatically set into the mountains. Amid scented pine forests is the picturesque little Berber village of **Toufliat**.

## 2–3

After 17km (10 miles) you'll reach the small alpine town of **Taddert**, surrounded by walnut trees and invaded by sellers of minerals and fossils, who also display their wares all along

the road. About 12km (7.5 miles) further on is a **viewpoint** with excellent views back over the valley, and a small café for refreshments. The **Col du Tichka**, 5km (3 miles) after this, is the highest road in Morocco, at 2,260m (7,400 feet). There is always a strong wind blowing at this altitude, but the view of the mountains is now obscured by the shops selling pottery and fossils.

## 3–4

Another 5km (3 miles) further on, take a small road to the left signposted to the village of **Telouet**, which you'll reach after 20km (12 miles; ▶ 153). Continue along the road and through the village to the Auberge de Telouet, which is on your left. Turn right here on a narrow track signposted to the kasbah, and after about 500m (550 yards) you will arrive on the small square in front of it. Look out for the caretaker outside the **Glaoui kasbah** to let you in for a look around, then return to the Auberge de Telouet for lunch or drinks.

## 4–5

Return through a windswept landscape with an occasional terraced village to the main

**Views from the Tizi n'Tichka Pass are unsurpassed**

Marrakech–Ouarzazate road and turn left. After 10km (6 miles) you'll reach **Irherm n'Ougdal**, a typical High Atlas village at 1,970m (6,460 feet), with low houses and a beautiful *irherm* or *agadir* (fortified communal granary). The next village of **Tiurdjal** (20km/12 miles), which seems to be sliding downhill, features a pretty marble minaret permanently topped with a stork's nest. The road now follows the Asif Imini River and becomes straighter and considerably

faster, with a panoramic view over some of the highest peaks in the Atlas. After about 8km (5 miles), just before **Agouim**, there are panoramas over some of the highest peaks in the Atlas; the village has a weaving co-operative set up by Franciscan friars, on road 6849, a dirt track on the right that leads to Sour.

**If you only see one kasbah, let it be well-maintained Aït Benhaddou**

Back on the main road, after 20km (12 miles) look out for the kasbah of **Tiseldei** on the left and, 2km (1 mile) further on, the ksar of **Ifilt**, a village set among olive groves. Some 8km (5 miles) to the south is **el-Mdint**, and another 2km (1 mile) outside the village, to the right, is a fine kasbah with ornate towers and the pretty **ksar of Taddoula**, both set in palm groves.

## 5–6

At a crossroads 10km (6 miles) further on, turn left on to the 6803 leading to the ksar of **Aït Benhaddou** in another 10km (6 miles; ➤ 150). The best view of this remarkable site is from a viewpoint 2km (1 mile) before the village. From here return to the main road and turn left to **Ouarzazate**, 25km (16 miles) away (➤ 153).

### TAKING A BREAK

The **Auberge de Telouet** (tel: (024) 89 07 17, open 7–7) serves a set lunch (fresh salad and excellent tagine) in a Berber tent overlooking the crumbling kasbah. The terrace of **La Kasbah** (➤ 158) commands great views over Aït Benhaddou and serves delicious Moroccan food or cool drinks near the pool.

### LORDS OF THE HIGH ATLAS

The powerful Glaoui family ruled over the Atlas from 1875 to 1956. They began as simple tribal leaders but came to control the important mountain road of Tizi n'Test (➤ 144–145). Unlike other mountain tribes, who fought against the French colonisers, the Glaouis made a pact with them. The French Marshal Lyautey appreciated their support and did nothing to stop their rise to power. The two brothers Madani and T'hami appointed themselves pashas of Marrakech and established other family members as *caïds* (tribal chiefs), who ruled as despots over all the main Atlas and desert cities. The brothers built many kasbahs in the region, and were notorious for their lavish parties.

# Practicalities

## BEFORE YOU GO

### WHAT YOU NEED

| | | UK | Germany | USA | Canada | Australia | Ireland | Netherlands | Spain |
|---|---|---|---|---|---|---|---|---|---|
| ● | Required | | | | | | | | |
| ○ | Suggested | | | | | | | | |
| ▲ | Not required | | | | | | | | |
| △ | Not applicable | | | | | | | | |
| Passport/National Identity Card | | ● | ● | ● | ● | ● | ● | ● | ● |
| Visa (regulations can change – check before you travel) | | ▲ | ▲ | ▲ | ▲ | ▲ | ▲ | ▲ | ▲ |
| Onward or Return Ticket | | ○ | ○ | ○ | ○ | ○ | ○ | ○ | ○ |
| Health Inoculations (tetanus, polio and malaria) | | ○ | ○ | ○ | ○ | ○ | ○ | ○ | ○ |
| Health Documentation | | ○ | ○ | ○ | ○ | ○ | ○ | ○ | ○ |
| Travel Insurance | | ● | ● | ● | ● | ● | ● | ● | ● |
| Driving Licence (national, International for US nationals) | | ● | ● | ● | ● | ● | ● | ● | ● |
| Car Insurance Certificate (included if car is rented) | | ● | ● | ● | ● | ● | ● | ● | ● |
| Car Registration Document | | ● | ● | ● | ● | ● | ● | ● | ● |

### WHEN TO GO

Rabat/Casablanca

High season          Low season

| JAN | FEB | MAR | APR | MAY | JUN | JUL | AUG | SEP | OCT | NOV | DEC |
|---|---|---|---|---|---|---|---|---|---|---|---|
| 17°C | 18°C | 19°C | 21°C | 23°C | 25°C | 28°C | 28°C | 27°C | 25°C | 20°C | 18°C |
| 63°F | 64°F | 66°F | 70°F | 73°F | 77°F | 82°F | 82°F | 81°F | 77°F | 68°F | 64°F |

☀ Sun          🌦 Sunshine and showers

Morocco is not called a cold country with a hot sun for nothing – **temperatures can vary dramatically** between night and day, depending on the season and the region. In summer the beaches will be hot but crowded, and on the Atlantic side the sky is very often overcast. The **coast is temperate** all year round, but the resorts will feel cool out of season. The summer months are excellent for visiting the High and Middle Atlas Mountains, but cities like Fez and Marrakech can be unbearably hot. The **best time to visit** the south and the Sahara region is in winter, from October to February, as the summer temperature here can easily soar to more than 45°C (113°F). For a general tour of Morocco **the best periods** are March to May and September to October, when it is cooler and there's less chance of rain.

### GETTING ADVANCE INFORMATION
**Websites**
- Moroccan Tourist Office www.visitmorocco.org
- Accommodation: www.riadsmorocco.com or www.ilove-marrakech.com

- General information www.al-bab.com/maroc
- Official information on Morocco: www.mincom.gov.ma

- Moroccan contemporary music www.maroccanmusic.com

## GETTING THERE

**By Air** Royal Air Maroc (tel: (020) 7439 4361; www.royalairmaroc.com) operates **direct, scheduled flights** from London Heathrow, Paris and other cities in France. New York and Montréal also have **direct flights** to Morocco. British Airways (tel: 0870 850 9850; www.ba.com) operates flights from London to Casablanca, Tangier and Marrakech. Budget airline Easyjet (www.easyjet.com) flies from several European airports to Marrakech, while Ryanair (www.ryanair.com) operates flights to Fez, Marrakech and Agadir. Atlas Blue (www.atlas-blue.com) has flights from several European cities to Agadir and Marakech. **Travel times** Direct flights from London to Casablanca take just over 3 hours, and to Marrakech 3 hours and 40 minutes.

**By Sea** Several ferry companies operate between France or Spain and Morocco. The **keenest prices** are available from Trasmediterranea in Algeciras, Spain (www. trasmediterranea.es) or Comanair (www.comanair.co.ma). There are **several crossings a day** between Algeciras in Spain and Ceuta by **vehicle ferry** (1hr 30 min), by **fast ferry** (40 min) or by **catamaran** (30 min). Passengers need to take a bus to the Moroccan border and then another one to their final destination.

**By Car** You can cross by ferry from **Spain or France**, but, as cars can face slow land border crossings from Ceuta into Morocco due to custom controls, it's better to arrive in Tangier.

## TIME

Morocco stays at Greenwich Mean Time all year, with no Daylight Saving Time in summer. However, Ceuta and Melilla keep Spanish time, which is GMT +1 in winter and GMT +2 in summer.

## CURRENCY AND FOREIGN EXCHANGE

**Currency** The monetary unit of Morocco is the dirham (dh), divided into 100 centimes. **Notes** are issued in 10, 20, 50, 100 and 200 dirhams. There are **coins** for 5, 10, 20 and 50 centimes and for 1 and 5 dirhams. Currency is labelled in Arabic and French.

**Exchange** Keep all exchange receipts and budget carefully as you will need them if you want to change any remaining dirhams back into your currency. **Eurocheques** are accepted in at least one bank in each major city, and both hotels and banks will change cash and traveller's cheques. Hotels usually offer slightly lower exchange rates than banks.

**Traveller's cheques** (sterling and US$) are easily exchanged in most banks, but there is usually a surcharge on each cheque. Hotels usually offer slightly lower exchange rates than banks. There are numerous **ATMs** (cash machines) in tourist areas and even in smaller towns.

**Credit cards** are widely accepted at banks, top hotels, restaurants and shops, but it is wise to check first.

| **In the UK** | **In the USA** | **In Canada** |
|---|---|---|
| 205 Regent Street | Suite 1201, 20 East 46th | Place Montréal, Trust 1800, |
| London W1B 4HB | Street, New York, | rue McGill, Suite 2450, |
| ☎ (020) 7437 0073 | NY 10017 | Montréal H3A 2A6 |
| | ☎ (212) 557 2520 | ☎ (151) 4842 8111 |

## WHEN YOU ARE THERE

### CLOTHING SIZES

| UK | Morocco | USA | |
|---|---|---|---|
| 36 | 46 | 36 | |
| 38 | 48 | 38 | |
| 40 | 50 | 40 | |
| 42 | 52 | 42 | Suits |
| 44 | 54 | 44 | |
| 46 | 56 | 46 | |
| 7 | 41 | 8 | |
| 7.5 | 42 | 8.5 | |
| 8.5 | 43 | 9.5 | |
| 9.5 | 44 | 10.5 | Shoes |
| 10.5 | 45 | 11.5 | |
| 11 | 46 | 12 | |
| 14.5 | 37 | 14.5 | |
| 15 | 38 | 15 | |
| 15.5 | 39/40 | 15.5 | |
| 16 | 41 | 16 | Shirts |
| 16.5 | 42 | 16.5 | |
| 17 | 43 | 17 | |
| 8 | 36 | 6 | |
| 10 | 38 | 8 | |
| 12 | 40 | 10 | |
| 14 | 42 | 12 | Dresses |
| 16 | 44 | 14 | |
| 18 | 46 | 16 | |
| 4.5 | 37.5 | 6 | |
| 5 | 38 | 6.5 | |
| 5.5 | 38.5 | 7 | |
| 6 | 39 | 7.5 | Shoes |
| 6.5 | 40 | 8 | |
| 7 | 41 | 8.5 | |

### NATIONAL HOLIDAYS

| | |
|---|---|
| 1 Jan | New Year's Day |
| 1 May | Labour Day |
| 23 May | National Day |
| 30 Jul | Feast of the Throne |
| 20 Aug | Revolution Day |
| 23 Aug | Birthday of King Mohammed VI/Youth Day |
| 6 Nov | Day of Green March |
| 18 Nov | Independence Day |

Morocco observes the traditional feast days of the Muslim year, such as Ramadan. The end of Ramadan is marked by the Eid es Seghir and, 40 days later, the Eid el Kebir. The dates of these change each year.

### OPENING HOURS

○ Shops
● Offices
● Banks
● Post Offices
● Museums/Monuments
● Pharmacies

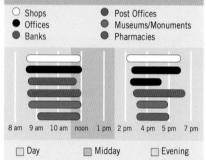

8 am  9 am  10 am  noon  1 pm  2 pm  4 pm  5 pm  7 pm

☐ Day     ▨ Midday     ☐ Evening

**Shops** Mon–Sat 9am–1pm and 3–7pm. Souks in the medinas are open 9am–7 or 8pm, sometimes longer in summer/high season. Some shops in the souks close for the Friday prayers.
**Banks** Mon–Fri 8:30–11:30am and 2:30–4:30pm.
**Post offices** Mon–Fri 8:30–noon and 2:30–6:30.
**Museums** Generally closed on Tuesday and between noon and 3pm on other days.
**Pharmacies** 9am–noon and 3–5pm.
All times may vary.

### TIME DIFFERENCES

| GMT 12 noon | Morocco 12 noon | USA (East) 7am | USA (West) 4am | Germany 1pm | Australia (Sydney) 10pm |
|---|---|---|---|---|---|

## PERSONAL SAFETY

- Watch out for *faux guides* posing as "students" or "friends"; extreme caution should be taken in accepting help from them. Use official tourist office guides or manage without. The grey-uniformed Sûreté police are tourist friendly.
- Do not accept offers of hashish cannabis (*kif*) – penalties for possessing drugs are high.
- Beware of pickpockets in crowded places.
- Keep money and passports out of sight.
- Do not walk alone at night in medinas.
- Women should dress modestly when away from the beach and hotel.

**Police assistance:**
 **19** from any phone

## ELECTRICITY

Moroccan power supply is 220 volts, but some areas are still on 110 volts. Sockets accept two-round-pin plugs, so an adaptor is advisable, as is a transformer for appliances operating on 100–120 volts.

## TELEPHONES

*Téléboutiques*, clearly marked in blue, are plentiful in towns. They give information and change, and are easy to operate. Card phones are increasingly available and are also easy to use. The cards can be bought at post offices, newsagents and tobacconists. Calls can be made from phone offices with operator assistance. The number is given to a telephonist who will dial the call number required and direct the caller to a cabin where the call is waiting. Although it is simpler to call from hotels, the charges can be double that paid elsewhere.

## POST

All cities and most towns have post offices (PTT). The postal service is reliable, but international post can be slow. Post to and from Europe can take up to a week; post to the USA, Canada and Australia takes two weeks. Letters are collected more frequently from post offices, so it's worth posting your letters in the box inside or just outside the buildings.

## TIPS/GRATUITIES

Tips are often expected by caretakers who open up attractions on demand. As a general guide:

| | |
|---|---|
| Restaurants (service incl.) | 10–15% |
| Cafés/bars | 10–15% |
| Taxis (agree price first) | Change |
| Museum and site guides | 20dh |
| Porters, hotel workers | 20dh |
| Hairdressers | 20dh |
| Filling station attendants | 5–105dh |
| Lavatories (in bars etc) | 5dh |

| | |
|---|---|
| **POLICE** | **19** |
| **FIRE** | **15** OR **(024) 43 04 15 (MARRAKECH)** |
| **AMBULANCE** | **15** OR **(024) 44 37 24 (MARRAKECH)** |
| **HIGHWAY EMERGENCY SERVICE** | **177** |

## HEALTH

 **Insurance** Morocco has well-qualified doctors in the larger towns and cities. State hospitals provide free or minimal charge emergency treatment, but full health insurance is essential.

 **Dental Services** Have a thorough check-up before leaving home. In case of emergency, ask a consulate in a major city to recommend a local dentist, who will be French-speaking. Medical insurance is essential.

 **Weather** The sun is very hot, so cover up with light cotton clothes, wear a hat, use high-factor sunscreen and drink plenty of bottled water. Avoid too much alcohol and caffeine as these contribute to dehydration.

 **Drugs** Although pharmacies are well supplied, check expiry dates as drugs deteriorate quickly in the heat. Drugs can be expensive, so bring a supply of painkillers, anti-diarrhoea pills and a sunburn remedy. Do not buy illegal drugs.

 **Safe Water** Drinking unboiled water can cause stomach problems. Use bottled water and do not eat raw food, especially salads washed in local water. Bilharzia, caused by blood flukes, can be caught by swimming in oases or slow-flowing rivers.

## WILDLIFE SOUVENIRS

Importing wildlife souvenirs sourced from rare or endangered species may be illegal or require a special permit. Check your country's customs rules.

## CONCESSIONS

**Students and Youths** Student cards are redundant in Morocco, but Royal Air Maroc gives a 25 per cent discount to under-26s on internal flights. InterRail passes for under-26s also extend to the Moroccan rail system.

**Senior Citizens** There are no general concessions for senior citizens, but beach-front hotels south of Agadir offer good rates for long-stay guests. However, many do not have lifts or ramps for wheelchairs.

## TRAVELLING WITH A DISABILITY

Facilities for visitors with disabilities are rare in Morocco, and medinas are tricky places to get around. Although Moroccans are usually helpful, it is still difficult to get around hotels, public transport and most of the monuments. Check with a specialist organisation for travellers with disabilities before travelling: Tripscope in the UK (tel: (08457) 585641; www.tripscope.org.uk), and AccessAbility in the USA (tel: 800/610-5640).
The AA *Disabled Travellers' Guide* gives details of accessible transport in Britain and abroad.

## CHILDREN

Moroccans love children and will welcome and entertain them wherever you go. While Western-style amusement parks are rare, most kids will be happy to stroll through the souks, or to enjoy the country's fabulous nature, mountains and beaches. The food is usually pretty child friendly, as well.

## LAVATORIES

Most hotels have Western-style lavatories, but almost everywhere else you will find the squat type, which are usually cleaner and more hygienic. Paper is not always provided in restaurants or public facilities.

## EMBASSIES AND HIGH COMMISSIONS

**UK/Ireland**
☎ (037) 63 33 33

**USA**
☎ (037) 76 22 65

**France**
☎ (037) 68 97 00

**Germany**
☎ (037) 70 96 62

**Canada/Australia**
☎ (037) 68 74 00

The official language in Morocco is Arabic, but it is quite different from classical Arabic. The country also has three different Berber dialects. French is widely taught in schools, and some Moroccans speak several languages fluently, including English and Spanish. The following is a phonetic transliteration from the Arabic script. Words or letters in brackets indicate the different form that is required when addressing, or speaking as, a woman.

## GREETINGS AND COMMON WORDS

Yes **Eeyeh, naam**
No **La**
Please **Min fadlak (fadlik) / Afek**
Thank you **Shukran / Baraka allah Oofeek**
You're welcome **Al Afow**
Hello to Muslims **As Salaam alaykum (formal)**
Response **Wa alaykum salaam**
Hello (informal) **La bes**
Response **Bikheer**
Welcome **Ahlan wa sahlan**
Response **Ahlan bik(i)**
Goodbye **Bislemah**
Good morning **Sbah l'khir**
Good evening **Msa l'khir**
Good night **Leela saieeda**
How are you? **La bes?**
Fine, thank you **Bikheer hamdulillaah**
God Willing **Inshallah**
Sorry **Esmeghli**
My name is… **Ismee…**
Do you speak English? **Itkelim Ingleezi?**
I don't understand **Mafhemsh**
I understand **Fhamt**
I don't speak Arabic **Ana Metkelimsh**

## NUMBERS

| 0 | sifr | 5 | khamsa |
|---|---|---|---|
| 1 | wahid | 6 | sitta |
| 2 | tnayn (formal) | 7 | sebaa |
| | zoos (common) | 8 | tmanya |
| | | 9 | tesa |
| 3 | tlaata | 10 | ashra |
| 4 | arbah | | |

## DAYS

| Monday | youm al-itnayn |
|---|---|
| Tuesday | youm at-talaat |
| Wednesday | youm al-arbah |
| Thursday | youm al-khamees |
| Friday | youm al-gumah |
| Saturday | youm is sabt |
| Sunday | youm al-hadd |

## EMERGENCY! Taari!

Help! **Atkooni!**
Thief! **Serrak / cheffar**
Police **Booleess**
Fire **Afia / nar**
Hospital **S'beetar**
Go away **Seer Fhalek!**
Where is the lavatory? **Feyn atoilet?**
I'm sick **Ana m'reed**
We want a doctor **B'gheet T'beeb**

## SHOPPING

Shop **Hanoot**
I would like… **B'gheet**
How much…? **Bech Hal? / Bekam?**
That's my last offer **Aakhir kelma**
That's too expensive **Ghali bezzaf**
Cheap **Rakhees**
Big / small **Kebeer / s'gheer**
Open / closed **Maftooh / mooglak**

## DIRECTIONS AND TRAVELLING

I'm lost **Ana T'left**
Where is…? **Feyn…?**
Airport **Mataar**
Boat **Babor / bato**
Bus **Kar**
Bus station **Mahattat el-ottobisat**
Embassy **Sifaara**
Market **Souk**
Mosque **Gaama; masjid**
Museum **Mathaf**
Square **Saaha**
Street **Zenka**
Taxi rank **Mahattat at taxiyat**
Train station **El gar**
Near / far? **baid / kreeb?**
How many kilometres? **Kam kilomet?**
Left / right **Yassar / yemeen**
Here / there **Hina / hinak**
Straight on **Toul / neeshan**
When does the bus/train leave **Waktash tren / kar yamshi?**
I want a taxi **B'gheet taxi**
Ticket **warka / tickita**
Car **tonobeel**
Train **Tren**

### RESTAURANT: Mattaam / restaurant

I would like to eat… **B'gheet akul…**
Alcohol / beer **Alcohol / birra**
Bread **Khobz**
Coffee / tea **Gahua / shay**
Meat **L'ham**
Mineral water **Mae maadini**
Milk **Halib**
Salt and pepper **Melh / filfil**
Wine red / white **Shrab rouge / blanc**
Breakfast **Ftoor**
Waiter **Garsson / serbaay**
Menu **La carte / menu**
Bill **L'hssab**

### MONEY: Flooss

Where is the bank? **Feyn el bank?**
Small change **Sarf**
Post office **Bosta**
Mail **Barid**
Cheque **Cheque**
Traveller's cheque **Traveller's cheque**
Credit card **Cart visa**

How much is that? **Bsh hal hadeek**

### GLOSSARY TO THE TEXT

**Aim** spring
**Aït** tribe
**Arabesque** geometrical and floral decoration, including caligraphy
**Bab** gate in city walls
**Babouche** traditional leather slipper
**Baraka** blessing of a saint, sought at his marabout
**Berbers** the first inhabitants of Morocco and North Africa
**Borj** fort/tower
**Caid** district administrator
**Caleche** horse-drawn carriage
**Caravanserai** lodgings for travellers and animals, around a courtyard
**Cherif (or shrif)** descendant of the Prophet Mohammed
**Djellaba (or Jellaba)** hooded outer dress worn by men and women
**Djemaa/jamaa** mosque
**Drar** house
**Ensemble artisanal** fixed-price government shop
**Eye** sand dune
**Fantasia** spectacular party traditionally held at Berber festivals
**Fassi** inhabitant of Fes
**Fondouk** inn, caravanserai
**Gnaoua** brotherhood descended from slaves from Mali and Senegal

**Haik** traditional veil
**Hammam** steam bath, usually near mosques for ablutions before prayers
**Harira** rich meat soup
**Jinn** genie, good or evil spirit
**Joutia** flea market
**Khanqah** Sufi monastery
**Kasbah** fortified village
**Kif** cannabis
**Kissaria** covered market where more expensive goods are sold
**Koran (Qu'ran)** Muslim holy book
**Koubba** tomb of a saint/dome (see marabout)
**Ksar** tribal stronghold
**Ksour** plural of ksar
**Makhzen** government
**Marabout** holy man, as well as his tomb (see koubba)
**Maristan** (Islamic) hospital
**Mechouar** large square for official gatherings
**Medersa** Koranic school
**Medina** old part of the city
**Mellah** Jewish quarter of a Moroccan town
**Midan** square
**Minaret** slender tower of a mosque
**Minzah** the garden in old Moroccan houses
**Moulay** descendant of Mohammed, title of Moroccan sultans
**Mouloud** birthday of the Prophet
**Moussem** pilgrimage and festival for a Muslim saint
**Mstani** Christian
**Muhayyem** campsite
**Oud** Moroccan music
**Oued** river or river bed
**Pisé** building material of packed clay and stones from river bed
**Ramadan** Islamic month of fasting
**Ras** source/head
**Sahn** courtyard of a mosque
**Sawiris** inhabitants of Essaouira
**Sharia** street
**Shereef** descendant of Mohammed
**Shouaf** witchdoctor
**Souk** street market/bazaar
**Sufi** Islamic brotherhood of ascetics and mystics
**Tagine** traditional stew of spiced meat or fish and vegetables or fruit
**Tizi** mountain pass
**Touareg** Berber nomad from the Western Sahara known for their blue clothes
**Vizier** chief minister of Islamic ruler
**Zaouia** a place of religious gathering

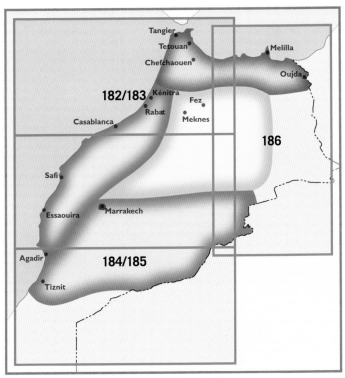

To identify the regions, see the map on the inside of the front cover

### Regional Maps

| | | | |
|---|---|---|---|
| ════ Major route | | ☐ | City |
| ═══ Motorway | | ▫ | Major town |
| ─── National road | | ○○ | Town/village |
| ─── Other road | | ✈ | Airport |
| ------ Track | | ▲ | Height in metres |
| –┼–┼– Tunnel | | ▣ | Featured place of interest |
| ─── Railway | | ▪ | Place of interest |
| –··– International boundary | | | National Park |

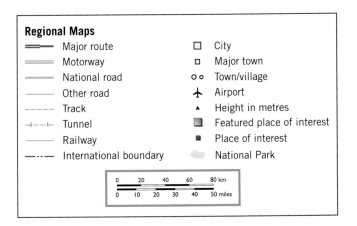

# Atlas

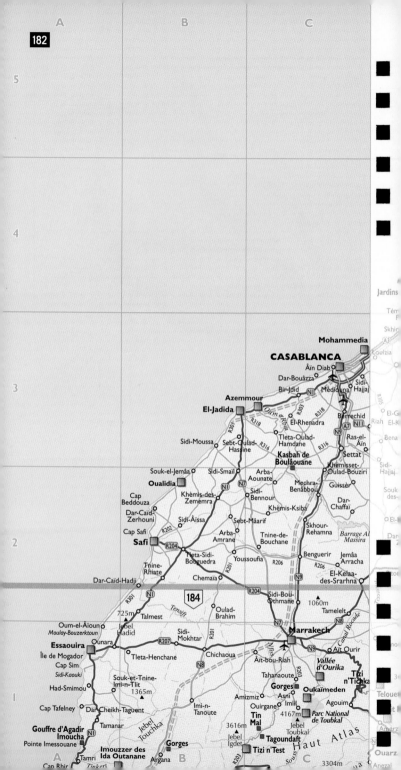

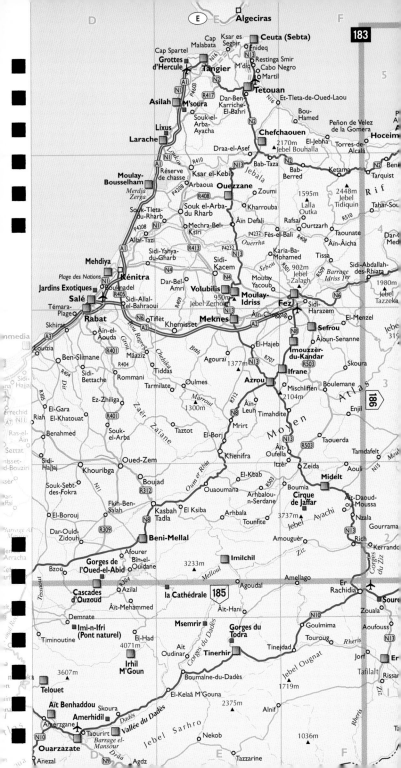

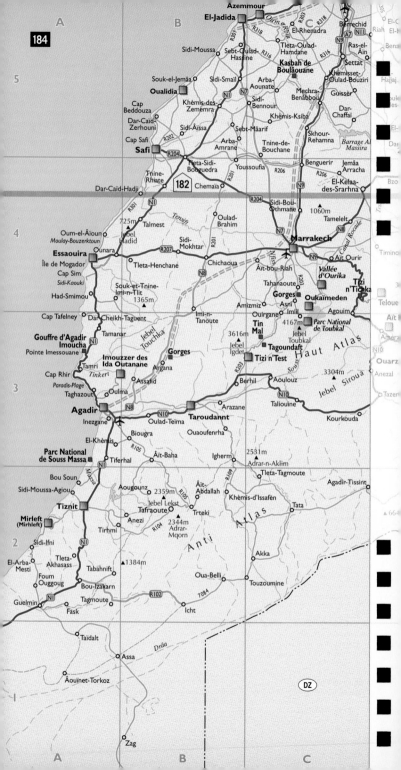

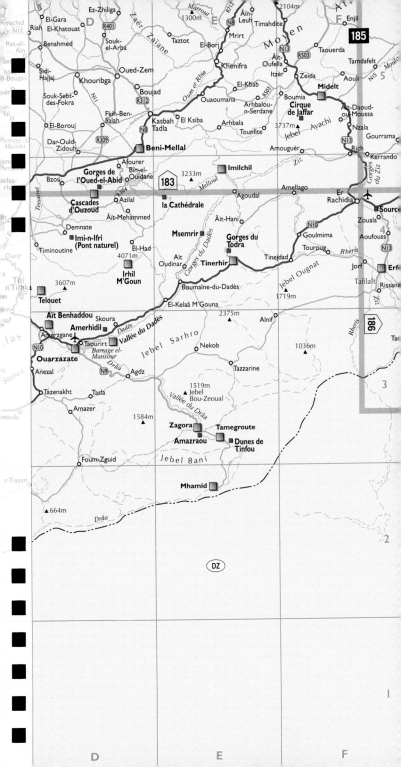

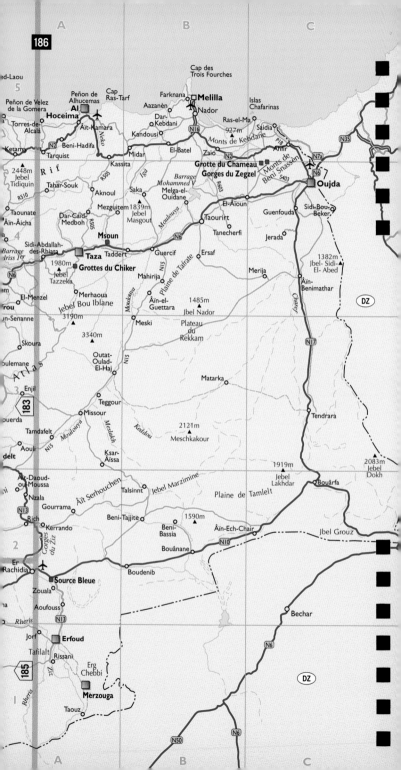

## Picture Credits/Acknowledgements

The Automobile Association wishes to thank the following photographers, libraries and museums for their assistance with the preparation of this book.

Abbreviations for terms appearing above: (t) top, (b) bottom, (l) left, (r) right, (c) centre

Front and back cover: (t) AA Photo Library/Paul Kenward; (ct) AA Photo Library/Ian Burgum; (cb) AA Photo Library/Ian Burgum; (b) AA Photo Library/Paul Kenward; Spine AA Photo Library/Paul Kenward.

2i AA/P Kenward; 2ii AA/A Mockford and N Bonetti; 2iii AA/A Mockford and N Bonetti; 2iv © Guenter Rossenbach/Zefa/Corbis; 3i AA/S McBride; 3ii AA/I Burgum; 3iii AA/A Mockford and N Bonetti; 3iv AA/A Mockford and N Bonetti; 5I AA/P Kenward; 5c AA/S McBride; 5r AA/A Mockford and N Bonetti; 6/7 AA/I Burgum; 8/9 Photolibrary Group; 10 AA/A Mockford and N Bonetti; 11 AA/A Mockford and N Bonetti; 12l AA/S McBride; 12r AA/I Burgum; 13 AA/A Mockford and N Bonetti; 14t AA/A Mockford and N Bonetti; 14b AA/A Mockford and N Bonetti; 15 AA/A Mockford and N Bonetti; 16 AA/S McBride; 17 AA/A Mockford and N Bonetti; 18 AA/I Burugum; 19 AA/P Kenward; 20l AA/I Burgum; 20r AA/A Mockford and N Bonetti; 21l AA/A Mockford and N Bonetti; 21r AA/I Burgum; 22l AA/A Mockford and N Bonetti; 22r AA/A Mockford and N Bonetti; 23 AA/I Burgum; 24 AA/A Mockford and N Bonetti; 24/25 AA/A Mockford and N Bonetti; 26 Photolibrary Group; 27 © Oliver Martel/Corbis; 28/29 Barbary Pirates Attacking A Spanish Ship (oil on canvas), Velde, Willem van de II, (1633-1707) (studio of)/Private Collection/Photo © Christie's Images/The Bridgeman Art Library; 30 Terrence Spencer/Time Life/Getty Images; 31 Philippe Wojazar/AFP/Getty Images; 32 AA/A Mockford and N Bonetti; 33l AA/A Mockford and N Bonetti; 33c AA/A Mockford and N Bonetti; 33r AA/A Mockford and N Bonetti; 45l AA/A Mockford and N Bonetti; 45c AA/A Mockford and N Bonetti; 45r AA/A Mockford and N Bonetti; 46 AA/A Mockford and N Bonetti; 46/47 AA/A Mockford and N Bonetti; 48 AA/A Mockford and N Bonetti; 49t AA/A Mockford and N Bonetti; 49b AA/A Mockford and N Bonetti; 50 AA/A Mockford and N Bonetti; 51 AA/A Mockford and N Bonetti; 52 AA/A Mockford and N Bonetti; 53 AA/A Mockford and N Bonetti; 54 AA/A Mockford and N Bonetti; 55 AA/A Mockford and N Bonetti; 56/57 AA/A Mockford and N Bonetti; 58 AA/A Mockford and N Bonetti; 59 AA/A Mockford and N Bonetti; 60 AA/A Mockford and N Bonetti; 61 AA/A Mockford and N Bonetti; 62 AA/A Mockford and N Bonetti; 63 AA/A Mockford and N Bonetti; 71l © Guenter Rossenbach/Zefa/Corbis; 71c AA/P Kenward; 71r AA/A Mockford and N Bonetti; 73 AA/A Mockford and N Bonetti; 74t AA/P Kenward; 74b Bruno Morandi/Robert Harding Picture Library; 75 AA/I Burgum; 76/77 AA/I Burgum; 78 © Gary Cook/Alamy; 79 Shaen Adey/Gallo Images/Getty Images; 80 AA/I Burgum; 81 AA/A Mockford and N Bonetti; 82 AA/A Mockford and N Bonetti; 83 AA/A Mockford and N Bonetti; 84 © Stephen Elson/Alamy; 85 AA/P Kenward; 86/87 Walter Biblkow/The Image Bank/Getty Images; 95l AA/S McBride; 95c Silvia Otte/Photonica/Getty Images; 95r AA/S McBride; 96/97 AA/S McBride; 97 AA/A Mockford and N Bonetti; 98 AA/I Burgum; 99t AA/S McBride; 99b Jean du Boiberranger/The Image Bank/Getty Images; 100/101 AA/S McBride; 101 AA/S McBride; 102 AA/S McBride; 103 AA/S McBride; 104 AA/S McBride; 105 Photolibrary Group; 106 AA/S McBride; 107 AA/S McBride; 108 © K.M. Westermann/Corbis; 109 Bruno Morandi/Robert Harding Picture Library; 110 AA/I Burgum; 117l AA/I Burgum; 118 AA/P Kenward; 119 AA/S McBride; 121 AA/P Kenward; 122/123 © Robert van der Hilst/Corbis; 123 © Robert van der Hilst/Corbis; 124 AA/I Burgum; 124/125 AA/I Burgum; 126 AA/I Burgum; 127 AA/I Burgum; 128 AA/S McBride; 129 AA/I Burgum; 130 AA/S McBride; 131 AA/I Burgum; 132 Walter Biblkow/The Image Bank/Getty Images; 133 AA/P Kenward; 139l AA/A Mockford and N Bonetti; 139c AA/A Mockford and N Bonetti; 139r AA/A Mockford and N Bonetti; 140 AA/A Mockford and N Bonetti; 141 AA/A Mockford and N Bonetti; 142 AA/S McBride; 143 AA/P Kenward; 144 AA/A Mockford and N Bonetti; 145 AA/A Mockford and N Bonetti; 147 © K. M. Westermann/Corbis; 148/149 AA/P Kenward; 150 AA/A Mockford and N Bonetti; 151 AA/A Mockford and N Bonetti; 152 AA/A Mockford and N Bonetti; 153 Maremagnum/Photographer's Choice/Getty Images; 155 AA/I Burgum; 163l AA/A Mockford and N Bonetti; 163c AA/A Mockford and N Bonetti; 163r AA/A Mockford and N Bonetti; 164 AA/A Mockford and N Bonetti; 165 AA/A Mockford and N Bonetti; 166 AA/A Mockford and N Bonetti; 167 AA/I Burgum; 168 AA/A Mockford and N Bonetti; 169 AA/I Burgum; 170 AA/A Mockford and N Bonetti; 171 AA/S McBride; 172 AA/A Mockford and N Bonetti; 173l AA/A Mockford and N Bonetti; 173c AA/A Mockford and N Bonetti; 173r AA/A Mockford and N Bonetti; 177t AA/A Mockford and N Bonetti; 177c AA/I Burgum; 177cr AA/A Mockford and N Bonetti

Every effort has been made to trace the copyright holders, and we apologise in advance for any accidental errors. We would be happy to apply the corrections in the following edition of this publication.

The author would like to thank the Moroccan National Tourist Office for its help in the preparation of this guide.

# SPIRALGUIDE
# Questionnaire

## Dear Traveller

Your comments, opinions and recommendations are very important to us. Please help us to improve our travel guides by taking a few minutes to complete this simple questionnaire.

You do not need a stamp (unless posted outside the UK). If you do not want to remove this page from your guide, then photocopy it or write your answers on a plain sheet of paper.

Send to: The Editor, Spiral Guides, AA World Travel Guides, FREEPOST SCE 4598, Basingstoke RG21 4GY.

## Your recommendations...

We always encourage readers' recommendations for restaurants, night-life or shopping – if your recommendation is used in the next edition of the guide, we will send you a FREE AA Spiral Guide of your choice. Please state below the establishment name, location and your reasons for recommending it.

_____

_____

_____

_____

_____

**Please send me AA Spiral** _____

(see list of titles inside the back cover)

## About this guide...

**Which title did you buy?**

_____ **AA Spiral**

**Where did you buy it?** _____

**When?** m m / y y

**Why did you choose an AA Spiral Guide?** _____

_____

_____

_____

**Did this guide meet your expectations?**

Exceeded ☐   Met all ☐   Met most ☐   Fell below ☐

**Please give your reasons** _____

_____

_____

_____

_____

continued on next page...

**Were there any aspects of this guide that you particularly liked?**

_____
_____
_____
_____
_____

**Is there anything we could have done better?**

_____
_____
_____
_____

## About you...

**Name (Mr/Mrs/Ms)** _____

**Address** _____

_____ **Postcode** _____

**Daytime tel no** _____ **email** _____

Please _only_ give us your email address and mobile phone number if you wish to hear from us about other products and services from the AA and partners by email or text or mms.

**Which age group are you in?**

Under 25 ☐   25–34 ☐   35–44 ☐   45–54 ☐   55–64 ☐   65+ ☐

**How many trips do you make a year?**

Less than one ☐   One ☐   Two ☐   Three or more ☐

**Are you an AA member? Yes ☐   No ☐**

---

**About your trip...**

**When did you book?** m m / y y       **When did you travel?** m m / y y

**How long did you stay?** _____

**Was it for business or leisure?** _____

**Did you buy any other travel guides for your trip?** ☐ Yes ☐ No

**If yes, which ones?** _____

**Thank you for taking the time to complete this questionnaire. Please send it to us as soon as possible, and remember, you do not need a stamp (unless posted outside the UK).**